ENGLISH LANGUAGE PROFICIENCY TESTING IN ASIA

As the demand for English language education grows in Asia, there has been a parallel growth in the development and implementation of standardized tests at the local level. Offering much-needed context on locally produced tests in Asia, contributors examine emerging models for English language assessment and the impact these large-scale tests have on the teaching and learning of English. Chapters address the following well-known and developing high-stakes tests in different regions across Asia: the GEPT, the TEPS, the VSTEP, the CET, the EIKEN and TEAP, and the ELPA.

Brought together by world-renowned testing assessment scholar Cyril Weir and the Language Training and Testing Center (LTTC), one of Asia's leading testing institutions based in Taiwan, this volume is a useful reference for evaluating, developing, and validating local tests of English and their societal impact. Comprehensive and research-based, chapters cover historic backgrounds, sociocultural contexts, test quality, international standing, and future considerations.

Ideal for graduate students, researchers, and scholars in language assessment, TESOL/ TEFL, and applied linguistics, this book will also be of interest to language teaching professionals, language test developers, and graduate students in Asian studies and international education, intercultural communication, and intercultural studies.

Lily I-Wen Su is a distinguished professor of the Graduate Institute of Linguistics at National Taiwan University and Executive Director of the LTTC, a non-profit educational foundation in Taiwan.

Cyril J. Weir (1950–2018) was Professor and Powdrill Chair in English Language Acquisition in CRELLA at the University of Bedfordshire, UK, and a Visiting Professor at the University of Reading, UK.

Jessica R. W. Wu holds a PhD in Language Testing and is the R&D Program Director at the LTTC.

ESL & Applied Linguistics Professional Series
Eli Hinkel, Series Editor

Pedagogies and Policies for Publishing Research in English
Local Initiatives Supporting International Scholars
James N. Corcoran, Karen Englander, and Laura-Mihaela Muresan

Teaching Chinese as a Second Language
The Way of the Learner
Jane Orton and Andrew Scrimgeour

Teaching Academic L2 Writing
Practical Techniques in Vocabulary and Grammar
Eli Hinkel

Quality in TESOL and Teacher Education
From a Results Culture Towards a Quality Culture
Juan de Dios Martínez Agudo

Language Curriculum Design, 2nd Edition
John Macalister and I.S.P. Nation

Teaching Extensive Reading in Another Language
I.S.P. Nation and Rob Waring

English Language Proficiency Testing in Asia
A New Paradigm Bridging Global and Local Contexts
Edited by Lily I-Wen Su, Cyril J. Weir, and Jessica R. W. Wu

For more information about this series, please visit: www.routledge.com/
ESL-Applied-Linguistics-Professional-Series/book-series/LEAESLALP

ENGLISH LANGUAGE PROFICIENCY TESTING IN ASIA

A New Paradigm Bridging Global and Local Contexts

Edited by Lily I-Wen Su, Cyril J. Weir, and Jessica R. W. Wu

NEW YORK AND LONDON

First published 2020
by Routledge
52 Vanderbilt Avenue, New York, NY 10017

and by Routledge
2 Park Square, Milton Park, Abingdon, Oxon, OX14 4RN

Routledge is an imprint of the Taylor & Francis Group, an informa business

© 2020 selection and editorial matter, Lily I-Wen Su, Cyril J. Weir, and Jessica R. W. Wu; individual chapters, the contributors

The right of Lily I-Wen Su, Cyril J. Weir, and Jessica R. W. Wu to be identified as the authors of the editorial material, and of the authors for their individual chapters, has been asserted in accordance with sections 77 and 78 of the Copyright, Designs and Patents Act 1988.

All rights reserved. No part of this book may be reprinted or reproduced or utilised in any form or by any electronic, mechanical, or other means, now known or hereafter invented, including photocopying and recording, or in any information storage or retrieval system, without permission in writing from the publishers.

Trademark notice: Product or corporate names may be trademarks or registered trademarks, and are used only for identification and explanation without intent to infringe.

Library of Congress Cataloging-in-Publication Data
A catalog record for this book has been requested

ISBN: 978-0-8153-6870-0 (hbk)
ISBN: 978-0-8153-6871-7 (pbk)
ISBN: 978-1-351-25402-1 (ebk)

Typeset in Bembo
by Apex CoVantage, LLC

 Printed in the United Kingdom by Henry Ling Limited

To Professor Cyril James Weir

CONTENTS

List of Tables	ix
List of Figures	x
Editor's Note	xi
Lily I-Wen Su	
Foreword: Localization	xiii
Barry O'Sullivan	
Notes on Contributors	xxix

1 Introduction
   Jessica R. W. Wu 1

2 The General English Proficiency Test in Taiwan:
   Past, Present, and Future
   Rachel Yi-fen Wu 9

3 TEPS and Its Family of Tests
   Yong-Won Lee, Heesung Jun, and Ja Young Kim 42

4 Vietnamese Standardized Test of English Proficiency:
   A Panorama
   Nguyen Thi Ngoc Quynh 71

5 Testing Tertiary-Level English Language Learners:
   The College English Test in China
   Yan Jin 101

viii Contents

6 EIKEN and TEAP: How Two Test Systems in Japan Have
Responded to Different Local Needs in the Same Context 131
Jamie Dunlea, Todd Fouts, Dan Joyce, and Keita Nakamura

7 The English Language Proficiency Assessment
for the Malaysian Public Service 162
Kadeessa Abdul-Kadir

8 Global, Local, or "Glocal": Alternative Pathways
in English Language Test Provision 193
Cyril J. Weir

Index 226

TABLES

0.1	Levels of Localization in the Aptis Test System	xxv
2.1	The GEPT Level Framework	10
2.2	Test Formats and Passing Standards of the GEPT	16
2.3	Summary of the Results of GEPT–CEFR Linking Studies	26
3.1	The TEPS and Its Family of Tests	45
3.2	Research on the Development of TEPS	58
3.3	Research on the Stabilization of TEPS	59
3.4	Research on the Maintenance of TEPS and Development of New Tests	61
3.5	Research on the Revision of the TEPS and Its Family of Tests	63
4.1	Test Formats of the VSTEP	76
5.1	The Three Stages of the CET Managerial System	103
5.2	The Input Materials Used in the CET in the Past Three Decades	104
5.3	The Latest Version of the CET (Since 2016)	105
5.4	Item Specifications and Assembly Models of the Three Speaking Tests	110
5.A1	Sub-Skills Assessed in the CET	129
6.1	Overview of Proficiency Levels of EIKEN Grades	140
6.A1	EIKEN Test Format	159
6.A2	TEAP Test Format	161
7.1	Comparison of ELPA 1.0 and 2.0	168
7.2	Interpretive Argument for a Trait Interpretation	178
7.3	Overall Interpretive Argument Evidence (Levels 1 to 4)	181

FIGURES

0.1	Revised Test Validation Model	xvii
0.2	Expertise Required for Local Test Development	xx
2.1	Overview of Selected GEPT Validation Studies	23
3.1	Pattern of Total Scale Scores	53
5.1	The Procedure of CET Item Writing	112
7.1	The Scoring Argument Structure: Level 1	179
7.2	Evidence Supporting Level 1 Inference	180
7.3	Evidence Supporting Level 4 Inference	184

EDITOR'S NOTE

According to the World Economic Forum (Torkington, 2016), 1.5 billion people around the world are learning English, and this figure is expected to reach 2 billion by 2020 (British Council, 2013). The increase in Asia is mainly due to the effect of globalization, as well as to the fact that English language ability is deemed indispensable in enhancing competitiveness in the international market.

In view of this increased need for English, most Asian countries have introduced policies to make English education compulsory, and significant portions of educational budgets and resources have been allocated accordingly (Kirkpatrick & Bui, 2016). These are largely used to evaluate the effectiveness of English language education, mostly by means of large-scale standardized tests, often used for high-stakes purposes such as gate-keeping in order to control access to employment, higher education, and other opportunities for upward social mobility.

In tandem with this trend towards globalization, the development of English tests tailored to specific educational and societal contexts has thus blossomed in hopes of offering nation-specific yet globally oriented alternatives to reliance on international English proficiency tests such as the International English Language Testing System (IELTS) and Test of English as a Foreign Language (TOEFL). The present book is written with this background in mind. We intend to discuss a highly important and timely issue: the broad and in-depth varieties of locally produced standardized English proficiency tests across Asia. All contributors address test-localization issues both common to Asian countries and specific to each unique context. Each chapter reiterates and resonates with the idea advanced by Ross (2008) that the scope of language testing goes far beyond the conventional technical concerns of reliability and validity, and that it has in fact complex social, economic, and educational implications.

xii Editor's Note

In my capacity as the Executive Director of the LTTC, and as an editor of this book, I would like to acknowledge a number of people, not limited to my co-editors and the authors, who have contributed to its publication. Without them, this book would not have been possible. First of all, I would like to acknowledge and thank my predecessor, Prof. Sebastian Hsienhao Liao, for taking the bold step of initiating the project, and Dr. Jessica R. W. Wu, for making the collaboration with Prof. Cyril Weir possible. I would also like to express my deep appreciation for the role played by Prof. Cyril Weir in the development of this book. His insightful redefinition of the local tests developed in the six Asian contexts has created a paradigm shift, viewing English language tests in the 21st century as a mode of *glocalization*. Sadly, Prof. Weir was not able to see this book published. His passing at the final stage of publication of this book came as a real blow to us and the whole language assessment community.

We at the LTTC would additionally like to express our heartfelt gratitude to several people who helped to shape the present book: to Prof. Barry O'Sullivan, for his foreword on localization, which establishes an illuminating theoretical framework as a backdrop for the chapters that follow; to the external reviewers, Prof. Antony Kunnan and Prof. Lynda Taylor, for providing constructive and valuable feedback on the final draft of the manuscript; to Karen Adler and her team at Routledge, Taylor & Francis Group, for their admirable commitment and much needed support throughout the process of producing this book; and to Ingrid Chao and Judy Lo, our LTTC colleagues, for their devoted editorial assistance.

The localization practices in each context sampled in this book reflect unique historical and cultural aspects, as well as commonalities evolving from the shared goal of introducing positive test impact to ultimately help learners. It is hoped that this book will bring to international readers a unique and comprehensive coverage of various issues related to standardized English proficiency tests in Asian contexts.

Lily I-Wen Su

References

British Council. (2013). *The English effect: The impact of English, what it's worth to the UK and why it matters to the world*. London: Author. Retrieved from www.britishcouncil.org/sites/default/files/english-effect-report-v2.pdf

Kirkpatrick, R., & Bui, T. T. N. (2016). Introduction: The challenges for English education policies in Asia. In R. Kirkpatrick (Ed.), *Language education policies in Asia*. London: Springer International Publishing Switzerland.

Ross, S. (2008). Language testing in Asia: Evolution, innovation, and policy challenges. *Language Testing, 25*(1), 5–13.

Torkington, S. (2016, August 8). *Which languages do most people want to learn?* Retrieved from www.weforum.org/agenda/2016/08/languages-most-people-speak-and-learn

FOREWORD: LOCALIZATION

Barry O'Sullivan

Background

The language-testing industry has grown from a minor cottage industry in the early part of the 20th century to the large-scale billion-pound juggernaut we now see in the early decades of the 21st century. In the early years of educational testing, the clear leaders, in terms of volume, were to be found in the U.S. with the Courtis Tests (see Courtis, 1914) selling over 13 million tests in the first decade after their launch in 1914 (Johanningmeier & Richardson, 2008, p. 235). At the same time, the University of Cambridge Local Examination Syndicate (UCLES, currently known as Cambridge Assessment English) became the first entrant into the world of English language testing with their Certificate of Proficiency in English (CPE), which was launched in 1913 to a population of just three test takers, a number which had only grown to 14 by the late 1920s (Weir, 2013, p. 30). While English language formed part of the university entrance testing system on both sides of the Atlantic at the time, the primary focus was on speakers of English as an L1 (first language). Growth in interest in studying overseas was not to begin in earnest until after World War II (see Weir & O'Sullivan, 2017, Chapter 3). During this period, the British Council advocated for a new test set at a higher level of proficiency than the CPE, while the U.S. Educational Testing Service (ETS) was founded in 1947. However, it was not until the early 1960s that what we now see as the modern language testing industry emerged.

In 1964, ETS launched its Test of English as a Foreign Language (TOEFL), and a year later the British Council introduced the English Proficiency Test Battery (EPTB), developed for them by Alan Davies at the University of Edinburgh. While both tests were heavily influenced by the psychometric-structuralist approach, which dominated educational testing in the U.S. at that time, the

xiv Foreword: Localization

EPTB was in many ways more contemporary. This was because the British Council/UCLES approach, as epitomized in the UCLES tests of the time, looked to the language learning literature for its theoretical basis. See Weir's (2013) excellent historical overview of the link between the UCLES tests and contemporary language learning theory. The British Council and UCLES soon reverted to their traditional approach (the EPTB was abandoned to be replaced by the British Council's truly innovative English Language Testing Service in 1980), while ETS remained faithful to their psychometric-structuralist approach for almost half a century.

From the 1990s, the tests developed by these two institutions were marketed as world-leading in terms of validity (particularly in the case of UCLES) and reliability (particularly in the case of ETS, who interpreted it as representing internal consistency). This marketing initiative proved successful in that tests such as the First Certificate in English (FCE) and TOEFL came to be seen as representing best practice in test development and administration. The FCE/TOEFL comparability study of 1989 caused UCLES to move somewhat in the direction of the indirect approach that typified ETS, to the extent that UCLES began to pay more attention in their literature to discussing the reliability of their tests.

Meanwhile, ETS was beginning the long process of updating TOEFL. When the new test emerged, it appeared to be a significant step towards the more direct approach of UCLES, though issues with delivery (it was the first major computer-based English language test) soon led to the experiment being abandoned. In its place, in 2007, ETS launched the internet-based TOEFL (iBT). This test was even more explicitly performance based and was generally recognized as a very British style test. While TOEFL's main rival, the International English Language Testing System (IELTS), remained unchanged from its 1995 revision, the two tests and their developers were considered the dominant forces in world testing.

The coming together of the language testing approaches of the two main protagonists in the world of English language testing is intriguing as it occurred at the same time as that world was beginning to fragment.

In my 2011 paper (O'Sullivan, 2011), I argued that the increasing professionalization of test developers and theorists outside of the traditional English test development countries (the UK and the U.S.) was leading to significant fragmentation of the English language testing industry. I based this argument on the fact that in the decades since the mid-1990s there has been a growth in the number of individuals studying for PhDs in language testing and allied fields both in the UK and the U.S. The interesting thing to note about this growth is that it has been filled almost (though not quite) entirely by "overseas" students. While some of these people chose to stay in their country of education beyond their studies, the majority moved back to their country of origin within a relatively short time of completing their studies—often having completed post-doctoral studies, internships, or full-time roles at major testing organizations. This injection of highly qualified and experienced expertise has set the scene for a move away from the traditional core bases of English language testing to the increasingly professionalized fringes. We are currently witnessing various manifestations of this shift in the increasing trend towards the development of "international" quality tests by locally based groups and the emergence of individuals with high-quality masters and PhDs in these same places. In particular, note the situation in China, where the recently launched China's Standards of English (CSE) were designed, developed, and operationalized entirely within country by over 150 researchers spread across the country—all experienced research-degree holders and their students.

These developments outlined saw the emergence, from the middle of the 1990s, of a number of tests that met or exceeded the standards of quality and consistency expected of their international counterparts. Examples of these tests include the COPE from Bilkent University, Turkey; the EXAVER suite of tests from Veracruz University, Mexico; and the GEPT from the Language Training and Testing Center, Taiwan. While these tests were, at one point in their development cycle, heavily influenced by experts from the UK or the U.S., the expertise gained by local or locally based colleagues soon meant that the tests came to reflect the needs of these local contexts of use.

Significantly, at the time these changes were happening, there was no established validation approach upon which their proposers could formulate a cohesive theoretical underpinning for the learner and for the context-of-use-based decisions they knew were needed. It was not until the development and operationalization of the socio-cognitive (SC) approach to test development and validation, initially by Weir (2005), later by O'Sullivan and Weir (2011) and O'Sullivan (2011, 2016b) that a truly useful model became available to serve as the theoretical basis for the kind of local tests mentioned earlier. In my application of the then-evolving SC model to a range of tests (including COPE, EXAVER, and others), I began to realize that my insistence on the test taker being recognized as the starting point for any test development and validation project would have significant consequences for test theory and practice. Essentially, if we genuinely start with the test taker, we are forced to immediately recognize the need for the proposed test to be appropriate to this individual or group. In the remainder of this foreword, I will further explore the theoretical and practical implications of this situation.

Unfortunately, for each of the positive cases reported in this book there are many more international and local tests out there that fail to meet even the basic expectations of quality. As I hope the reader will discover while reading this foreword, there can be no excuse for poor quality, no excuse for inappropriate usage, no excuse for unprofessional practice.

Theoretical Basis

I first became aware of the centrality of the test taker in test design when writing my MA dissertation at the University of Reading in 1993 (O'Sullivan, 1995).

xvi Foreword: Localization

Inspired by the work of Don Porter (1991a, 1991b), who was also my supervisor at that time, my initial research into speaking test performance clearly demonstrated an affective reaction on the part of candidates to their interlocutors. The candidates typically performed differently depending on the relative age of their interlocutor. This suggested that the social structure of this interaction was critical to the construct being tested. My later PhD studies (O'Sullivan, 2000, 2007) confirmed and extended this view by including additional variables such as gender, level of acquaintanceship, relative personality type, and language ability. In undertaking this research, it became clear that test developers and theorists paid lip service to the centrality of candidates, claiming that they were a starting point of both the theoretical and development processes, but essentially ignoring them in the development process and in their theoretical discussions. This was probably because at this point in time the prime focus of many of these people was on large-scale international tests, where the population tended to be heterogeneous and problematic in terms of definition. Mislevy et al. (2002, 2003) pointed to the need for a "student model" in their *Evidence Based Design* approach but failed to clarify what this model might look like, despite the fact that I had proposed such a model in 2000, building on the work of J. D. Brown from 1996.

As I have indicated, the development of the SC frameworks in the early years of the 21st century offered developers a systematic and clearly articulated approach to the creation of appropriate and *efficient* tests (in the sense used by Wiseman, 1969). The SC frameworks presented a series of checklists focused on all aspects of the development and validation process, which it saw as a single entity. These checklists were supported by a clearly articulated vision of how these multi-element aspects linked together to define the construct (see Weir, 2005). Over the course of the first decade of the century, I focused on the application of the SC frameworks to a series of development and validation projects (see O'Sullivan & Weir, 2011). During this time, I also worked to identify and further define a basic underlying model of development and validation (see O'Sullivan, 2011; O'Sullivan & Weir, 2011). By 2016 this work had identified and offered solutions to those problematic issues I had identified in the early frameworks (O'Sullivan, 2011). These issues were

- the claim that development/validation was temporal in nature. O'Sullivan (2011) argued that it was in fact an iterative process and that taking a temporal approach would result in critical elements being considered too late in the process—I was particularly concerned with issues such as scoring and consequence; and
- the lack of a clear definition of how consequence fits into the approach. I argued that it should not be seen as an *a posteriori* validation issue, as it needed to be taken into account from the beginning of the process and impacted on all elements of the process (O'Sullivan, 2011). However, at that

time, I failed to satisfactorily explain how this might be operationalized and only attempted to do so in a systematic way in my later work on the model (2016b).

It is this later work that drove the creation of the British Council's Aptis test service, the first test to be developed from conception through to administration on the SC model. While a full discussion of current thinking around the SC model can be found in Chalhoub-Deville and O'Sullivan (in press), I will present here an overview in order to demonstrate how the model can be argued to form the theoretical basis of the localization concept.

The test element of the SC model can be summarized as follows:

1. **The test taker featured centrally.** The test taker model would then require

    a. a multi-faceted definition of the candidate such as my own suggestion (O'Sullivan, 2000), to incorporate physical, psychological, and experiential characteristics. Without this, it would not be possible to interpret the complex interactions that characterize communication;

    b. a cognitive model of language progression. Without this, it would not be possible to adequately define what a typical, successful candidate should be able to do with the language at particular stages of development; and

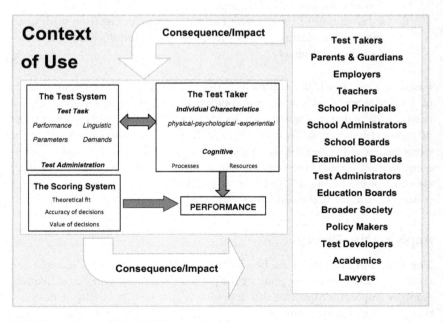

FIGURE 0.1   Revised Test Validation Model

Source: O'Sullivan, 2016b

xviii Foreword: Localization

    c.   a social model of how the candidate's language being tested facilitates social communication.

2. **The test system was fully described** to include

    a.   a description of the performance parameters that govern the test and that have been made clear to the candidate, such as timing, test structure, scoring criteria, score meaning;

    b.   a description of how the underlying cognitive and social models are operationalized in the test (i.e., how the test tasks and items reflect the construct); and

    c.   a description of the administrative procedures that are in place to ensure that the test is systematically and fairly administered.

3. **The scoring system is sufficiently defined** to include

    a.   a description of how the score is awarded—an answer key in the case of the receptive skills and a rating scale in the case of the productive skills. It is critical that the link between the scale used and the construct being tested (including level) is explicitly stated;

    b.   a description of how examiners, raters, and markers are trained and monitored;

    c.   a description of the efficiency of the test scoring system (reliability, consistency, and accuracy); and

    d.   a description of the value of the test score in comparison with other appropriate measures and in terms of the stated decisions the test is designed to support.

Based on this model, the argument is that for a test to be used appropriately in a specific social or educational context, it must be shown to *fit* with the needs of that context. For almost a decade now, I have referred to this concept of appropriateness as *localization* (see O'Sullivan, 2011). For a test to meet the expectations of localization, the validation argument must specifically address considerations around the operationalization of the construct across all three elements of the SC model. Put succinctly, localization is the reflection of the context of test use in the validation argument.

Applying the Theory

The first thing to consider when interpreting the SC model is that the test taker is seen as the starting point of the process of development and validation. Another important aspect of this approach is that test development does not take place in a vacuum. In fact, we should always consider two aspects of context; the first is the context of test development, and the second is the context of test use. In the traditional approach, the contexts were typically detached, with expert developers either developing tests remotely or advising on local development procedures. As we move away from this approach, the contexts merge, so that the context of development and use are unified. This merging of contexts provides the basis for tests that are more context (and therefore test taker) specific. The two contexts can be briefly described as follows:

- The context of test development will primarily focus on the three central elements of the SC model (Test Taker, Test System, Scoring System) in that the focus here is on developing a test that complies with technical and educational standards—or that is, to use Borsboom's (2012, 2014) interpretation of the term, "valid."
- The context of test use refers to the social and educational context in which the test will be administered. O'Sullivan (2016b) argues that this context should be defined as representing the expectations and interests of key stakeholder groups (as listed in the right-hand panel in the SC model shown in Figure 0.1).

To provide evidence that the test that emerges from the development process is appropriate to the context of use, it is necessary to either ensure that the contexts are merged (i.e., the tests are developed by professionals who are familiar with both contexts) or by establishing evidence that the test reflects the context of use. This evidence can be gathered post operationalization, see the work of Berry, O'Sullivan, and Rugea (2012) in evidencing the appropriateness of the use of IELTS as a language measure in the selection of medical practitioners in the UK—though it is best done prior to operationalization in order to avoid the embarrassing, expensive, and business-threatening situation in which the test proves to be unsuitable for use in a particular context (other than that for which it has been designed) when a decision to use the test in this context has already been made.

Context of Development

The most realistic and practical way to ensure that the contexts are merged is to ensure that the development work is undertaken by individuals with considerable contextual awareness (i.e., of the context of use), subject matter expertise, and technical language test development experience (see Figure 0.2). We are assuming, of course, that these individuals will also have first-hand knowledge of the test development context, for example, knowing the key stakeholders who make up that context, their interrelationships, and also the internal politics of the developing organization or department. The extent to which this is practically achievable is clearly an important issue. Hence, the reliance on external experts to provide support and/or advice, particularly where a developer is entering the arena for the first time, seems inevitable. Of course, having gained the experience and the expertise required to develop a major test instrument or service, this need would reduce or disappear.

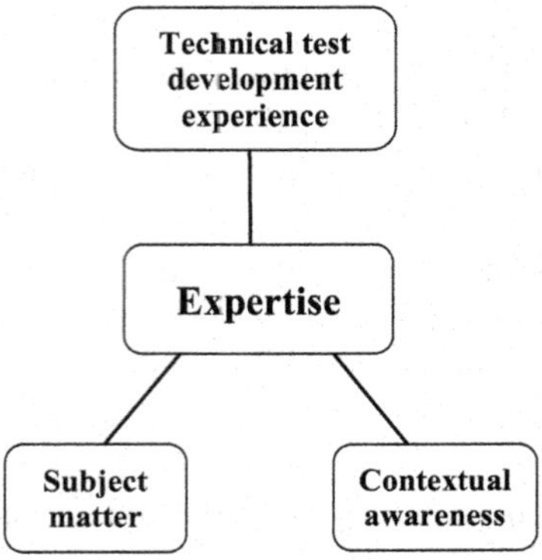

xx Foreword: Localization

FIGURE 0.2 Expertise Required for Local Test Development

Context of Use

The second aspect to be considered is that of the test's context of use. O'Sullivan (2016b) argues that this context will always be defined by the people who make up the key stakeholder groups within that context (see Figure 0.1). In order to ensure the success of a test development initiative, the developer must interact with these key stakeholders, as any consideration of test consequence will be meaningless without the input of these groups. One major criticism of test developers has been that they are remote from the reality of test administration and the impact on local societies of the tests for which they are responsible. By communicating fully with key stakeholder groups, developers can help these groups to understand the rationale behind specific development and administration decisions and in turn learn from the stakeholders about their main concerns. This latter understanding will then feed into how the developers operationalize the construct or how they explain this operationalization to stakeholders. It will also help to shape their validation arguments.

These two contexts are clearly linked in any local test development project, with the developers fully aware of the requirements and the expectations of those stakeholders who define the context of use. In fact, without this symbiotic relationship the construct cannot be adequately defined within the context of test use.

Features of Localization

Localization can be seen to impact on three different situations:

- When a test is designed and built to meet specific needs in a specific context
- When an existing test is altered to meet specific needs in a specific context
- When an existing test is shown to meet specific needs in a specific context

Foreword: Localization **xxi**

The tests discussed in this book all reflect the first of these three categories, while the following example of Aptis reflects the second. As I indicated earlier, the final category will always be the most problematic for a test developer, as there is always a chance that a test simply does not fit the needs of a particular context of use. In fact, it could well be argued that the final category is not strictly localization at all, but an attempt to demonstrate local appropriateness (since the test does not actually change in any way). However, a broader understanding of test localization would suggest that this final category is apposite as the test developer must engage directly with the context of use in establishing evidence of appropriateness.

The Aptis General is a test of general proficiency in English. The original conceptualization of the test was that it should be accessible, flexible, and afford-able. The first of these features allows for the test to be systematically reviewed before each specific use to ensure local appropriateness, and where this was not found to be the case, a systematic program of work would be set in place to ensure appropriateness. In other words, the test was designed to be localizable. When developing the Aptis localization approach, it became clear that localization worked on a number of levels. Perhaps the most important of these is the construct definition level. For example, when developing a test for use in Japan, the British Council took into account the way in which the underlying construct was defined in the Japanese course of studies. This is because, in the SC approach, construct can only be fully described in relation to the test population.

Localization is most obviously realized in the test task element within the SC model. Here, it can be described under three broad headings: linguistic, social, and experiential. These are operationalized as follows:

Linguistic   Is the language usage appropriate for the target population? An example of this might be appropriate vocabulary in a test of language for engineers, or in a test for Chinese high school students (i.e., reflecting their course of study). It might also extend to presenting the rubrics (or instructions) to the test takers in their own language—there is an obsession with presenting these in English even to relatively low-level candidates in what seems to be an attempt to establish some type of face validity. This aspect can also extend to including local (or locally heard) accents in the test (particularly listening and speaking).

Social   Are the topics and themes (both linguistic and visual, e.g., images) appropriate to the population? This can mean quite surface level changes, such as changing character or place names from those typical of the UK/the U.S. to those more locally used.

Experiential   Are the people taking the test likely to be familiar with the contents of the test? An example of this is where I have observed teachers preparing materials for their students in an Indian school

xxii Foreword: Localization

for writing and speaking tasks about Christmas, Santa, and snow because these were likely to be tested in a well-known international test. Another aspect of this relates to the visuals used in a test. It is critical that these be treated in the same way as any input language. Images should reflect the social norms of the target population as well as the likely experiences of that population.

It is only by fully understanding the test takers that we can fully respond to the elements described earlier. So, we can see that it is critically important to first define the test-taking population as fully as possible. Because language is a cognitive phenomenon operationalized in a social context, we can utilize candidate definition (or profile) as well as both social and cognitive models of language knowledge and language use in order to define the underlying construct.

Of course, localization extends beyond the test taker and the test task. It should also be seen as relating to the scoring system, including score generation and interpretation. This will be operationalized right across the scoring system, including the following aspects:

Rating scale The scale should take into account specific local language usage. Where the decisions to be made are specifically local in nature (e.g., university entrance or exit), this may emphasize specific criteria such as pronunciation, grammatical appropriateness, or specific error types within these (or other) criteria. Where the test is focused on a specific purpose (e.g., academic), this might also extend to the inclusion of specific rhetorical structures and specific representation of voice.

Rater selection Raters should be selected on the basis of their familiarity with local language usage. It might be that they should be familiar with local pronunciation or other variants (e.g., typical lexical errors) or that they should be fully unfamiliar with these— thus offering an external perspective on the language usage of candidates. We are thereby controlling context familiarity.

Standardization Just as rating scales should be locally appropriate, rater standardization (i.e., training) should take into account the need to focus on the locally specific features of the scale, thus ensuring that these features are appropriately evaluated in the scoring process.

Score reporting It goes without saying that for a test to be appropriate to a specific context of use it should report performance in a way that is meaningful to that context (i.e., that local people can readily interpret). This goes beyond the need for test scores to be locally interpretable to include the local interpretability of test validation arguments.

In addition, the concept of localization can be extended to reflect the local expectations of validation reporting. As I have previously argued (Chalhoub-Deville & O'Sullivan, in press; O'Sullivan, 2016a, 2016b), the extremely limited focus of test theorists and developers of the audience for their validation arguments and of the message included in these arguments has critically undermined their global effectiveness. By ignoring local needs and expectations in the past, we as a community of practice have failed the vast majority of our stakeholders. Instead of our current one-size-fits-all approach to validation, we should be communicating with local stakeholders to explore how to transmit and target these messages more effectively in terms of language, medium, and focus.

Implications of Localization

Perhaps the principal implication of the concept of localization is that the current use of tests across large international markets, with little or no evidence of the local appropriateness of these tests, is not supportable. Tests that claim to test English language proficiency (specific or general) but are not supported by either a coherent language or test taking population model can never expect to be recognized as being validated for use in a specific context. The implications of the various element of this chapter are that:

1. The SC model suggests that no convincing validation argument can be postulated for a language test that is not supported by a clearly defined model of language.
2. No convincing validation argument can be postulated for a language test that claims to be test taker agnostic. The argument proposed here means that for language and other tests, the argument that one-size-fits-all is not supportable.

This is not to say that a test such as the FCE from Cambridge is always going to be inappropriate for local use. It simply says that, for such a test to be used in a specific context, evidence of its appropriateness is first required. One example of this is the decision to continue to use IELTS as a language gatekeeper for medical doctors entering the UK's National Health Service (NHS). Despite regular criticism of this use of the test (it was clearly not designed for this purpose), the fact is that the only major independent study that explored the question of its use (in addition to the IELTS grade levels expected) found that there was significant support amongst the medical community; including from consultants, doctors, nurses, other NHS employees, and patients (see Berry et al., 2012; Berry & O'Sullivan, 2016a, 2016b). Moore et al. (2015) examined the appropriateness of using IELTS with candidates involved in a range of occupational areas as well as those in the academic domain. Though they found that there were some similarities across the needs of both groups, the

xxiv Foreword: Localization

"highly transactional nature of professional communications" (Moore et al., 2015) suggested that one test could not meet the needs of the different groups. In these two examples we see that it cannot be taken for granted that even a well-known and highly regarded test such as IELTS can be used for various purposes. Instead, empirical evidence is needed to either support (as in the former case) or reject (as in the latter case) such usage.

Other Implications

The shift in balance from the traditional English language test developing nations (the UK and the U.S.) to new, or relatively new, developers such as those represented in this volume, will continue. As local test developers increasingly professionalize their operations, the tests they develop will come to be recognized internationally as reflecting best practice. This will lead to the situation where internationally recognized locally developed tests will become the norm instead of the exception. This has already begun to happen, as we can see with the increasing (though still relatively limited) recognition of tests such as the GEPT from Taiwan or EIKEN from Japan (see Chapters 2 and 6, respectively).

Another important implication to consider is inspired by the British Council's Aptis test service. In a true example of research by design, the British Council's Assessment Research Group (ARG) realized that Aptis would be used across the world to offer an estimate of language proficiency for different candidates working in different contexts. With this in mind, the test was designed with the concept of localization as one of its core principles. Aptis was designed to be as fully accessible to stakeholders as feasible. This not only meant that the service should be affordable, but that the test itself could be localized for specific populations and uses: the realization being that a one-size-fits-all approach to language (or other) assessment was no longer appropriate given the changes to the global context described here.

According to the Aptis General Technical Manual (O'Sullivan & Dunlea, 2015, p. 7), Table 0.1 is

> intended to provide a general framework to guide the discussion of assessment options for localised needs in a principled way, and to facilitate communication between the Aptis development team and test users by giving broad indications of the degree of time, effort and resources that might be required at each level of localisation.

The Aptis service was designed not only to allow for varying levels of localization but also to involve test users in the process of test selection and localization. Prospective users were, and are, encouraged to research the appropriateness of the existing test papers to the proposed population before making informed decisions concerning the level of localization required. On many occasions, this research led the prospective user to decide that no localization would be

TABLE 0.1 Levels of Localization in the Aptis Test System

Level	Description	Examples
Level 0	Aptis General (or other existing variant) in a full, four-skills package	User selects a four-skills package of any Aptis (General or variant) available for use.
Level 1	Options for localisation are limited to selection from a fixed range of pre-existing features, such as delivery mode and/or components	User is able to select the skills to be tested and/or the mode of delivery that is appropriate. For example, the Reading package (Core component + Reading component) of Aptis General, taken as a pen-and-paper administration.
Level 2	Contextual localisation: lexical, topical modification	Development of specifications for generating items using existing task formats but with topics, vocabulary, etc. relevant for specific domains (e.g. Aptis for Teachers).
Level 3	Structural reassembly: changing the number of items, proficiency levels targeted, etc., while utilising existing item-bank content.	Developing a test of reading targeted at a specific level, e.g. B1, using existing task types and items of known difficulty calibrated to the Aptis reading scale.
Level 4	Partial re-definition of target construct from existing variants. Will involve developing different task types to elicit different aspects of performance.	Developing new task types that are more relevant for a specific population of test-takers, while remaining within the overall framework of the Aptis test system (e.g. Aptis for Teens).
Level 5	The construct and/or other aspects of the test system are changed to such an extent that the test will no longer be a variant within the system.	For example, developing a matriculation test for uses within a formal secondary educational context; developing a certification test available to individuals rather than organisations, etc.

Source: O'Sullivan and Dunlea 2015, p. 8

required. However, there have been occasions when they have requested some changes, or declined to use the test. On other occasions the British Council has suggested that, based on the research findings, the test was not fully appropriate to the specific context for some reason and recommended an alternative course of action.

It is worth noting that where an international test is making a claim for valid use in a particular local context, it will clearly not be sufficient to present evidence of a link to a locally used (and validated) test though such a claim of a link to a local test will obviously form part of any validation process. Neither is

xxvi Foreword: Localization

it sensible to consider that a claim of a link to a framework such as the CEFR is in itself sufficient to ensure local appropriateness (in the case of Aptis in Taiwan for example) or global appropriateness (in the case of the GEPT or EIKEN for use in an international context). Of course, evidence of a link to a set of standards or a reference framework will form part of any validation claim.

Conclusions

In this foreword, I have presented a comprehensive overview of my thinking on the concept of localization. Broadly speaking, I see the concept as forming a critical element of test use and by extension of validation. In administering a test within a specific context with the intention of making claims or decisions about a specific group of people, it is imperative that the test should be shown to be appropriate to the specific people and to the context. Where a test is developed locally, we would expect that careful and detailed consideration be given to the test population and to the context of test development and use (e.g., the learning system, broader social attitudes, and expectations). Without meeting these requirements, any test is open to question. Just because a test is locally developed does not automatically grant its local appropriateness. For a test developed outside of a specific context or domain, the situation is somewhat different. Large-scale international tests need to work hard to evidence their local appropriateness where they are being used for purposes or in contexts other than those for which they were originally designed. Examples of good practice with regard to this can be found in the groundbreaking work undertaken by the British Council on the Aptis service. This test has been designed from the outset with the concept of localization in mind.

Localization projects have been undertaken in a number of places, for example with a private university in Canada and for a school system in the Kingdom of Saudi Arabia. In both of these cases, the British Council's ARG worked with local experts (in teaching and assessment) to identify appropriate ways in which the existing test might be changed to make it more locally appropriate. These changes were primarily focused on candidates' L1, the society in which they live, and their experiences learning English (both formal and informal), though aspects of test scoring and reporting were also explored.

It is possible that localization will be seen by some as an extension of the traditional status quo: large-scale international test developers simply carrying on with their imperialist ways, looking to continue to dominate the language testing industry from both business and cultural perspectives. I see things differently. I see the localization agenda as the realization of years of significant shift in the language testing world. Local tests can and should be seen to have the potential to be at least as good as global products, and where the developers of global test products see the need to genuinely localize their products, this should be seen as a positive sign that they recognize this potential. While it may fit with political ideology to reject localization, the reality is that localization can only lead to better testing practice at the local level.

Localization is not a "get out of jail free" card for any test. It must be recognized that to be considered for legitimate use in a particular context, a test must meet all of the highest international standards of development, administration, and reporting. While there was once a time when local tests were not thought to be capable of meeting these standards, the various tests discussed in this volume demonstrate that this should no longer be perceived as the case (see, for example, the discussions across Chapters 2 to 7 in this volume on the topic of establishing and maintaining test quality). Though local tests reflect the changes in the language testing world that I first wrote about in 2011 (professionalization, localization, and fragmentation), they also remind us that any lack of human or financial resources cannot be used to excuse the demand for quality. The commitment of the developers of the tests reported in this volume to invest in the professionalization of their approach over a period of years or even decades emphasizes the fact that it is the responsibility of test developers to ensure that the highest expectations for quality are met at all times. The important message here is that whether we are talking about large-scale international tests or tests that operate on a smaller scale, such as regional, national, or institutional tests and including tests devised by higher education institutions to allow for the entry of overseas students, we must demand that they meet the stringent requirements of localization and validation.

References

Berry, V., & O'Sullivan, B. (2016a). Language standards for medical practice in the UK: Issues of fairness and quality for all. In C. Docherty & F. Barker (Eds.), *Language assessment for multilingualism: Proceedings of the ALTE Paris Conference, April 2014* (pp. 268–285). Studies in Language Testing, 44. Cambridge, UK: UCLES/Cam bridge University Press.

Berry, V., & O'Sullivan, B. (2016b). Setting language standards for international medical graduates. In J. Banerjee & D. Tsagari (Eds.), *Contemporary second language assessment*. London: Continuum.

Berry, V., O'Sullivan, B., & Rugea, S. (2012). *Identifying the appropriate IELTS score levels for IMG applicants to the GMC register*. London: University of Roehampton/ The General Medical Council. Retrieved from www.gmc-uk.org/Identifying_ the_appropriate_IELTS_score_levels_for_IMG_applicants_to_the_GMC_register. pdf_55197989.pdf

Borsboom, D. (2012). Whose consensus is it, anyway? Scientific versus legalistic conceptions of validity. *Measurement, 10*, 38–41.

Borsboom, D. (2014). *Validity as the realist views it*. Keynote presentation at the 36th Language Testing Research Colloquium, Amsterdam.

Brown, J. D. (1996). *Testing in language programs*. Upper Saddle River, NJ: Prentice Hall Regents.

Chalhoub-Deville, M., & O'Sullivan, B. (in press). *Validity: Theoretical development and integrated arguments*. Sheffield: Equinox.

Courtis, S. A. (1914). Standard tests in English. *The Elementary School Teacher, 14*(8), 374–392.

Johanningmeier, E. V., & Richardson, T. (Eds.). (2008). *Educational research, the national agenda, and educational reform: A history.* Charlotte, NC: Information Age Publishing.

Mislevy, R. J., Steinberg, L. S., & Almond, R. G. (2002). Design and analysis in task-based language assessment. *Language Testing, 19*(4), 477–496.

Mislevy, R. J., Steinberg, L. S., & Almond, R. G. (2003). On the structure of educational assessments. *Measurement: Interdisciplinary Research and Perspectives, 1*(1), 3–62.

Moore, T., Morton, J., Hall, D., & Wallis, C. (2015). *Literacy practices in the professional workplace: Implications for the IELTS reading and writing tests* (IELTS Research Reports Online Series 2015/1). IELTS Partners: Australia and the UK.

O'Sullivan, B. (1995). *Factors that affect performance in tests of speaking* (Unpublished MA dissertation). University of Reading, UK.

O'Sullivan, B. (2000). *Towards a model of performance in oral language testing* (Unpublished doctoral dissertation). University of Reading, UK.

O'Sullivan, B. (2007). *Modelling performance in tests of spoken language.* Frankfurt am Main: Peter Lang.

O'Sullivan, B. (2011). Introduction—Professionalisation, localisation and fragmentation in language testing. In B. O'Sullivan (Ed.), *Language testing: Theories and practices* (pp. 1–12). Basingstoke: Palgrave Macmillan.

O'Sullivan, B. (2016a). Adapting tests to the local context. *New Directions in Language Assessment, special edition of the JASELE Journal*, 145–158. Tokyo: Japan Society of English Language Education & the British Council.

O'Sullivan, B. (2016b). Validity: What is it and who is it for? In Y. N. Leung (Ed.), *Epoch making in English teaching and learning: Evolution, innovation, and revolution.* Taipei: Crane Publishing.

O'Sullivan, B., & Dunlea, J. (2015). *Aptis general technical manual 1.0.* London: British Council.

O'Sullivan, B., & Weir, C. J. (2011). Test development and validation. In B. O'Sullivan (Ed.), *Language testing: Theories and practices* (pp. 13–32). Basingstoke: Palgrave Macmillan.

Porter, D. (1991a). Affective factors in language testing. In J. C. Alderson & B. North (Eds.), *Language testing in the 1990s* (pp. 32–40). London: Macmillan.

Porter, D. (1991b). Affective factors in the assessment of oral interaction: Gender and status. In S. Arnivan (Ed.), *Current developments in language testing* (pp. 92–102). Anthology Series 25. Singapore: SEAMEO Regional Language Centre.

Weir, C. J. (2005). *Language testing and validation: An evidence-based approach.* Oxford: Palgrave.

Weir, C. J. (2013). An overview of the influences on English language testing in the United Kingdom 1913–2012. In C. J. Weir, I. Vidaković, & E. D. Galaczi (Eds.), *Measured constructs: A history of the constructs underlying Cambridge English Language (ESOL) examinations 1913–2012* (pp. 1–102). Studies in Language Testing, 37. Cambridge, UK: Cambridge University Press.

Weir, C. J., & O'Sullivan, B. (2017). *Assessing English on the global stage: The British Council and English language testing, 1941–2016.* Sheffield: Equinox.

Wiseman, S. (1969). *Examinations and English education.* Manchester: Manchester University Press.

CONTRIBUTORS

Lily I-Wen Su is a distinguished professor of the Graduate Institute of Linguistics at National Taiwan University (NTU) and Executive Director of the Language Training and Testing center (LTTC), a non-profit educational foundation in Taiwan. Her research interests include discourse analysis, pragmatics, and cognitive linguistics. In addition to her research interests in linguistics, she is highly devoted to language learning and teaching. In addition to taking charge of several government-funded projects that promote English learning in Taiwan, she is also the founding director of the Academic Writing Education Center at NTU.

Cyril J. Weir (1950–2018) was Professor and Powdrill Chair in English Language Acquisition in CRELLA at the University of Bedfordshire and a Visiting Professor at the University of Reading. He was the series editor for Studies in Language Testing and member of the Editorial Board of Language Testing. His research resulted in an innovative socio-cognitive framework for language test development and validation, whose impact on English language testing has been invaluable. He advised and working tirelessly with examination boards and ministries of education in over 50 countries to improve the quality of language proficiency tests. Among his many accolades, he received the Cambridge/ILTA distinguished achievement award in 2014. In 2015, he was awarded the OBE for his services to English Language Assessment.

Jessica R. W. Wu holds a PhD in Language Testing. She is the R&D Program Director at the Language Training & Testing Center (LTTC), a non-profit educational foundation in Taiwan. She also serves as an adviser to the government on the development and administration of L1 tests. She has published

xxx Contributors

numerous articles and book chapters in the field of language testing and has presented her work at conferences around the world. She is currently the President of the Asian Association for Language Assessment (AALA, 2018–2019).

Kadeessa Abdul-Kadir (PhD) has extensive experience in English Language training and assessment. Currently she heads the Cluster for Language Excellence at Malaysia's National Institute of Public Administration (INTAN), Public Service Department, where she oversees the planning, coordinating, implementing and monitoring of the delivery of Language training and assessment for the Malaysian Public Service. Her areas of expertise include language measurement and evaluation, and ELT and ESP language teaching and assessment. She completed her doctorate in Educational Psychology at the University of Illinois, Urbana-Champaign, U.S., in 2008.

Jamie Dunlea is a Senior Researcher and Manager of the British Council's Assessment Research Group, based in London. He works on a range of language-test development and validation projects for assessment systems designed and developed by the British Council, and he collaborates on projects with researchers and organizations internationally. Jamie joined the British Council in 2013 and was previously Chief Researcher at the Eiken Foundation of Japan. He has 25 years of experience working in EFL education, first as a teacher, then in test development and production and assessment research.

Todd Fouts is a managing editor at the Eiken Foundation of Japan. He was involved in the development of the Test of English for Academic Purposes (TEAP) and currently oversees a team of content specialists who create content for the TEAP and EIKEN tests. He has lived and worked in Japan since 1990 as a teacher, writer, and test developer.

Yan Jin is professor of applied linguistics at School of Foreign Languages, Shanghai Jiao Tong University in China. She has been researching and working for the College English Test since the late 1980s and has been chair of the National College English Testing Committee since 2004.

Dan Joyce is a senior editor at the Eiken Foundation of Japan. He was involved in the development of the Test of English for Academic Purposes (TEAP) and is currently responsible for content development for the test. Prior to this project, he was involved in production of the EIKEN tests and carried out validation research.

Heesung Jun is a Senior Researcher at the TEPS Center, Language Education Institute, Seoul National University, where she works on the development and validation of English proficiency tests, including the TEPS and its family of tests. Her research interests are integrated writing assessment tasks and computer-assisted language testing.

Ja Young Kim is a Psychometrician at Gyeonggi Institute of Education, a government-affiliated research institute in Korea. She analyzes test data to evaluate item performance, conducts linking and equating, and designs test blueprints. She gained her PhD in Educational Measurement and Statistics from the University of Iowa.

Yong-Won Lee is Professor of English Linguistics in the Department of English Language and Literature at Seoul National University. He served as TEPS Center Director for years and directed, or participated in, various research and development projects for the revised TEPS and its family of tests.

Keita Nakamura is a researcher in the Research and Test Development Section at the Eiken Foundation of Japan. He has been involved in several language-test development and validation projects. His current main research area is test washback.

Barry O'Sullivan is the Head of Assessment Research & Development at the British Council where he was responsible for the design and development of the Aptis test service. He has undertaken research across many areas on language testing and assessment and its history and has worked on the development and refinement of the socio-cognitive model of test development and validation since 2000. He is particularly interested in the communication of test validation and in test localization and has presented his work at many conferences around the world, while almost 100 of his publications have appeared in a range of international journals, books, and technical reports. He has worked on many test development and validation projects over the past 25 years and advises ministries and institutions on assessment policy and practice. He is the founding president of the UK Association of Language Testing and Assessment (UKALTA) and holds honorary and visiting chairs at a number of universities globally. He was awarded a fellowship by the Academy of Social Science in the UK in 2016 and was awarded another fellowship by the Asian Association for Language Assessment in 2017.

Thi Ngoc Quynh Nguyen (also known as Quynh Nguyen) holds a PhD in Applied Linguistics from the University of Melbourne, Australia. She plays a key role in the research and development of the Vietnamese Standardized Test of English Proficiency (VSTEP). She also participates in many national and international projects on education and assessment. She reviews for some journals on second language acquisition and teacher education and has presented and published on second language education and assessment. She is

xxxii Contributors

currently the 2nd Vice President of the Asian Association for Language Assessment (AALA).

Rachel Yi-fen Wu is the Head of Testing Editorial Department at the Language Training and Testing Center (LTTC), a non-profit educational foundation in Taiwan. She has been closely involved in the research and development, test production and validation of the General English Proficiency Test (GEPT), Taiwan's first island-wide English language proficiency test. Her research interests include reading assessment, language test development and validation, and methodological approaches to linking examinations to the CEFR.

1

INTRODUCTION

Jessica R. W. Wu

Purpose of This Volume

This work aims to provide in a single volume previously unavailable access to in-depth analyses of six high-stakes English language tests, all of which have been developed and used in particular educational and cultural contexts in Asia. We will take a detailed look at the General English Proficiency Test (GEPT), the EIKEN/Test of English for Academic Purposes (TEAP), the College English Test (CET), the Test of English Proficiency developed by Seoul National University (TEPS), the Vietnam Standardized Test of English Proficiency (VSTEP), and the English Language Proficiency Assessment (ELPA) for the Malaysian Public Service. As O'Sullivan suggests in his foreword, these tests represent a radical paradigm shift in approaches to language testing. They illustrate the increasing trend towards the development of quality tests by locally based groups; that is, they are made by locals, for locals, in a specified local context. They contrast with the broad-spectrum global tests developed for worldwide use by language-testing agencies, such as the Test of English as a Foreign Language (TOEFL) and the International English Language Testing System (IELTS) (see Chapter 8).

Tests of this kind are referred to in the literature as "locally produced," "localized," or simply "local" tests. However, these terms need to be interpreted differently according to the diverse contexts within Asia. This is, in fact, one of the key messages shared in the current book, where the definition of a locally produced test will be further discussed by the various contributors. In this introduction, "locally produced" refers to a test which is produced within a specific geographical scope and is developed by a local team composed primarily of non-native speakers of English (Dunlea, 2013; Wu, 2014, 2016), albeit

2 Jessica R. W. Wu

often with input from external experts, usually native speakers of English. By contrast, an international test, such as the IELTS or TOEFL, is intended to assess learners around the world and is typically developed by native speakers of English (see further discussion of this in Chapter 8).

The enormous growth in numbers of EFL or ESL learners in these six regions has greatly increased the need to assess learners' levels of English proficiency. In addition, in reaction to the forces of globalization, many governments in Asia have incorporated locally developed English language exams into their strategic plans for enhancing their citizens' English skills. The growing need to assess learners' English language proficiency in Asia has occasioned discussion, most notably in a special issue of the *Journal of Language Testing* (2005) which promoted greater understanding of language assessment policies and practices. It presented six different Asian contexts, and provided a window into "language assessment issues both common across the varied cultural milieu in Asia and specific to each national context" (Ross, 2008, p. 5). However, it should be noted that the content of the special issue focused solely on language assessment policies and their consequences. Moreover, the cases presented in the special issue included both tests developed by local teams and those developed by international testing institutions such as the Educational Testing Service or Cambridge Assessment English. All the articles in the special issue were authored by scholars. What this volume wishes to add are the voices and practical experiences of test developers.

Given the increasing trend of developing and using locally produced tests of English in Asia, the contributors to this volume believe that the time is ripe for a volume dedicated to presenting important endeavors in the development of English language tests for high-stakes purposes in their own local context, as well as the key issues and problems that are involved. Yet this book by no means intends to present a crude comparison of the test quality or testing services provided by locally produced and international tests or to promote competition between them. Instead, it aims to provide readers with further insight into test localization arising out of the experience of test developers from the aforementioned Asian contexts. We hope that by sharing the knowledge and expertise drawn from their experiences in developing tests of English tailored to local needs, this book can engender a greater understanding of the theory and practice of test localization.

Why the LTTC Supports This Volume

This volume was commissioned by the Language Training and Testing Center (LTTC) and represents the LTTC's enduring commitment to enhancing foreign language teaching, learning, and assessment. Aside from our obvious interest in this matter as developer of the GEPT, the LTTC's long-term engagement in the Academic Forum on English Language Testing in Asia (AFELTA), whose membership is currently composed of nine testing institutions,[1] has strengthened our awareness of the pressing need to facilitate additional academic dialogues and discussions focused on the development of locally produced tests and related issues. When the LTTC hosted the AFELTA annual meeting in 2010, the theme "Language Testing in Asia: Continuity, Innovation and Synergy" was chosen to foster exchanges among AFELTA institutional members on how to meet the challenge of improving testing services to more fully support English language education within their respective contexts.

Furthermore, between 2012 and 2013 the LTTC welcomed visiting delegations from the University of Languages and International Studies, Vietnam National University, Hanoi (ULIS), who sought to learn from our GEPT experience as they developed the first-ever made-in-Vietnam standardized EFL test, later named the VSTEP, as part of the country's NFL 2020 Project. The LTTC's consultancy to ULIS continued, providing three workshops in 2014 and 2016, in which in-depth know-how concerning test development, validation, and administration were communicated to approximately 30 ULIS faculty members and research staff involved in the test development project.

As a result of the LTTC's frequent exchanges with both AFELTA members and the ULIS regarding our common interest in developing language assessment to suit local needs, we found "locally produced tests" to be a fascinating research area that has yet to be explored fully. By supporting this volume, we hope to draw more attention to this paradigm shift and continue making contributions to the language testing community, locally as well as globally.

Localization

Every test is designed for a different purpose and a different population, and its developers may view and assess language traits differently as well as describe test-taker performance in different ways (Davies, Brown, Elder, Hill, & McNamara, 1999, p. 199). Therefore, it is essential to build a more thorough appreciation of the salient characteristics that distinguish a locally produced test of English from a broad-spectrum international test of English. This localization is carried out through the process of contextual mediation in test design and development (Saville, 2009, 2010; Wu, 2016). Contextual mediation is the core strength of a locally produced test of English, representing its developers' understanding of learners' cultural backgrounds, learning experiences, world knowledge, and social needs. In other words, as Dendrinos (2013, p. 14) suggests, when developing a local test, "attention is relocated from the language itself (as an abstract meaning system) to the user (as a meaning-maker)." Such localization efforts are intended to result in the development of tests that are appropriate for local learners linguistically, visually, and even conceptually

(O'Sullivan, 2014). This explains why each of the aforementioned locally produced tests is distinctive in its own right in terms of the localization features that influence test construction and administration, as each test reflects the test-taker's communicative needs in the educational and societal systems within its intended context. Inevitably, each of these locally produced tests has its own context-specific problems and challenges. In short, localization remains the central concern with regard to the evolution, innovation, and impact of each of these locally produced language tests.

Glocalization

In addition to a focus on test localization, the notion of glocalization is also discussed as essential to understanding the dynamics and complexities that underlie the trend of using locally produced tests in Asia. Glocalization is a combination of the words "globalization" and "localization." It has been described as the process of creating a product or service with a global perspective in mind, while adjusting it to accommodate the user or consumer in a local market (see Chapter 8). Hence, the expression "think globally, act locally" has become a common principle applied to organizations, business, education, and governance. It asks that employees, students, and citizens consider the global impact of their actions. In an effort to address the impact of glocalization on language education, the LTTC has called for a paradigm shift in how English is taught to EFL or ESL learners and how their English proficiency is assessed. "Globalization and Local Interventions" was therefore the main theme chosen for the LTTC's international conference in 2016, where critical reflections on foreign language education were advocated. It is this thread that is being followed up in the current volume.

We do not intend to categorize language tests dichotomously as local or global, because the distinction between these domains is fuzzy. As Weir rightly suggests in the final chapter of this volume, glocalization may be indeed viewed as an alternative pathway in English language test provision; moreover, the glocal phenomenon in English language testing seems to manifest itself in two distinct ways in English language testing: Glocal Type 1 and Glocal Type 2. In Weir's definition of glocal tests, Glocal Type 1 refers to an international test that aims for a good fit with a particular local context (e.g., Aptis). In contrast, the case studies presented in Chapters 2–7 of this volume are Glocal Type 2 tests in that they are localized in certain ways but global in others (e.g., compliance with international standards). Although these two types of tests differ in the direction of their glocalization, Weir reminds us that both tests should establish their suitability for local use and demonstrate validity for the local context.

Therefore, by inviting the authors to review their Glocal Type 2 tests in terms of both local and global features, we can gain a better understanding of how to strike a balance between globalization and local interventions when designing a test that is more appropriate for its intended purpose and target learners.

Structure of the Book

This volume consists of eight chapters. Chapters 2–7, written by colleagues who represent their respective test bodies, cover the aforementioned English language tests developed and used in Asia. The tests are categorized into three groups in accordance with their target test-takers, from a wider range to a narrower one: tests for general public (Chapters 2–4), tests targeting the tertiary level (Chapters 5 and 6), and tests for a specific group of people (Chapter 7). A brief description of each test is provided in the following paragraphs.[2]

Chapter 2 introduces the GEPT, a five-level testing system developed and administered by the LTTC since 2000. It targets English learners at all levels in Taiwan. The test is designed to correspond to Taiwan's English education framework and meet the specific self-assessment needs of English learners in Taiwan, as well as provide institutions and schools with a reference for evaluating the English proficiency levels of their job applicants, employees, and students. The test has been widely recognized in Taiwan, and in recent years it has also been recognized by a growing number of educational institutions worldwide.

Chapter 3 introduces the TEPS, developed and administered by Seoul National University's Language Education Institute since 1999. The TEPS is a large-scale, paper-based, standardized English test that is intended to measure the English language proficiency of Korean learners of English. TEPS scores are recognized by many governmental and non-governmental organizations, schools, and universities in Korea.

Chapter 4 introduces the VSTEP, the specifications and format of which were developed by the University of Languages and International Studies, Vietnam National University, Hanoi (ULIS). It was released nationally under the auspices of the Ministry of Education and Training in 2015. The VSTEP is intended for general purposes and targets adult test-takers aged 18 years or older in Vietnam.

Chapter 5 introduces the CET, which is designed to assess the English proficiency of undergraduate and postgraduate students in China. It consists of two levels, CET-4 and CET-6, and is meant to ensure that students reach the required English levels specified in the National College English Teaching Syllabuses. The CET has been administered in China for about 30 years.

Chapter 6 introduces two proficiency testing programs produced in and for the context of Japan. EIKEN is a seven-level testing system developed and widely administered by the Eiken Foundation of Japan since 1963. The development of EIKEN will thus provide a historical framework for the discussion of both tests in this chapter. The TEAP was introduced in 2012 as a collaborative

6 Jessica R. W. Wu

project between the Eiken Foundation and Sophia University with the specific intention of contributing to the reform of university entrance exams in Japan.

Chapter 7 introduces the ELPA, originally developed through a collaborative project between National Institute of Public Administration (INTAN) and the British Council. The ELPA was first launched in 1998 as a test assessing the workplace use of English by junior- and middle-level management officers in the Administrative and Diplomatic Service in Malaysia. It is administered by INTAN's English Language Unit and is among the requirements for career development and advancement.

To help readers compare the similarities and differences among these tests, each chapter has the same structure and contains the following content:

- a history of the particular locally produced test, covering the origins of the test and milestones in its development;
- reasons that the test is considered more appropriate to its specific context than an international test which may serve a similar purpose—namely, in what ways the test is localized to make it more appropriate for its test-takers. In addition, a number of concerns (e.g., the test's relationship to the educational system; the needs of target test-takers; specific task or text parameters such as lexis, structure, discourse, content, topic, and evaluative criteria) that were taken into consideration when the test was developed are discussed;
- intended and unintended societal impacts of the test that have been observed;
- innovative features that the test is associated with in both practical and research contexts (i.e., how they have contributed to the field of language testing);
- evidence that has been generated to support claims that the test meets international standards or codes of practice (i.e., what procedures have been employed to enhance the quality and fairness of the test, and whether the test has been empirically linked to a framework of reference such as the CEFR); and
- critical reflection on future improvement.

The book is intended for a broad audience, including researchers in the fields of language testing and assessment, language education, and intercultural studies; language test developers, teaching material developers, and curriculum designers who are preparing localized materials for learners in particular contexts; and instructors and graduate students involved in courses on language testing, bilingual education, and intercultural communication.

Final Remarks

The locally produced tests of English collected in this volume represent the perspectives and initiatives of professionals who endeavor to enhance the relevance of English language assessment to learners' needs, education policy, and cultural values within their respective local contexts. However, as illustrated in their respective chapters, the authors do not merely confine their efforts to their own local contexts. Instead, they are open to interaction with the global testing community. We hope that this volume can serve as a catalyst for further inquiries into appropriate localization in English language testing when it is used to make specific claims about a particular population in the context for which it has been developed (O'Sullivan, 2011).

Last but not least, we agree with Weir's conclusion in the end of this book that the expertise gained in the positive impact and legacy of these locally produced English language tests in Asia is transferable to other L2 tests. Therefore, we trust (or hope) that the content of this volume can also be of benefit to other L2 language testing research and test development which also aims to bridge test localization and global standards.

Notes

1. The nine AFELTA members (in alphabetical order): College Entrance Examination Center (CEEC), College English Test Committee (CET), Eiken Foundation (EIKEN), Hong Kong Examinations & Assessment Authority (HKEAA), Korea English Language Testing Association (KELTA), Korea Institute for Curriculum and Evaluation (KICE), Language Training & Testing Center (LTTC), Singapore Examinations and Assessment Board (SEAB), and University of Languages and International Studies, Vietnam National University, Hanoi (ULIS).
2. The official websites of the tests (in alphabetical order) covered in this work are: CET (http://cet.neea.edu.cn/), EIKEN (www.eiken.or.jp/eiken/en/eiken-tests/), ELPA (www.intanbk.intan.my/iportal/en/elpa-elpa), GEPT (www.gept.org.tw/), TEPS (http://en.teps.or.kr/index.html), VSTEP (http://vstep.vnu.edu.vn/).

References

Davies, A., Brown, A., Elder, C., Hill, K., & McNamara, R. (1999). *Dictionary of Language Testing.* Studies in Language Testing, 7. Cambridge, UK: Cambridge University Press.

Dendrinos, B. (2013). Social meanings in global-glocal language proficiency exams. In D. Tsagari, S. Papadima-Sophocleous, & S. Ioannou-Georgiou (Eds.), *International experiences in language testing and assessment* (pp. 33–57). Frankfurt am Main: Peter Lang.

Dunlea, J. (2013, November). *Recognition for locally developed tests: An overview of regional approaches.* Plenary presentation at the 1st British Council New Directions in English Language Assessment conference, Beijing, China.

O'Sullivan, B. (2011). Language testing. In J. Simpson (Ed.), *Routledge handbook of applied linguistics.* Oxford: Routledge.

O'Sullivan, B. (2014, September). *Adapting tests to the local context.* Plenary presentation at the 2nd British Council New Directions in English Language Assessment conference, Tokyo, Japan.

Ross, S. (2008). Language testing in Asia: Evolution, innovation, and policy challenges. *Language Testing, 25*(1), 5–13.

Saville, N. (2009). *Developing a model for investigating the impact of language assessment within educational contexts by a public examination provider* (Unpublished doctoral dissertation). University of Bedfordshire, UK.

Saville, N. (2010). Developing a model for investigating the impact of language assessment. *Research Notes, 42*, 2–8.

Wu, J. (2014, April). *Ensuring quality and fairness in the Asian EFL context: Challenges and opportunities*. Plenary presentation at the 5th ALTE International Conference, Paris, France.

Wu, J. (2016, October). *A locally appropriate English language test—locality, globality & validity*. Plenary presentation at the 4th British Council New Directions in English Language Assessment conference, Hanoi, Vietnam.

2

THE GENERAL ENGLISH PROFICIENCY TEST IN TAIWAN

Past, Present, and Future

Rachel Yi-fen Wu

Introduction

The General English Proficiency Test (GEPT) is a level-based criterion-referenced EFL testing system tailored to learners of English in Taiwan. The GEPT was developed by the Language Training and Testing Center (LTTC)[1] and was first administered in 2000. The key objectives of the GEPT are to encourage continued learning and the balanced development of listening, reading, speaking, and writing abilities. Each GEPT level is targeted at learners whose English proficiency level corresponds to that expected at every major educational stage in Taiwan. The GEPT Elementary Level is intended to provide an attainable target for students in lower secondary education (typically aged 12 to 15), the Intermediate Level for students in upper secondary education (aged 15 to 18), the High-Intermediate Level for tertiary level students who major in subjects other than English, and the Advanced and Superior Levels for those tertiary level students who major in English in Taiwan. The test places equal weight on listening, reading, speaking, and writing at all levels. To provide further information for the interpretation of scores and validation evidence for the GEPT level framework, the GEPT has been linked with the *Common European Framework of Reference for Languages: Learning, teaching, assessment* (CEFR, Council of Europe, 2001). The Elementary, Intermediate, High-Intermediate, and Advanced Levels of the GEPT tests largely corresponded to CEFR levels A2, B1, B2, and C1, respectively (Brunfaut & Harding, 2014; Green, Inoue, & Nakatsuhara, 2017; Knoch, 2016; Wu & Wu, 2010); see Table 2.1.

The GEPT has received extensive recognition of its quality both domestically and internationally since its launch and is now the most widely taken English proficiency examination in Taiwan. As of December 2016, more than

10 Rachel Yi-fen Wu

TABLE 2.1 The GEPT Level Framework

GEPT Level	General Level Descriptors	Targeted Educational Stage	CEFR
Elementary	Test takers who pass this level have basic ability in English and can understand and use rudimentary language needed in daily life.	Lower secondary	A2
Intermediate	Test takers who pass this level can use basic English to communicate about topics in daily life.	Upper secondary	B1
High-Intermediate	Test takers who pass this level have a generally effective command of English and can handle a broader range of topics.	Tertiary (those who major in subjects other than English)	B2
Advanced	Test takers who pass this level have English language abilities that enable them to communicate fluently with only occasional errors related to language accuracy and appropriateness, and to handle academic or professional requirements and situations.	Tertiary (those who major in English)	C1 and above
Superior	Test takers who pass this level have English language abilities almost equivalent to the linguistic competence of a native speaker who has received higher education. They can use English effectively and precisely under all kinds of circumstances.		

Note. The Superior Level was not addressed by the CEFR linking studies as it is only administered intermittently, at the request of sponsoring schools or institutions.

seven million Taiwanese learners of English, almost a third of Taiwan's total population, have taken the GEPT. The test results are used by hundreds of government sectors and private enterprises and over 400 schools for various purposes, including:

- by the Directorate-General of Personnel Administration for certification of the English language abilities of civil servants seeking promotion;
- by the Ministry of Education (MoE) for selection of qualified students and teachers for government sponsored study overseas and of qualified teachers who wish to apply for English-teaching positions in schools;
- by private organizations and enterprises for evaluation of the English abilities of employees and job applicants;
- by more than 100 higher education institutions as a criterion for admission, placement, or graduation, and for the selection of local students for international exchange programs; and
- by secondary schools nationwide to evaluate learning outcomes.

Following this brief introduction, an overview of how the GEPT has been developed is provided. I then examine how it is used to bring about changes in the teaching and learning of English in its social context. Selected GEPT validation activities are presented in terms of Weir's (2005) socio-cognitive validation framework[2] to exemplify the sustained effort to establish and maintain the reliability and validity of the GEPT. The impact of the GEPT on EFL education in Taiwan is then examined. The chapter concludes with a discussion of challenges that lie ahead for the GEPT and future directions for the research and implementation of the test.

Overview of GEPT Development

In Taiwan, English first became a compulsory subject at the higher secondary school level in 1949. The policy was extended to the lower secondary school level in 1968 and further to the primary school level in 2001. Before the MoE implemented *The Grade 1–9 Integrated Coordinated Curriculum* in 2001, formal English education at the secondary level emphasized reading skills with a heavy focus on grammar and vocabulary, due to large class sizes and pressure stemming from highly competitive high school and college entrance examinations. Success in these examinations hinges upon knowledge of grammar and vocabulary, as well as reading skills. As examination-oriented learning and a "teaching to the test" approach have prevailed in formal education, students have naturally placed more emphasis on developing reading skills, while other skills of the English language have generally been neglected. The implementation of additional large-scale listening and speaking tests has been relatively challenging since test administration requires a high level of logistical support. Thus, college entrance examinations in Taiwan did not include a listening component until 2013, and senior high school entrance examinations did not do so until 2014. At the tertiary level, there has been no core English curriculum to guide teachers in deciding what to teach. The grammar-translation and audiolingual approaches have remained dominant in classrooms. Consequently, students'

12 Rachel Yi-fen Wu

abilities to write and speak English are largely underdeveloped and undervalued. Most Taiwanese students have been unable to communicate in the language they have spent years learning.

The GEPT as a Means to Bring About Changes in EFL Education in Taiwan

With the intention of shifting English learning to a more communicative orientation, in 1997 the LTTC initiated a project to develop a level-based testing system, now officially known as the LTTC GEPT. The GEPT was a revolution in mainstream English language exams in Taiwan at that time because it assessed all four language skills. At the beginning of the GEPT project, the LTTC invited scholars and experts in English language teaching and testing from tertiary institutions around Taiwan to assist it in forming a Testing Research Committee and a Testing Advisory Committee, comprised of a total of 22 professors representing English learning and teaching contexts from different regions of Taiwan to ensure a fair reflection of ideological inclinations and geographical areas during the process of defining the constructs of the GEPT. The Committees met on a regular basis to share expertise and work towards the common goal of developing an English language proficiency testing system specifically tailored to the local learning context and linguistic needs in terms of learning objectives and communication needs.

Before the GEPT was introduced, learners of English in Taiwan relied on international examinations, such as the Test of English as a Foreign Language (TOEFL), the International English Language Testing System (IELTS), and the Test of English for International Communication (TOEIC), to demonstrate their English proficiency. The landscape for the use of English language examinations changed drastically after the GEPT came into operation. In 2005, five years after the GEPT was launched, the MoE implemented an English language proficiency benchmark under *MoE Major Policy Objectives for 2005–2008* (教育部未來四年施政主軸行動方案; Ministry of Education, 2004), and GEPT passing rates were used as an indicator to measure the effectiveness of this policy (Chu & Yeh, 2017, p. 1063). The MoE called for 50% of university students to pass the GEPT Intermediate Level and 50% of technical college students to pass the GEPT Elementary Level by 2007. Although the policy did not meet the MoE's expectations to enhance the overall English proficiency of students in higher education, and its washback on teaching and learning has been limited (Chu & Yeh, 2017, p. 1070), teachers and students maintain positive and supportive attitudes towards the policy (Chu & Yeh, 2017, p. 1066–1067; Wu & Lee, 2017), and the implementation of the policy has led to a greater awareness of the importance of learning English after graduation from high school (Chen & Liu, 2007; Cheng et al., 2014; Liao, 2016; Vongpumivitch, 2012a).

Government Support for the GEPT Project and Alignment With CEFR

Due to budgetary constraints, the LTTC initially allotted 10 years for the development and launch of the testing system. In 1999, the MoE recognized that the goal of the GEPT project was aligned with its mission titled *Towards a Learning Society* (邁向學習社會), which aimed to advance Taiwanese society in the 21st century through continuing education. Thus, the MoE decided to provide a three-year subsidy to the LTTC to expedite the R&D process for the GEPT. With the MoE's financial support, the GEPT development project came to completion in July 2002; the first GEPT level, Intermediate, was launched in 2000, followed by the Elementary and High-Intermediate Levels in 2001, the Advanced Level in 2002, and the Superior Level in 2004.

In 2004, the Executive Yuan, Taiwan's main cabinet-level government agency, issued a policy titled *Measures to Enhance the English Proficiency of Civil Servants* (提升公務人員英語能力改進措施),[3] which set a goal for 50% of civil servants to pass the GEPT Elementary or Intermediate Levels or other certified English exams within three years. At that time, there were various English exams in use besides the GEPT. In 2005, the MoE decided to adopt an international yardstick, the CEFR, and requested that all major large-scale standardized English exams administered in Taiwan be mapped against it for comparative purposes. That same year, the LTTC registered with the Council of Europe and followed the procedures proposed by the *Manual* (Council of Europe, 2003) to relate the GEPT to the CEFR levels (Wu & Wu, 2010). The results showed that the Elementary, Intermediate, High-Intermediate, and Advanced Levels of the GEPT tests largely corresponded to CEFR levels A2, B1, B2, and C1, respectively.

Recognition of GEPT Scores by International Institutions

The GEPT has been administered at nearly 200 different venues in Taiwan, as well as to Taiwanese students outside Taiwan, for example in Korea since 2016, allowing examinees to choose the test location most convenient for them. The LTTC has also endeavored to expand the international recognition of the GEPT. Currently, GEPT scores are used by over 100 prestigious universities in Hong Kong, Japan, France, Germany, the UK, and the U.S. when admitting Taiwanese students to degree, exchange, and summer programs. For tertiary-level students who have taken the GEPT to demonstrate that their English language proficiency meets universities' English language requirements, they do not have to take additional English tests such as TOEFL and IELTS when they seek further studies or apply for exchange programs at these overseas universities.

14 Rachel Yi-fen Wu

Local Features of the GEPT

The GEPT is locally developed and operated. Since the GEPT design process was initiated, the LTTC's in-house R&D team has been working closely with the GEPT Research and GEPT Advisory Committees, which consist of external scholars and experts in English language teaching and testing from tertiary institutions across Taiwan, to develop the test's five-level framework. All professionals and academics involved in developing and administering the exams are familiar with the Taiwanese educational context and with local testing practices, which enables the GEPT to address the specific needs of local learners of English.

In addition to the guidance of local academics from the Committees, the GEPT benefits from the insight of international scholars in the field of language testing and assessment. Professor Cyril Weir joined the GEPT Research Committee in 2001 when the Advanced and Superior Levels were under development, and later continued to assist with validation of the GEPT as an external consultant. In 2008, Professors Charles Alderson, Lyle Bachman, Antony Kunnan, and Tim McNamara accepted the LTTC's invitation to provide consultancy and share their expertise on matters including diagnostic assessment, criterion-referenced test validation, test fairness, and performance-based testing.

GEPT content and scoring are based on a common language core of traditionally standard forms of English. In Taiwan, this means standard American English since local learners receive much greater exposure to American English textbooks and media than to other standard varieties. As such, the content of the GEPT mostly reflects standard American English conventions with regard to grammar, spelling, punctuation, and accents in listening tests. Nevertheless, in terms of assessment criteria for speaking and writing tasks, examinees' responses to GEPT speaking tasks are acceptable in all varieties and accents of English, provided they do not interfere with communication, and various Standard English writing conventions are accepted if used consistently for GEPT writing tasks.

Localization of the GEPT is also evidenced in other important ways. The following section outlines how localization of the GEPT is manifested in task design, topic selection, and lexical choice.

Task Design

The GEPT task design reflects assessment activities with which Taiwanese learners at different stages are familiar. For the first two levels of the GEPT, Elementary and Intermediate, the test content is guided by the MoE's curriculum objectives for junior and senior high schools, respectively. Because there is no such curriculum at the tertiary level, the upper levels of the GEPT were developed on the basis of the expectations of stakeholders in English education in Taiwan as identified through textbook analysis, needs analysis, and teachers' forms (the Language Training and Testing Center, 1997, 1999, 2000a, 2000b, 2002a, 2002b).

At the initial stage of the GEPT design process, the LTTC in-house R&D team worked closely with the GEPT Research and GEPT Advisory Committees to develop the five-level framework and can-do descriptors corresponding to different levels of the GEPT. Based on the can-do descriptors, the LTTC R&D team developed test specifications and pilot versions of test tasks. These tasks were administered to representative samples selected from the target population at each specified level, in order to assess whether the tasks were at an appropriate level of difficulty. During this stage, stakeholder perception surveys were given to students, teachers, and administrators to collect their views regarding various aspects of the GEPT. Overall, more than 80% of students and teachers perceived that the content of the reading tests was highly relevant to what they learned or taught in school, and that the test results accurately reflected students' English abilities. Based on the pilot test performances and survey results and through consultation with the GEPT Research and Advisory Committees, the satisfactory level of proficiency and the cut scores corresponding to each GEPT level were determined. For the formats and passing standards of the different levels of the GEPT, see Table 2.2.

One of the unique features of the GEPT, compared to other large-scale international examinations, is that its tasks measure translation competence. Translation is considered a fifth skill alongside listening, reading, speaking, and writing in English language education in Taiwan. Chinese-to-English translation is not only an integral part of Taiwan's English curriculum, as a means to develop intercultural communicative competence, it is also included in major English examinations in Taiwan, such as college entrance and civil service examinations. The GEPT Writing Tests at the Intermediate and High-Intermediate Levels include two parts, *Part 1 Chinese to English Translation*, and *Part 2 Guided Writing*. In completing Guided Writing tasks, examinees may engage in circumlocution to avoid the need to use words or structures that they do not know. In *Part 1 Chinese to English Translation*, source texts are designed to examine grammar, vocabulary, sentence structures, cohesive devices, and other language points that Taiwanese learners at the Intermediate and High-Intermediate Levels may not yet have assimilated. After each test administration, common mistakes are reported online along with score summary statistics in order to raise learners' awareness of the differences between the target and their native languages and thereby counteract L1 (first language) interference in English language learning.

Topic Selection

Learners' ages, prior learning experience, cultural experience, and world knowledge have been taken into account in the development of GEPT tasks at different levels. To encourage examinees' engagement with these tasks

TABLE 2.2 Test Formats and Passing Standards of the GEPT

GEPT Level	Module	Test Format	Test Time	Max. Score	Passing Standard
Elementary	Listening	Picture description Answering questions Conversations	Approx. 20 minutes	120	The total score is equal to or above 160, with each subtest score no lower than 72.
	Reading	Sentence completion Cloze Reading comprehension	35 minutes	120	
	Speaking	Repeating Reading Aloud Answering questions	Approx. 10 minutes	100	80
	Writing	Sentence writing Paragraph writing	40 minutes	100	70
Intermediate	Listening	Picture description Answering questions Conversations	Approx. 30 minutes	120	The total score is equal to or above 160, with each subtest score no lower than 72.
	Reading	Sentence completion Cloze Reading comprehension	45 minutes	120	
	Speaking	Reading aloud Answering questions Picture description	Approx. 15 minutes	100	80
	Writing	Chinese–English translation Guided writing	40 minutes	100	80

High-Intermediate	Listening	Answering questions Conversations Short talks	Approx. 35 minutes	120	The total score is equal to or above 160, with each subtest score no lower than 72.
	Reading	Sentence completion Cloze Reading comprehension	50 minutes	120	
	Speaking	Answering questions Picture description Discussion	Approx. 15 minutes	100	80
	Writing	Chinese–English translation Guided writing	50 minutes	100	80
Advanced	Listening	Short conversations & talks Long conversations Long talks	Approx. 55 minutes	120	The total score is equal to or above 150, with each subtest score no lower than 64.
	Reading	Expeditious reading Careful reading	20 minutes 50 minutes	120	
	Speaking	Warm-up questions Information exchange and discussion Presentation	Approx. 25 minutes	Band 5	Band 3
	Writing	A 250-word essay based on 2 articles A 250-word essay based on 2 charts	60 minutes 45 minutes	Band 5	Band 3
Superior	Integrated Writing	A 750-word essay based on a 10–15 min. multimedia program and a 3,000-word article	3 hours	—	Pass
	Integrated Speaking	Face-to-face presentation Follow-up questions & answers	Approx. 50 minutes	—	Pass

18 Rachel Yi-fen Wu

(Bachman, 1996, pp. 25–26), each GEPT test paper includes topics that are relevant to the life and cultural experiences of the target examinees. Item writers are instructed to select topics that are interesting, informative, and educational. While they are encouraged to write about contemporary issues in Taiwanese contexts and on themes related to local culture, items on foreign cultures and global issues are also welcome.

GEPT Wordlists

The lexical needs of L2 learners may "differ across contexts, proficiency levels, L1 and cultural backgrounds, and personal aims" (Plonsky & Oswald, 2014, p. 766). The LTTC developed the GEPT Wordlists at the Elementary, Intermediate, and High-Intermediate Levels in consultation with local academics. One of the main purposes of the GEPT Wordlists is to guide item writers to maintain a consistent level of difficulty in the test tasks they produce. The GEPT Elementary Level Wordlist, composed of 2,263 words, was compiled from Collins COBUILD English Dictionary frequency bands 1 and 2 (totaling around 1,900 words), the *Senior High English Wordlist for Reference* (Chang et al., 1998; Jeng, Chang, Cheng, & Gu, 2002), published by Taiwan's College Entrance Examination Center, Levels 1 and 2 (totaling 2,160 words), and *2000 Common English Words for Elementary and Junior High School Students*, published by Taiwan's MoE in 2003. The GEPT Intermediate Level Wordlist, composed of 4,947 words, was compiled from Collins COBUILD English Dictionary frequency bands 1 to 4 (totaling around 6,600) and Taiwan's *Senior High English Wordlist for Reference* Levels 1 and 4 (totaling 4,320 words). The GEPT High-Intermediate Level Wordlist, composed of 8,238 words, was compiled from Collins COBUILD English Dictionary frequency bands 1 to 5 (totaling around 14,700 words) and the *Senior High English Wordlist for Reference* Levels 1 and 6 (totaling 6,480 words). The GEPT R&D team prepared a draft list of words that appear in more than one source, and local consultants then manually selected, on the basis of their pedagogical usefulness, those that are likely to be encountered by learners of English in Taiwan at the specified level. For example, words of very low frequency in the *Collins COBUILD English Dictionary* (e.g., Mandarin, mango, mosquito, pineapple, and typhoon) were identified by local academics as commonly used words for everyday life in Taiwan and were therefore included in the GEPT Elementary Wordlist. Lexical items are labeled with word class (e.g., noun, verb, and adjective) and placed in alphabetical order. In case of words with different British and American spelling, the American spelling is given as the headword, and the British spelling alternate is provided in a separate column. In writing test items, writers are instructed to use no fewer than 95% of the words from the relevant wordlist. The GEPT Wordlists are also publicly available on the official LTTC website at www.lttc. ntu.edu.tw/wordlist.htm.

Quality Control and Test Fairness

The LTTC follows a detailed code of practice that ensures quality and fairness throughout the testing process. The following section describes the GEPT quality assurance and quality control procedures in test production, the scoring process, test delivery, and testing services.

Test Paper Production

To maintain test reliability and score dependability, the content of all tests is based on the LTTC GEPT Specifications at the relevant level, and stringent guidelines are followed throughout the test production process to ensure all test papers conform to the specifications. The GEPT test materials are written by those who have experience in English teaching and have a clear understanding of the local English-learning environments. Item writers are required to sign an agreement protecting the confidentiality of the items they submit. Before they begin, they undertake item-writing training and receive instructions to guide them through the process of preparing the assigned test materials. Once the first drafts have been written, editors review them to check whether they are technically accurate and clearly worded, and to ensure they are not misleading, deliberately tricky, or biased in any aspect, particularly with regards to gender, residential location, and educational background. After editing changes are made, the items are reviewed and approved by a small team of internal technical reviewers to ensure the content matches the specifications; the distractors are plausible but not possibly correct; and that there is only one correct answer. Once reviewed, edited, and approved, items are tagged with the cognitive processes targeted (e.g., main idea, specific details, and inferences), contextual features (e.g., text type, language function, and topic), and estimates of item difficulty, and then placed in an item bank. Thereafter, items are selected from the item bank and compiled into pre-test papers according to the test specifications. Pre-test papers are then administered to a representative sample of the target population, and statistical attributes of the test items are obtained. Data such as item difficulty, item discrimination, and differential item functioning (DIF) statistics are then reviewed to determine whether the items have performed as intended. Items with unsatisfactory statistics are flagged for review by content experts to resolve the problems. They are then saved in the item bank for use in a future pre-test. To ensure consistency in operational examinations (i.e., equivalence of each test form at both the content and measurement level), items are drawn from the item bank based on their statistical attributes, in terms of item difficulty and discrimination power, and the test specifications, in terms of text length, average sentence length, topic coverage, genre, range of vocabulary, and cognitive processing, ensuring that the test content is a fair reflection of the constructs. Before they are formally administered,

20 Rachel Yi-fen Wu

the test papers are again carefully reviewed using both expert judgement and Wordsmith (Scott, 2008) and edited.

Satisfaction surveys are routinely distributed to stakeholders in order to evaluate the quality of test administration and check whether the tests meet public expectations. When collecting and processing personal data, the LTTC strictly adheres to the Personal Information Protection Act of Taiwan to protect and secure personal information.

Scoring

After each test administration, answers to fixed-response questions from the listening and reading tests are machine-scored, and responses to open-ended questions, as well as the writing and speaking tests, are marked by human raters. In the case of machine scoring, test statistics, including the mean, standard deviation, standard error of measurement, highest and lowest scores obtained, percentage of candidates passing, test reliability (Cronbach's alpha), Classical Test Theory (CTT) and Item Response Theory (IRT) item analysis, Confirmatory Factor Analysis (CFA), and DIF are obtained and examined for the purpose of monitoring the consistency of test papers. In the case of human rating, all responses are double-marked to reduce subjectivity in marking and ensure reliability of results. Raters of the GEPT Speaking and Writing Tests are in-service English language teachers at the secondary and tertiary levels or those in adult education who have a clear understanding of the local English-learning environments. To ensure that raters understand and apply the scoring criteria accurately and consistently, each official marking session begins with raters attending training sessions and completing a set of calibration tests to demonstrate that their scoring is on track. For the marking sessions, the GEPT on-screen marking system randomly pairs two raters. Meanwhile, "scoring leaders," comprised of members of the LTTC R&D teams, evaluate raters' performances online based on summary statistics provided by the marking system, which includes the mean, standard deviation, distribution of band scores, and correlations. If the difference between an individual rater's average ratings and the average of the overall rating statistics exceeds an acceptable range (i.e., greater than or equal to 0.5 band score on a scale of 0 to 5), the rater is flagged. The rater then receives a notice to confer with a scoring leader. In addition, when scores from two raters differ by more than one band score, they are considered discrepant, and resolution by a senior rater is required before scores are reported. Individual raters are also flagged if their exact agreement rate is significantly lower or higher than that of other raters. Scoring leaders mentor these raters; if raters are consistently scoring off target, their scores may be cancelled and their responses rescored by a third rater. Average agreement rates (i.e., the percentage of double-rated responses with acceptable difference in the two ratings) for the GEPT Speaking and Writing Tests are 85–95%.

Ongoing Quality Monitoring

To ensure the validity and reliability of the GEPT and align it with international standards, a variety of in-house studies have been conducted through collaboration (e.g., Chan, Wu, & Weir, 2014; Wu, Yeh, Dunlea, & Spiby, 2016) and through contracts with external researchers (e.g., Bax & Chan, 2016; Brunfaut & Harding, 2014; Green et al., 2017; Knoch, 2016; Kunnan & Carr, 2015; Qian, 2014; Weir, Chan, & Nakatsuhara, 2013; Yu & Lin, 2014). The LTTC established the LTTC–GEPT Research Grants Program in 2010, and since then it has allocated funding for educational institutions and independent researchers with relevant expertise and experience to undertake various GEPT validation projects. Over the years, researchers from Australia, Hong Kong, the U.S., and the UK have conducted studies on GEPT–CEFR linking (Brunfaut & Harding, 2014; Green et al., 2017; Knoch, 2016), cognitive validity (Bax & Chan, 2016; Yu & Lin, 2014), criterion-related validation (Kunnan & Carr, 2015; Weir et al., 2013) and register analysis (Qian, 2014). Research findings have been reported to professionals and lay audiences through a variety of channels, such as in newspapers, magazines, books, and research reports published in academic journals and on the LTTC website (www.lttc.ntu.edu. tw/thesis.htm), as well as conference papers presented at the Academic Forum on English Language Testing in Asia (AFELTA), the Asian Association for Language Assessment (AALA), the Japan Language Testing Association (JLTA), the Association of Language Testers in Europe (ALTE), the European Association for Language Testing and Assessment (EALTA), the Language Testing Research Colloquium (LTRC), and New Directions English and Global Education Dialogue. These efforts reflect Dendrinos' (2013, p. 41) view of glocalization, which "involves locally operated schemes, set up to serve domestic social conditions and needs, which are informed by international research and assessment practice." By interacting frequently with other testing and expert bodies, the LTTC aims to continuously improve the quality of its research and administration in the field of language testing.

In keeping with this objective, the LTTC regularly reviews and updates the GEPT, ensuring that the testing system meets the current needs of stakeholders and reflects the latest findings in English language teaching and assessment practices. For example, following Wu and Wu's (2007) GEPT Reading–CEFR linking study, Ma and Li (2009) conducted textbook analysis and a survey of university teachers in Taiwan. The results showed that longer texts and a greater variety of text types were necessary in order to assess higher levels of cognitive processing. Thus, these features were introduced in the GEPT High-Intermediate Level Reading Test in 2010. In December 2012, the LTTC adopted the ISO 9001 Quality Management System standard, and in 2013 the GEPT testing service was awarded the ISO 9001:2008 certification, the first language test developed in Taiwan to receive such a certification.

A Posteriori Validation of the GEPT

The LTTC continually collects empirical evidence to establish various aspects of the validity of the GEPT. To provide an overview of GEPT validation activities, selected studies are outlined in the following paragraphs in terms of the key components of the socio-cognitive framework for test validation that Weir (2005) proposed and further explicated (Khalifa & Weir, 2009; O'Sullivan & Weir, 2011). The socio-cognitive validation model conceptualizes the relationships among examinee characteristics, the contextual characteristics of target language use (TLU) tasks, language knowledge, the cognitive processing skills of language users, scoring within and across test administrations, and external criterion measures coupled with interpretation of test scores. As language users play a central role in the model, this makes it well-suited to guiding the data collection and research agendas of validation studies of glocal examinations, whose attention is "relocated from the language itself to the user" (Dendrinos, 2013, p. 48). The GEPT validation studies exemplified here cover research on the five validation components of the socio-cognitive validation framework (see Figure 2.1).

Context and Cognitive Validity

In the socio-cognitive validation framework, context and cognitive validity are concerned with the extent to which test tasks, performed under specified conditions that approximate those in real life, can elicit the cognitive operations required in real-life language processing (Weir, 2005, pp. 17–21). This section outlines studies by Chan et al. (2014) and Bax and Chan (2016), which exemplify the LTTC's efforts to provide evidence for the context and cognitive validity of the GEPT.

Chan et al. (2014) examined the relationship between the GEPT Advanced Level (CEFR C1) Writing Test and real-life academic writing tasks in university courses in the UK in terms of contextual features and the cognitive processes elicited. The GEPT Advanced Level Writing Test measures examinees' ability to write in an academic environment. The scope of this study was limited to Task 1, in which examinees first summarize the main ideas from two articles that express opposing points of view on the same topic, and then express their personal opinions. To examine the degree of correspondence between the overall task setting and input text features of the target academic writing tasks and those of the GEPT writing tasks, both expert judgment (to evaluate the overall task setting of the real-life and GEPT tasks) and automated textual analysis (to analyze the features of the input texts, including lexical complexity, syntactic complexity, and degree of coherence) were applied. The results showed that the overall task setting and difficulty level were comparable between the GEPT and real-life input texts. The cognitive processes elicited by

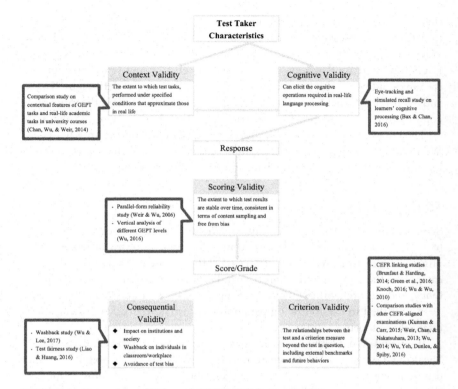

FIGURE 2.1 Overview of Selected GEPT Validation Studies

Source: Adapted from Weir's (2005) framework

the GEPT writing task were compared to the real-life academic writing tasks through a cognitive processing questionnaire. Both the questionnaire results and exploratory factor analyses showed that the GEPT writing task was largely able to elicit the same underlying cognitive processes as the real-life tasks did. The high degree of similarity between test and real-life conditions in the findings of this study supports claims about the context and cognitive validity of the GEPT Advanced Writing Task 1.

Bax and Chan (2016) investigated the cognitive validity of the GEPT Reading Tests at the High-Intermediate (CEFR B2) and Advanced (CEFR C1) Levels, using eye-tracking technology and stimulated recall interviews and surveys. Representative reading tasks were selected from the GEPT High-Intermediate and Advanced Level Reading Tests. Taiwanese students studying in graduate-level programs at UK universities were recruited to complete the tasks on a computer, and their gaze behavior was tracked. Immediately after each student had completed each individual task, they reported the cognitive processes

24 Rachel Yi-fen Wu

they employed by using a Reading Process Checklist, and some participated in a further investigation using a stimulated recall interview while viewing video footage of their gaze patterns. The results showed that while the GEPT High-Intermediate Reading Tests successfully elicited and tested an appropriate range of lower- and higher-level cognitive processes, as defined by Khalifa and Weir (2009), the Advanced Reading Tests not only elicited the same set of cognitive processes as the High-Intermediate Tests but also evinced the highest level, and therefore the most difficult cognitive operation, in Khalifa and Weir's (2009) model. The findings supported claims about the cognitive validity of the GEPT High-Intermediate and Advanced Reading Tests.

Scoring Validity

Scoring validity in the socio-cognitive validation model concerns "the extent to which test results are stable over time, consistent in terms of content sampling and free from bias" and covers reliability, which has traditionally been categorized as test-retest reliability, parallel forms reliability, internal consistency, and rater reliability (Weir, 2005, pp. 23–24). Weir and Wu 2006 and Wu 2016, outlined in the following paragraphs, illustrate the LTTC's attention to establishing scoring validity.

Weir and Wu (2006) focused on a horizontal comparison of the GEPT Speaking Tests at the Intermediate Level and investigated the extent to which different speaking test forms were comparable in terms of code complexity (lexical and syntactical difficulty), cognitive complexity (content familiarity and information processing), and communicative demand (time pressure). In this study, GEPT Intermediate Level target examinees were recruited from those who registered for the operational GEPT Intermediate Speaking Tests. Their responses were scored by accredited GEPT raters. Test results were compared, and correlation, factor analysis, ANOVA, and MFRM (multi-facet Rasch measurement) analyses were performed. In addition, expert judgment was collected using two checklists: one to elicit raters' views on task difficulty in terms of code complexity, cognitive complexity, and communicative demand; and the other to compare predicted and actual test task performance. Both qualitative and quantitative results supported claims that different versions of the GEPT Intermediate Level Speaking Test were parallel.

Wu (2016) focused on a vertical comparison of four levels of the GEPT Listening and Reading Tests and examined the degree of differentiation across levels. Scores on the GEPT Elementary, Intermediate, High-Intermediate, and Advanced Level Listening and Reading Tests were vertically linked into two separate scales. The common-item non-equivalent groups design was employed to scale both dichotomously scored (multiple-choice and matching) questions and polytomously scored (constructed-response) test items based on Rasch model estimation. Examinees' performance on the items that were common between adjacent levels was used to establish a linking chain to place all levels onto the same vertical scale. The findings suggested that the higher the GEPT level, the more difficult the test was, which validated the projected increase in difficulty across the GEPT levels.

Criterion-Related Validity

Criterion-related validity is concerned with the relationships between the test and a criterion measure beyond the test in question, including external benchmarks and future behaviors (Weir, 2005, pp. 207–209). The following GEPT validation studies have been conducted to generate evidence for the relationships between the GEPT and external criteria, including the CEFR, other English proficiency examinations, and language use in real-life situations.

CEFR linking studies have been prioritized in the LTTC's research agenda in order to provide further information for interpreting GEPT scores and also to gather evidence to validate the GEPT level framework. Four of these studies (Brunfaut & Harding, 2014; Green et al., 2017; Knoch, 2016; Wu & Wu, 2010) used the procedures recommended by the *Manual: Relating Language Examinations to the CEFR* (Council of Europe, 2003, 2009) and exercises and materials provided by the Council of Europe to investigate the linking relationships between the GEPT and the CEFR. Three studies (Brunfaut & Harding, 2014; Green et al., 2017; Knoch, 2016) employed the twin-panel approach: one panel consisting of teachers, researchers, and item developers based in Taiwan, whose panelists were familiar with the GEPT, and the other consisting of language teaching, testing, and standard-setting experts based in the UK or Australia who had no prior knowledge of the GEPT. In this way, both insider and outsider perspectives were included. Based on the results of these studies, the GEPT Elementary, Intermediate, High-Intermediate, and Advanced Levels have been situated at the CEFR A2, B1, B2, and C1 levels, respectively, in terms of test content and task design. However, cut-scores resulting from the panelists' judgments of examinees' writing and speaking performances indicate that the existing GEPT passing score for the writing tests across the four levels may need to be set slightly lower and the passing score for speaking tests at the High-Intermediate and Advanced Levels may need to be set slightly higher in order to reflect the relevant CEFR level benchmarks. See Table 2.3 for a summary of the results of GEPT–CEFR linking studies.

In addition to the CEFR linking, comparison studies were conducted with other CEFR-aligned examinations, including the IELTS (Weir et al., 2013), Cambridge English PET and FCE (Wu, R. Y. F., 2014), TOEFL (Kunnan & Carr, 2015), and Aptis (Wu et al., 2016). These studies investigated the comparability of the GEPT and external referents both quantitatively and qualitatively.

Weir et al. (2013) compared the reading and writing components of the GEPT Advanced Level with those of the IELTS, as well as with real-life

26 Rachel Yi-fen Wu

TABLE 2.3 Summary of the Results of GEPT–CEFR Linking Studies

	No. of Panelists	GEPT			
		Elementary	Intermediate	High-Intermediate	Advanced
Reading (Wu & Wu, 2010)	15	A2+	B1	B2-	C1
Listening (Brunfaut & Harding, 2014)	Twin-panel 6 + 6	A2	B1	B2	B2+
Writing (Knoch, 2016)	Twin-panel 8 + 7	A2/A2+	B1/B1+	B2/B2+	C1/C1+
Speaking (Green et al., 2017)	Twin-panel 12 + 6	A2	B1	B2/B1+	C1/B2+

academic activities, in terms of test results and predictive power. Undergraduate students studying in the UK were recruited. Their IELTS scores, real-life writing assignments, one in-class test, and an end-of term examination were compared with their scores on the GEPT Advanced Level Reading and Writing Tests. In addition, a questionnaire was given to the students in which they self-assessed their reading and writing abilities based on their university learning experience. The results showed moderate to high correlations between GEPT and IELTS scores and between the GEPT scores and the participants' academic performances. Nevertheless, it was harder to pass the GEPT Advanced Tests than to score 6.5, which is roughly at the C1 level, on the IELTS Tests. The results of the self-assessment survey suggested that the GEPT Reading and Writing Tests covered the essential skills and abilities necessary for studying in English-medium universities.

Wu, R. Y. F. (2014) compared the reading component of the GEPT and Cambridge English at CEFR levels B1 and B2, in terms of contextual characteristics, examinees' cognitive operations, and test results. Contextual features that may affect the comprehensibility and difficulty of the tests were analyzed using both expert judgment and automated tools. Cognitive operations were examined from both experts' and examinees' perspectives. The results showed that the GEPT and Cambridge Reading Tests at the B1 level were comparable, but those at the B2 level were significantly different. The Cambridge English level B2 tests were significantly more difficult than the GEPT counterpart in terms of examinees' performance and cognitive demands, but the reading texts in the Cambridge tests were significantly less complex than those of the GEPT in terms of contextual features.

Kunnan and Carr (2015) compared the reading and writing components of the GEPT Advanced Level and iBT TOEFL, both of which are used by undergraduate and graduate programs in North America for admission and selection purposes. One past paper of the GEPT Advanced Test and three practice iBT TOEFL Reading and Writing Tests published by Educational Testing Service for test preparation purposes were analyzed in terms of the textual features of the reading passages, test constructs, response formats, and examinees' performances. Students recruited in Taiwan and in the U.S. took the GEPT Advanced Level Reading and Writing Tests. Participants recruited in the U.S. were also asked to complete a questionnaire to provide information about their iBT TOEFL scores and their perception of the difficulty of the GEPT Advanced Level Tests and relevance of the test content and tasks to their academic studies. Automated tools were used to analyze the cohesion, syntax, and vocabulary of the reading passages. Test constructs were analyzed using expert judgment and factor analysis. Analysis of the textual features suggested that the two reading tests were very similar in most respects. The factor analysis results suggested that the two tests assessed the same constructs. Although the response formats of the two tests were very different, analysis of test performances showed medium-to-high correlations between the GEPT and iBT TOEFL Reading and Writing Tests. Regression analyses between the two tests suggested that a GEPT Advanced Level Reading Test score of 68 corresponded to an iBT TOEFL Reading score of 24 and a Writing score of 3 corresponded to an iBT TOEFL Writing score of 24, both situated at the CEFR C1 Level. In terms of relevance to their academic studies, most agreed the GEPT Writing Test was relevant, whereas they were neutral regarding the GEPT Reading Test.

Consequential Validity

Consequential validity concerns whether the interpretation or use of test scores supports the intended testing purposes (Messick, 1989, p. 18). The socio-cognitive model covers three aspects of consequential validity, namely "impact on institutions and society," "washback on individuals in classroom/workplace," and "avoidance of test bias" (Khalifa & Weir, 2009, p. 169). This section outlines Wu and Lee's (2017) study exploring the washback effects of the GEPT on college students' English language learning and Liao and Huang's (2016) study on test fairness.

Wu and Lee (2017) investigated university students' views on the GEPT at the Intermediate and High-Intermediate Levels. In Taiwan, the MoE's implementation of the English language proficiency benchmark policy in universities since 2005 has encouraged students to enhance and demonstrate their English ability through taking an external standardized English test, such as the GEPT, TOEFL, IELTS, or TOEIC, before they graduate. The relationships among students' perceptions of the requirement, test value, test anxiety, learning motivation, and test performance were examined using Structural Equation Modeling (SEM). The results showed that university students held a positive attitude towards the GEPT. The SEM results showed that students'

28 Rachel Yi-fen Wu

attitudes towards the English language proficiency benchmark policy positively affected perceived test value and learning motivation, and perceived test value was positively correlated with learning motivation. However, there was no significant relationship between attitudes towards the policy and test performance, whereas test anxiety has a negative effect on test performance.

Liao and Huang (2016) investigated the effects of differential item functioning (DIF) and differential bundle functioning (DBF) on students' performance on the GEPT Intermediate Level Listening and Reading Tests in terms of gender and residential location. DIF and DBF analyses are used to determine test fairness by investigating potential bias at the item and subtest (also referred to as "bundle") level, respectively. They were concerned with identifying whether examinees at the same level of proficiency, but from different demographic groups, had an unequal probability of answering an individual item or a subset of items correctly. Score data from 3,500 examinees randomly selected from northern, middle, southern, and eastern Taiwan were analyzed. The results of the study suggested that gender and residential location minimally influenced test performance.

Impact of the GEPT on EFL Education in Taiwan

The GEPT has a significant impact on not only learners of English but also teachers and researchers in Taiwan. Because an exam-oriented culture remains predominant in Taiwan, learners are accustomed to relying on tests to motivate themselves to learn. The GEPT has therefore become a useful tool for encouraging desired EFL learning behaviors. Listening and speaking previously received little attention in classroom teaching and assessment. Over the years, the existence of the GEPT has resulted in an increased emphasis on communicative competence and the nurturing of listening and speaking skills throughout Taiwan (Wu, 2008, p. 8). Most teachers consider that the GEPT leads to more balanced study of the various aspects necessary for mastering the English language (Wu, J. R. W., 2014). There is evidence that Taiwanese learners' English listening comprehension has improved significantly; according to a statistical analysis of the GEPT Intermediate Level Listening Tests, the scores of upper secondary school students (totaling around 630,000) increased by an average of 8 points over the first decade of the GEPT (Wu, 2013, pp. 14–15). The GEPT has also been used by the MoE to raise the English proficiency of local teachers, and the policy appears to have had a positive impact on the proficiency level of English teachers (Department of Education of the Taipei City Government, 2009). To equip teachers with the knowledge and skills to integrate assessment with instruction, the LTTC has been hosting workshops and seminars to promote the professional development of assessment literacy for teachers, focusing on the most common challenges that teachers face, that is, developing useful classroom assessment tasks and advising students on how to choose external tests (Wu, 2008, 2012). For researchers, the GEPT has stimulated interest in examining language assessment and increased research capacity in Taiwan. An increasing number of local researchers have been publishing research papers on the GEPT in reputable journals (e.g., Huang, 2016; Liao, 2016; Tseng, 2016). The following section discusses the impact that the GEPT has had on learning, teaching, and research in Taiwan.

Promoting Assessment for Learning

As the internationalization of higher education has grown in importance, most universities and colleges in Taiwan have set their own English language requirements. GEPT scores have been widely used for this purpose (Wu, 2012; Pan & Roever, 2016): technological and vocational colleges commonly set the minimum standard at the GEPT Elementary Level or CEFR A2 level, while universities set it at the GEPT Intermediate Level or CEFR B1 level. In addition to being used as a measure of accountability, the GEPT has also been used by teachers to identify the strengths and weaknesses of individual students and to develop appropriate learning interventions and adapt instructions to meet students' learning needs. For example, National Taiwan University has integrated the GEPT into its curriculum design and aligned course objectives with GEPT High-Intermediate level descriptors (the Language Training and Testing Center, 2012; Wu, 2012, p. 17; Yeh & Wang, 2014). As a result, teachers have more specific teaching goals in mind when planning instruction, and students, for their part, have clearer learning objectives that keep them motivated to learn English.

To encourage autonomous learning, the LTTC provides a wide range of test preparation materials and learning resources, including the GEPT Past Papers, GEPT Writing Companion Series, LTTC Dr. Writing, and GEPT Self-Assessment Scales and Tests. Given that writing is considered the most difficult skill within Taiwan's EFL context, the LTTC set up the GEPT Outstanding Essay Awards in 2009. Selected winning essays are edited and published in the GEPT Writing Companion Series as a resource for learners seeking to improve their writing skills. In addition, the LTTC developed Dr. Writing, a blended learning course. Those who attend the course receive individualized feedback on their writing online and have the option of face-to-face instruction, with a teacher to further diagnose their writing problems and provide consultancy. The GEPT Self-Assessment Scales and Tests are intended to help learners develop language awareness and engage in more self-directed learning. The GEPT Self-Assessment Scales consist of can-do statements, which have been validated empirically (Wu & Lee, 2010; Wu, Lee, & Lo, 2014). The Self-Assessment Tests are composed of test questions selected from item banks based

30 Rachel Yi-fen Wu

on GEPT test constructs. Learners are encouraged to use these self-assessment results when registering for the GEPT level that best matches their ability.

Monitoring the Effectiveness of Policy Implementation

The MoE has long been engaged in efforts to raise teachers' English proficiency. The Ministry encourages teachers at all levels of instruction to demonstrate adequate English proficiency by presenting scores from standardized English exams.[4] GEPT scores have been used as a criterion to certify teachers (Education Bureau, Taichung City Government, 2014). Teachers of subjects other than English in elementary and secondary schools are expected to achieve passing scores on standardized English tests equivalent to the GEPT Intermediate Level, CEFR B1 Level, or above; teachers of English in these schools are expected to achieve passing scores equivalent to the GEPT High-Intermediate Level, CEFR B2 Level, or above. According to official statistics (Department of Education, Taipei City Government, 2009), the ratio of elementary school English teachers with qualified English teaching expertise, that is, English proficiency at the B2 Level or above, increased from 97.5% in 2008 to 99.1% in 2009. This provides evidence of the policy's success in improving the quality of English instruction at the primary level.

Supporting the Professional Development of Assessment Literacy

The importance of promoting assessment literacy is increasing with the growth of the role of testing and assessment in Taiwan. The need has emerged for teachers of English in Taiwan to undergo professional training to build up a working knowledge of language testing and assessment, especially after the introduction of English proficiency requirements and the adoption of the CEFR as a tool to interpret test results and students' language proficiency (Wu, J. R. W., 2014). Universities across Taiwan have taken the controversial step of allowing students to choose to either pass an external exam (i.e., GEPT, TOEFL) or an in-house English test as part of their English language proficiency requirements, which may confuse stakeholders as to how to adhere to the CEFR benchmark. To make better use of assessment tools, relevant stakeholders need an appropriate level of assessment literacy so that they are able to communicate their goals and needs, critically evaluate tests, and interpret test results. Over the years, the LTTC has been hosting workshops and seminars on assessment literacy to enable stakeholders to make informed decisions based on assessment results. Every summer, the LTTC hosts a series of teacher workshops that provide resources for language testing and assessment, as well as hands-on classroom assessment techniques, across Taiwan. As part of its efforts to promote assessment literacy in Taiwan, the LTTC also invites in-service teachers to attend training to become raters for the GEPT Speaking and Writing Tests. To date, over 400 teachers have received GEPT rater training. By bringing teachers into the GEPT rating process, the GEPT rating mechanism and classroom assessment practices mutually reinforce each other, leading to positive feedback loops that bridge assessment and instruction.

Stimulating Interest in Language Assessment Research

Since the GEPT was first administered in 2000, the GEPT has attracted extensive research interest. Over the years, hundreds of postgraduate students have written their thesis on the GEPT; the earliest was by Huang Shuming, who wrote a master's thesis titled *A Comparative Analysis of the Listening Test Items of GEPT, STEP and PETS* in 2003. Local academics have conducted in-depth investigations on various aspects of the GEPT, including test anxiety (Huang, 2016), critical features and error types of expository essays (Tseng, 2016), score and decision dependability (Liao, 2016), test fairness (Huang & Lee, 2011), and washback effects (Shih, 2008, 2009; Vongpumivitch, 2012a, 2012b). In 2013, the LTTC established LTTC Language Teaching & Testing Research Grants Program. The program is open exclusively to local teachers at all levels and postgraduate students in Taiwan to promote research in the areas of language testing and assessment. An increasing number of local researchers supported by the LTTC Language Teaching & Testing Research Grants Program have been publishing research papers in high-quality journals, such as *English Teaching & Learning, Language Assessment Quarterly*, and *System*.

Innovation

The GEPT, as a test developed in the early 21st century, has the advantage of incorporating the latest developments in L2 research, pedagogy, and language testing into its test design and services. The next section outlines the LTTC's efforts to sustain continuous improvement in test design, score usefulness, and the quality of marking.

Introducing New Concepts to Task Design

Performance conditions, such as response format, time constraints, and the linguistic demands of the input, influence how examinees engage with test tasks (Weir, 2005). Roever and Pan (2008, p. 408) note "the GEPT appears to be a solid, traditional test battery with a focus on high practicality at the three lower levels, whereas the two upper levels resemble more recent generations of academically and communicatively oriented tests." In terms of response format, due to the large number of examinees for each test administration, the lower three levels of the GEPT Listening and Reading Tests use the traditional multiple-choice-only format, and the Speaking Tests at these three levels are

32 Rachel Yi-fen Wu

audio-recorded for raters to mark in a secure central location at a later time. The upper levels, having a relatively small number of examinees, are able to include diverse response formats. For example, the Advanced Level Listening and Reading Tests cover both selected-response (multiple-choice and matching questions) and short-constructed response (short-answer and note-completion) formats, and the Speaking Test is a paired oral interview, comprising self-introduction, information exchange and discussion between the candidates, and presentation on a given topic (see Table 2.2). In addition to diverse question types, the GEPT Advanced Level Reading Test takes into account Urquhart and Weir's (1998, p. 123) view on the componentiality of reading and assesses careful reading and expeditious reading separately (see Table 2.2), as well as the hierarchical levels of cognitive processes proposed in Khalifa and Weir's (2009) model of reading. At the Advanced Level, GEPT examinees are to apply different reading strategies according to various reading purposes. In Part 1 of the Reading Test, examinees are to read quickly and selectively to extract the gist of multiple texts and to integrate information across texts in order to elicit the highest level of cognitive operations, "creating an intertextual representation," as defined by Khalifa and Weir (2009). In Part 2, examinees are to thoroughly read long and complex texts in order to comprehend main ideas, supporting details, and implied meanings. The GEPT Advanced Writing Test adopts an integrated-skills approach and incorporates intertextuality in the form of knowledge transformation into task design. The reading-into-writing tasks assess examinees' ability to utilize strategic knowledge to extract information from two articles in Task 1 and two graphs in Task 2 and to transform what they have read into the form of arguments that can effectively meet the expectations of their audience. Examinees are to identify themselves in the role of writer *(who)*, and to write, based on text prompts *(why, what, and how)*, to the specified audience *(to whom)*. Text prompts are provided as a resource for examinees to draw upon in order to minimize the effect of background knowledge, the possession of which cannot be presumed to be equally common to all examinees. For example, in Task 2 of GEPT Advanced Level Test Past Paper-1 (LTTC, 2009, W-6), examinees are presented with the scenario of a nationwide increase in credit card debts and are required to write to the Opinion Section of a local English-language newspaper to discuss possible reasons for the increase and make suggestions on how these problems can be avoided. While the GEPT Advanced Level Writing Test integrates reading into the writing tasks, the Superior Level Test integrates four skills: Task 1 is an integrated writing task, in which examinees are required to summarize and organize the main points from both a video/radio program of between 10 and 15 minutes and a 3000-word article, and then integrate these points with their opinions into an essay of around 750 words; and Task 2 is an integrated speaking task, which requires examinees to orally present the essays they have written and answer questions posed by interlocutors.

Constructing the LTTC English Learner Corpus

The potential applications of learner corpora have attracted considerable interest in language pedagogy and interlanguage research since the 1990s. The LTTC has been sampling written and spoken data from examinees' responses to the Writing and Speaking Tests of each GEPT administration since 2001. Starting in 2008, the LTTC collaborated with the Graduate Institute of Linguistics at National Taiwan University to compile the LTTC English Learner Corpus (LTTC–ELC). The LTTC–ELC project, completed in 2014, created a corpus consisting of over two million tokens (i.e., running words) of written production data. The LTTC–ELC is a computer-readable learner corpus. The Corpus is free and publicly available at www.lttcelc.org.tw/. Teachers and researchers can perform three types of searches in the Corpus, including keyword search (for a target word), collocation search (for a target word and its collocates), and Ngram search (for multiple words, such as phrases). This Corpus serves as a useful reference for teachers and researchers to identify the frequency and patterns of errors made by Taiwanese learners at different levels of English. If the errors are caused by L1 interference, the teachers may draw students' attention to the differences between their L1 and the target language in order to avoid negative transfer from the L1.

In addition to its pedagogical potential, a variety of studies have been conducted using the LTTC–ELC, including research into easily confused near-synonyms (Hsieh & Chung, 2009), the effect of topic variation (Chung & Wu, 2009), and automatic essay scoring (Gao, 2014).

Vertically Linking Scores From Different Levels Into a Common Score Scale

The LTTC has been continuously working to enhance the usefulness of GEPT scores and score reporting mechanisms. While the GEPT is designed to provide accessible attainment targets for English learners at different stages, the LTTC is currently exploring the feasibility of presenting vertical scale scores, together with GEPT scores by level, to enrich interpretations of test results. GEPT scores have been widely used in school settings to measure learning outcomes and evaluate students' progress in learning English. Students who pass one level of the GEPT are often motivated to take the test at the next highest level. However, their learning progress cannot be measured by directly comparing scores from different levels because the units of measurement are not necessarily the same. Vertical scale scores based on Item Response Theory (IRT) make it possible to establish the comparability of measurements and visualize incremental changes across levels, and thus provide additional information to complement GEPT scores by level. Based on the results reported by Wu and Liao (2010), Wu and Wu (2015), and Wu (2016), the LTTC published a GEPT score concordance table (see www.gept.org.tw/WebFile/DOC/ScoreForm_Eng.pdf) in

2015. Examinees can use the concordance table to predict the scores they might receive at an adjacent level. Once the relationships between the current GEPT scoring and the IRT-based scaling are further validated, vertical scale scores can be presented in the official GEPT score report, together with the operational GEPT scores by level. This will enable teachers and students to visualize learning progress directly.

Extending the GEPT Level Framework to CEFR A1 Level

The beginning of compulsory English instruction in Taiwan was lowered from Grade 7 (aged 12 to 13) to Grade 5 (aged 10 to 11) in 2001. In 2005, it was further lowered to Grade 3 (aged 8 to 9) island-wide and Grade 1 (aged 6 to 7) in a few major cities. To address the growing need for assessment measures that can monitor and track young students' progress in learning English, GEPT Kids, a CEFR A1 level test, was added to the GEPT testing system in 2015. Following the GEPT model, GEPT Kids assesses four language skills: listening, reading, writing, and speaking. The test is learning-oriented and its design reflects local educational practices and the learning and cultural experiences of young Taiwanese learners. Examinees' overall performance is represented by a number of suns, instead of numerical scores. Each examinee receives diagnostic feedback that shows his or her learning strengths and weaknesses based on can-do statements, which can serve as a reference for future teaching and learning.

Exploring the Feasibility of Adopting Automated Scoring

Automated scoring systems have made substantial progress since their beginnings in the 1960s. Over the years, studies have been conducted to assess the appropriateness of using automated systems to replace or supplement human rating assessment. Following its introduction of the onscreen marking and computer-based GEPT[5] in 2017, the LTTC has begun to explore the possibility of applying artificial intelligence to support GEPT rating processes. While automated scoring technologies have been gaining wider acceptance in recent years, public suspicion of the performance of automated scoring remains high, especially regarding the ability of computers to understand the semantics of human responses. Before machine scoring receives high acceptability among local stakeholders, instead of replacing human rating, an automated scoring system would most likely be incorporated as a means of improving the quality of rater training and moderation and of reducing rater workloads without compromising fairness and consistency.

Challenges: The Way Forward

The key objectives of the GEPT are to support learners of English at different stages in setting learning goals and to promote the balanced development of listening, reading, speaking, and writing abilities. Since its inception, the GEPT has evolved to tackle the challenges posed by changing trends in English language education in Taiwan while maintaining professional quality standards in testing. The following sections outline selected items on research agendas for the GEPT to support pedagogical reform and to better reflect the sociocultural contexts of English education in Taiwan.

Aligning GEPT With the Updated Local Curriculum

In 2019, the MoE introduced a major curriculum reform in Taiwan, the Framework for the Twelve-Year Basic Education Curriculum (Ministry of Education, 2014). Compared to the earlier nine-year curriculum formally implemented in 2001, the twelve-year curriculum moves from knowledge to competency orientation and focusses more on the development of core competencies, broadly categorized in three areas: spontaneity, communicative interaction, and social participation (Ministry of Education, 2014). The new curriculum aims to develop students' lifelong learning potential and enable them to acquire essential competences to cope with real-life challenges and opportunities. In view of the recent education reform, the GEPT is currently under review to assess whether there is a need to introduce new tasks to better reflect the concepts and skills contained in the revised English curriculum (such as critical thinking and problem solving) to further enhance its cognitive and context validity, as defined in Weir's (2005) model.

Enhancing Transparency and Quality of GEPT by Aligning It With International Language Proficiency Frameworks

To present evidence in support of the validity of the GEPT level framework and to provide further information for interpreting GEPT scores, GEPT–CEFR linking studies have been prioritized in the LTTC research agenda. The results of earlier GEPT–CEFR linking studies (Brunfaut & Harding, 2014; Green et al., 2017; Knoch, 2016; Wu & Wu, 2010) have shown the GEPT is well-aligned with the CEFR in terms of test content; however, the existing passing scores for the GEPT Writing and Speaking Tests across the four levels may need to be adjusted to better reflect the relevant CEFR levels (Green et al., 2017; Knoch, 2016). The findings may be attributed to differences between the GEPT rating scales and CEFR assessment grids (Knoch, 2016, p. 20), limited samples (Green et al., 2017, p. 1), and the fact that not all parts of the tests were included in the benchmark studies (Green et al., 2017, pp. 1, 32; Knoch, 2016, p. 20). The Council of Europe (2018) released extended CEFR descriptor scales for mediation, making it possible for the Chinese-English translation tasks that form part of the GEPT Intermediate and High-Intermediate level tests to be included in future linking studies, thereby facilitating further investigation of the causes of discrepancy in alignment. Although the Ministry has no intention

36 Rachel Yi-fen Wu

of aligning the new English curriculum with the CEFR levels or other international language proficiency scales, research on criterion-related validity will continue to remain a high priority in LTTC's research agenda in order to promote transparency of the GEPT and good practice.

Improving Test Score Reporting to Support Self-Directed Learning

To promote learner autonomy, the LTTC is planning to introduce an updated score reporting practice that places more emphasis on self-directed learning and learning-oriented assessment. In addition to providing test scores that inform learners of their current status on the basis of their test performance, the new score reporting service aims to provide feedback that can empower test takers to take the necessary action to further enhance their abilities. The LTTC is exploring possibilities for providing personalized feedback that not only diagnoses learners' strengths and weaknesses but also offers constructive advice. The feedback is intended to support test takers to more closely monitor their learning progress and to prioritize future learning objectives.

This chapter has provided an overview of the historical background and work of the GEPT project. Special focus has been placed on the sociocultural contexts of the development and use of the GEPT level framework, as well as on a systematic approach to collecting empirical evidence on test validation based on Weir's (2005) socio-cognitive validation framework. Over the past twenty years, the GEPT has made a positive impact on EFL education in Taiwan, while supporting the government's policy of promoting lifelong learning. In the GEPT's third decade, the LTTC will continue its endeavors to maintain the relevance and usefulness of the test in contemporary contexts while meeting international quality standards (e.g., AERA, 2014; ALTE, 2001; ILTA, 2007).

Notes

1. The Language Training and Testing Center (LTTC) was first established in 1951. The Center is a non-profit educational foundation under a mandate to meet the needs of social and economic development through research, development, and administration in language training and testing. For details, please see www.lttc. ntu.edu.tw/aboutthelttc.htm.
2. Weir's framework has been further explicated by Khalifa and Weir (2009) and O'Sullivan and Weir (2011). It has become an increasingly influential model for test development and validation (e.g., Field, 2012; Geranpayeh & Taylor, 2013; Green, 2013; McCray & Brunfaut, 2018; Owen, 2016; Taylor, 2011).
3. Source: Document Number Jen-Li 0950061619 issued by the Executive Yuan on April 4, 2006 (行政院民國95年4月4日院授人力字第0950061619號)
4. Source: Document Number Tai-Jiao-Shou-Guo 1060028215 issued by Ministry of Education on April 18, 2017 (教育部106年4月18日臺教授國字第1060028215號)

5. The GEPT tests are currently administered in both paper-based and computer-based modes. Due to limited technological capacity of schools to support computer-based tests, only a very limited number of CBT registrations are accepted at present.

References

American Educational Research Association, American Psychological Association, & National Council on Measurement in Education. (2014). *Standards for educational and psychological testing*. Washington, DC: Author.

Association of Language Testers in Europe. (1993/2001). *Principles of good practice for ALTE examinations*. Retrieved from www.testdaf.de/fileadmin/Redakteur/PDF/TestDaF/ALTE/ALTE_good_practice.pdf

Bachman, L. F., & Palmer, A. S. (1996). *Language testing in practice*. Oxford: Oxford University Press.

Bax, S., & Chan, S. H. C. (2016). *Researching the cognitive validity of GEPT high-interme diate and advanced reading: An eye tracking and stimulated recall study* (LTTC–GEPT Research Report No. RG-07). Taipei: The Language Training and Testing Center.

Brunfaut, T., & Harding, L. (2014). *Linking the GEPT listening test to the Common European Framework of Reference* (LTTC–GEPT Research Report No. RG-05). Taipei: The Language Training and Testing Center.

Chan, H. C., Wu, R. Y. F., & Weir, C. (2014). *Examining the context and cognitive validity of the GEPT advanced writing task 1: A comparison with real-life academic writing tasks* (LTTC–GEPT Research Report No. RG-03). Taipei: The Language Training and Testing Center.

Chang, W. C. et al. [張武昌、陳坤田、史嘉琳、黃訴、顧英秀、王專色、張淑媖] (1998). 八十四年度基礎科目英文考科試題研發工作計畫研究報告：高中常用字彙表[Senior high English wordlist for reference]. Taipei: College Entrance Examination Center.

Chen, S. W., & Liu, G. Z. (2007). The impact of English exit policy on motivation and motivated learning behaviors. In Y. N. Leung (Ed.), *Proceedings of the twenty-fourth international conference on English teaching and learning in the Republic of China* (pp. 104–110). Taipei: Crane Publishing.

Cheng, L., Klinger, D., Fox, J., Doe, C., Jin, Y., & Wu, J. (2014). Motivation and test anxiety in test performance across three testing contexts: The CAEL, CET, and GEPT. *TESOL Quarterly, 48*, 300–330.

Chu, H., & Yeh, H. (2017). English benchmark policy for graduation in Taiwan's higher education: Investigation and reflection. *Journal of Language Teaching and Research, 8*(6), 1063–1072. doi:10.17507/jltr.0806.06

Chung, S. F., & Wu, C. Y. (2009). *Effects of topic familiarity on writing performance: A study based on GEPT intermediate test materials*. Paper presented at the 2009 LTTC International Conference on English Language Teaching and Testing, Taipei.

Council of Europe. (2001). *Common European Framework of Reference for Languages: Learning, teaching, assessment*. Cambridge, UK: Cambridge University Press.

Council of Europe. (2003). *Relating language examinations to the Common European Framework of Reference for Languages: Learning, teaching, assessment: Manual, preliminary pilot version*. Strasbourg: Council of Europe.

Council of Europe. (2009). *Relating language examinations to the Common European Framework of Reference for Languages: Learning, teaching, assessment (CEFR)*. Strasbourg: Council of Europe.

Council of Europe. (2018). *Common European Framework of Reference for Languages: Learning, teaching, assessment, companion volume with new descriptors.* Strasbourg: Council of Europe. Retrieved from https://rm.coe.int/cefr-companion-volume-with-new-descriptors-2018/1680787989

Dendrinos, B. (2013). Social meanings in global-glocal language proficiency exams. In D. Tsagari, S. Papadima-Sophocleous, & S. Ioannou-Georgiou (Eds.), *International experiences in language testing and assessment* (pp. 33–57). Frankfurt am Main: Peter Lang.

Department of Education, Taipei City Government. (2009). 臺北市98學年度國小合格英語師資現況調查 Retrieved from https://sec.gov.taipei/News_Content.aspx?n=4 9B4C3242CB7658C&sms=72544237BBE4C5F6&s=F48D2E050207314D

Education Bureau, Taichung City Government. (2014).臺中市國民小學提升合格英語教師授課比率實施計畫 Retrieved from www.tjes.tc.parents.tw/include/download.php?target=a_news&id=MTA0NDA=&f=2

Field, J. (2012). The cognitive validity of the lecture-based question in the IELTS listening paper. In L. Taylor & C. Weir (Eds.), *IELTS collected papers 2: Research in reading and listening assessment* (pp. 391–453). Studies in Language Testing 34. Cambridge, UK: Cambridge University Press.

Gao, Z. M. (2014). Automatic extraction of English collocations and their Chinese-English bilingual Examples: A computational tool for bilingual lexicography. *Concentric Studies in Linguistics, 40*(1), 95–121.

Geranpayeh, A., & Taylor, L. (2013). *Examining listening: Research and practice in assessing second language listening.* Studies in Language Testing, 35. Cambridge, UK: Cambridge University Press.

Green, A. (2013). *Exploring language assessment and testing: Language in action.* London: Taylor & Francis Ltd.

Green, A., Inoue, C., & Nakatsuhara, F. (2017). *GEPT speaking—CEFR benchmarking* (LTTC–GEPT Research Report No. RG-09). Taipei: The Language Training and Testing Center.

Hsieh, Y. C., & Chung, S. F. (2009). *'Do' and 'Make': A corpus-based study.* Paper presented at the American Association for Corpus Linguistics Conference. University of Alberta, Canada.

Huang, H. (2016). Exploring strategy use in L2 speaking assessment. *System, 63,* 13–27.

Huang, S. S., & Lee, C. L. (2011). *The differential item functioning analysis of the GEPT: A case study.* Paper presented at the 20th International Symposium on English Teaching, Taipei.

International Language Testing Association. (2007). *Guidelines for practice.* Retrieved from www.iltaonline.com/page/ITLAGuidelinesforPra

Jeng, H., Chang, S., Cheng, Y., & Gu, Y. (2002). 高中英文參考詞彙表 [Senior high English wordlist for reference]. Taipei: College Entrance Examination Center.

Khalifa, H., & Weir, C. J. (2009). *Examining reading: Research and practice in assessing second language reading.* Studies in Language Testing, 29. Cambridge, UK: UCLES/Cambridge University Press.

Knoch, U. (2016). *Linking the GEPT writing sub-test to the Common European Framework of Reference (CEFR)* (LTTC–GEPT Research Report No. RG-08). Taipei: The Language Training and Testing Center.

Kunnan, A., & Carr, N. (2015). *Comparability study between the General English Proficiency Test—Advanced and the Internet-Based Test of English as a Foreign Language (iBT TOEFL)* (LTTC–GEPT Research Report No. RG-06). Taipei: The Language Training and Testing Center.

The Language Training and Testing Center. (1997). 英語能力分級檢定測驗研究第一、二階段研究報告 [The GEPT research and development project: Phases 1 & 2 research report]. Unpublished internal report.

The Language Training and Testing Center. (1999). 全民英語能力檢定測驗：中級測驗研究報告 [The GEPT intermediate level research report]. Taipei: Author. Retrieved from www.lttc.ntu.edu.tw/thesis.htm

The Language Training and Testing Center. (2000a). 全民英語能力檢定測驗：初級測驗研究報告 [The GEPT elementary level research report]. Taipei: Author. Retrieved from www.lttc.ntu.edu.tw/thesis.htm

The Language Training and Testing Center. (2000b). 全民英語能力檢定測驗：中高級測驗研究報告 [The GEPT high-intermediate level research report]. Taipei: Author. Retrieved from www.lttc.ntu.edu.tw/thesis.htm

The Language Training and Testing Center. (2002a). 全民英語能力檢定測驗：高級測驗研究報告 [The GEPT advanced level research report]. Taipei: Author. Retrieved from www.lttc.ntu.edu.tw/thesis.htm

The Language Training and Testing Center. (2002b). 全民英語能力檢定測驗：優級測驗研究報告 [The GEPT superior level research report]. Taipei: Author. Retrieved from www.lttc.ntu.edu.tw/thesis.htm

The Language Training and Testing Center. (2009). 全民英語能力分級檢定測驗正式測驗考題(高級-1) [The GEPT advanced level test past paper-1]. Taipei: Author.

The Language Training and Testing Center. (2012). *The GEPT information brochure.* Taipei: Author. Retrieved from www.lttc.ntu.edu.tw/E_LTTC/E_GEPT/files/GEPT_Information_Brochure.pdf

Liao, C. H. Y., & Huang, S. S. (2016). *Examining differential item functioning and differential bundle functioning for the GEPT.* Paper presented at the 25th International Symposium on English Teaching, Taipei.

Liao, Y. F. (2016). Investigating the score dependability and decision dependability of the GEPT listening test: A multivariate generalizability theory approach. *English Teaching & Learning, 40*(1), 79–111.

Ma, M., & Li, S. F. (2009). *Bridging test construct and beneficial washback effects: Revising the GEPT high-intermediate reading test.* Paper presented at the 26th International Conference of English Teaching and Learning in the R. O. C., National Tsing Hua University, Hsinchu.

McCray, G., & Brunfaut, T. (2018). Investigating the construct measured by banked gap-fill items: Evidence from eye tracking. *Language Testing, 35*(1), 51–73.

Messick, S. (1989). Validity. In R. L. Linn (Ed.), *Educational measurement* (3rd ed., pp. 13–103). New York, NY: Macmillan.

Ministry of Education. (2004). 教育部未來四年施政主軸行動方案 [Major policy objectives for 2005–2008]. Retrieved from http://163.32.134.10/mintsu/edu-trend/2005-8/next-4.doc

Ministry of Education. (2014). 十二年國民基本教育課程綱要總綱 [General guidelines of the twelve-year curriculum]. Retrieved from www.naer.edu.tw/files/15-1000-7944,c1174-1.php?Lang=zh-tw

O'Sullivan, B., & Weir, C. J. (2011). Test development and validation. In B. O'Sullivan (Ed.), *Language testing: Theories and practices* (pp. 13–32). Basingstoke: Palgrave Macmillan.

Owen, N. (2016). *An evidence-centred approach to reverse engineering: Comparative analysis of IELTS and TOEFL iBT reading sections* (Unpublished doctoral dissertation). University of Leicester, UK.

Pan, Y., & Roever, C. (2016). Consequences of test use: A case study of employers' voice on the social impact of English certification exit requirements in Taiwan. *Language Testing in Asia, 6*(6), 1–21.

Plonsky, L., & Oswald, F. L. (2014). How big is "big"? Interpreting effect sizes in L2 research. *Language Learning, 64*, 878–912.

Qian, D. (2014). *A register analysis of the GEPT advanced level examinees' written production* (LTTC–GEPT Research Report No. RG-04). Taipei: The Language Training and Testing Center.

Roever, C., & Pan, Y. (2008). Test review: GEPT: General English Proficiency Test. *Language Testing, 25*(3), 403–418.

Scott, M. (2008). *WordSmith Tools version 5.* Liverpool: Lexical Analysis Software.

Shih, C. M. (2008). The General English Proficiency Test. *Language Assessment Quarterly, 5*, 63–76. doi:10.1080/15434300701776377

Shih, C. M. (2009). How tests change teaching: A model for reference. *English Teaching: Practice and Critique, 8*(2), 188–206.

Taylor, L. (Ed.). (2011). *Examining speaking: Research and practice in assessing second language speaking.* Studies in Language Testing, 30. Cambridge, UK: Cambridge University Press.

Tseng, C. C. (2016). Subsumable relationship among error types of EFL writers: A learner corpus-based study of expository writing at the intermediate level. *English Teaching and Learning, 1*(40), 113–151.

Urquhart, A. H., & Weir, C. J. (1998). *Reading in a second language: Process, product and practice.* New York, NY: Longman.

Vongpumivitch, V. (2012a). Motivating lifelong learning of English? Test takers' perceptions of the success of the General English Proficiency Test. *Language Assessment Quarterly, 9*(1), 26–59.

Vongpumivitch, V. (2012b). English-as-a-foreign-language assessment in Taiwan. *Language Assessment Quarterly, 9*(1), 1–10.

Weir, C. J. (2005). *Language testing and validation: An evidence-based approach.* Basingstoke: Palgrave MacMillan.

Weir, C. J., Chan, S. H., & Nakatsuhara, F. (2013). *Examining the criterion-related validity of the GEPT advanced reading and writing tests: Comparing GEPT with IELTS and real-life academic performance* (LTTC–GEPT Research Report No. RG-01). Taipei: The Language Training and Testing Center.

Weir, C. J., & Wu, J. (2006). Establishing test form and individual task comparability: A case study of semi-direct speaking test. *Language Testing, 23*, 167–197.

Wu, J. R. W. (2008). Views of Taiwanese students and teachers on English language testing. *Research Notes, 34*, 6–9. Retrieved from www.cambridgeenglish.org/images/23153-research-notes-34.pdf

Wu, J. R. W. (2012). GEPT and English language teaching and testing in Taiwan. *Language Assessment Quarterly, 9*(1), 11–25.

Wu, J. R. W. (2014). Investigating Taiwanese teachers' language testing and assessment needs. *English Teaching & Learning, 38*(1), 1–27.

Wu, J. R. W., & Lee, C. (2010). The development of the GEPT self-assessment statements. *English Teaching & Learning, 34*(1), 99–142.

Wu, J. R. W., & Lee, C. (2017). The relationships between test performance and students' perceptions of learning motivation, test value, and test anxiety in the context of the English benchmark requirement for graduation in Taiwan's universities. *Language Testing in Asia, 7*(9), 1–21.

Wu, J. R. W., Lee, M., & Lo, J. (2014). *Development and validation of the self-Assessment scales for Taiwanese EFL learners.* Paper presented at the 36th Language Testing and Research Colloquium, Amsterdam, Netherlands.

Wu, J. R. W., & Wu, R. Y. F. (2007). *Using the CEFR in Taiwan: The perspective of a local examination board.* Paper presented at the Fourth European Association for Language Testing and Assessment (EALTA) Conference, Sitges, Spain.

Wu, J. R. W., & Wu, R. Y. F. (2010). Relating the GEPT reading comprehension tests to the CEFR. In W. Martyniuk (Ed.), *Aligning tests with the CEFR* (pp. 204–224). Studies in Language Testing, 33. Cambridge, UK: Cambridge University Press.

Wu, J. R. W., & Wu, R. Y. F. (2015). *Constructing a common scale for a multi-level test to enhance interpretation of learning outcomes.* Paper presented at the 37th Language Testing and Research Colloquium, Toronto, Canada.

Wu, R. Y. F. (2013). The General English Proficiency Test. *The Way of Language, 1,* 13–15.

Wu, R. Y. F. (2014). *Validating second language reading examinations: Establishing the validity of the GEPT through alignment with the Common European Framework of Reference.* Studies in Language Testing, 41. Cambridge, UK: Cambridge University Press.

Wu, R. Y. F. (2016). Creating a common score scale for the GEPT to support interpretation of learning progress. In Y. N. Leung (Ed.), *Epoch making in English language teaching and learning* (pp. 223–236). Taipei: Crane Publishing.

Wu, R. Y. F., & Liao, C. H. Y. (2010). Establishing a common score scale for the GEPT elementary, intermediate, and high-intermediate level listening and reading tests. In T. Kao & Y. Li (Eds.), *A new look at language teaching and testing: English as subject and vehicle—Selected papers from the 2009 LTTC International Conference on English Language Teaching and Testing* (pp. 309–329). Taipei: The Language Training and Testing Center.

Wu, R. Y. F., Yeh, H. Y., Dunlea, J., & Spiby, R. (2016). *Aptis–GEPT test comparison study: Looking at two tests from multi-perspectives using the socio-cognitive model.* London: British Council. Retrieved from www.britishcouncil.org/sites/default/files/aptis-gept_trial.pdf

Yeh, T. D., & Wang, S. S. (2014). 混成式補救教學對全民英檢測驗呈現之英語能力之影響 [Investigating the effects of English remedial instruction designed on a blended learning basis]. Taipei: LTTC. Retrieved from www.lttc.ntu.edu.tw/lttc-grants/doc/YeWang_all.pdf

Yu, G., & Lin, S. (2014). *A comparability study on the cognitive processes of taking graph-based GEPT–advanced and IELTS–academic writing tasks* (LTTC–GEPT Research Report No. RG-02). Taipei: The Language Training and Testing Center.

3

TEPS AND ITS FAMILY OF TESTS

Yong-Won Lee, Heesung Jun, and Ja Young Kim

Introduction

The TEPS (Test of English Proficiency developed by Seoul National University) is a large-scale, paper-based, standardized English proficiency test that is intended to measure the English language proficiency of ESL/EFL (English as a second/foreign language) learners, primarily Korean learners of English. The TEPS Center, which is housed under the Language Education Institute (LEI) at Seoul National University (SNU), is currently in charge of writing/editing test items, assembling test forms, scoring test-taker responses, and conducting psychometric analysis of test data for both regular and special administrations, while the TEPS Council (or the Division of TEPS Marketing and Operation within the Seoul National University Foundation) is responsible for registration, test administration, and the notification/mailing of score reports to test-takers. The regular administrations of TEPS are currently conducted 18 times annually, with some additional special administrations carried out when requested by client organizations.

During the 12 years since its first administration in January 1999, the TEPS achieved rapid growth and expansion, although it is facing myriad new challenges now. The TEPS online registration system was launched a year after its first administration in January 2000, and soon after in 2003, TEPS obtained national certification as a test of private qualification from the Korea Research Institute for Vocational Education and Training (KRIVET) in South Korea. The number of regular administrations for the TEPS increased from six to 12 and then to 16 during this period, with the annual number of test-takers rising dramatically from approximately 27,000 to more than 400,000. These are an amazing array of achievements attained by the TEPS testing program in the face of the strong presence and market share of international English proficiency tests, such as TOEIC and TOEFL, in the South Korean context. It was also during this period that computer-based tests, such as TOP (Test of Oral Proficiency) and *i*-TEPS, were developed and successfully launched along with the paper-based TWP (Test of Written Proficiency). TOP and TWP were later renamed to TEPS-Speaking and TEPS-Writing, respectively, in 2008, and began to be administered more regularly from then on. The testing volumes of these tests, however, remained rather small, compared to that of TEPS. Most recently in 2018, TEPS was revised and relaunched in response to the new demands and requests from test-takers, English teaching professionals, and other major stakeholders of TEPS in South Korea.

TEPS and its family of tests seem to be occupying a unique place as one of the local tests of English in Asia in terms of its localized features. TEPS, for example, is basically a locally developed English proficiency test that is designed to be sensitive to the needs of Korean learners of English. However, TEPS is also intended to be a general English proficiency test for Korean EFL learners built on the ideology of English for international communication and global intelligibility, rather than an English achievement test directly tied with Korea's national curricula for elementary, secondary, or tertiary English education. For these reasons, TEPS may have both localized and international test features at the same time. Thus, it would be helpful to see TEPS and its family of tests in a broadened framework of localization that allows for some degree of variability and flexibility on the localized spectrum instead of imposing a purely monolithic localization view on the tests.

With this in mind, our discussion in this chapter is centered around six major aspects of TEPS and its family of tests. First, we provide readers with a brief overview of the process of initial development, and recent revision, of TEPS by reflecting upon under what social and educational contexts a decision was made to develop the TEPS and how it is related to the other tests in the TEPS family. Second, we attempt to identify some of the important components and characteristics of TEPS exemplifying its localized nature. Third, we examine a number of security and quality control measures adopted for TEPS and its family of tests in order to maintain high standards of score reliability, validity, and fairness. Fourth, we go over the social consequences of introducing the TEPS in Korean society and its impact on the teaching and learning of English. Fifth, we review the research that has been undertaken for the TEPS and its family of tests and discuss some technological and psychometric innovations attempted for the TEPS family of tests, including the computer-based tests and the online scoring of speaking and writing responses for TEPS-Speaking and TEPS-Writing. Finally, we will outline some necessary and promising avenues for future research and assessment development in relation to the TEPS family of tests.

Overview of Development and Revision of TEPS

The TEPS was first administered in January 1999 after a series of research and development projects was conducted to develop, pilot-test, and validate it for several years at the Language Research Institute (LRI). Soon after, the LRI changed its name to Language Education Institute (LEI) to better reflect its expanded missions (comprising language research, teaching, and assessment). Several years earlier, in 1992, a research and development team was formed at the LRI to investigate the feasibility of developing and administering a large-scale English language proficiency test in Korea.

When the TEPS development project was undertaken, the research team consisted of the researchers of LRI and the faculty members of related departments at SNU. As a first step, a research effort was made to examine the feasibility of creating and administering a large-scale English proficiency test in the South Korean context. At that time, it was initially called SNUCREPT (Seoul National University Criterion Referenced English Proficiency Test) (Choi, 1993a, 1995). An item database was created to make it possible for the assessment development staff to input, edit, and store a large number of items created and submitted by internal/external item writers. In October of 1998, the name TEPS was given to the test being piloted at that time. Not long after the test was launched in 1999, the test scores began to be accepted by many governmental and non-governmental organizations (e.g., Ministries of Education, Foreign Affairs, Personnel Management, and Defense; Bureau of Military Manpower; Korean National Police Agency), high schools and universities, and major business conglomerates/companies, such as Hyundai, LG, Lotte, POSCO, KT, Shinhan Bank, KBS, MBC, and Korean Air.

Even long before the first administration of TEPS, LRI had been in charge of developing and administering small-scale tests of numerous foreign languages for various government and business organizations. These tests were administered under a big umbrella name of SNULT (Seoul National University Language Tests), which came to include Chinese, French, German, Japanese, Russian, and Spanish, in addition to English. In fact, the history of SNULT dates back to the late 1960s, when some of these tests were first created upon request from external organizations and administered to Korean students and personnel dispatched abroad for either study or business/work. Beginning in August 2008, these tests began to be administered as part of regular administrations. Unfortunately, however, the SNULT's English test was discontinued in 2017 partly due to its overlapping nature with the TEPS and some of its family of tests, while the SNULT tests in the other six languages continue to be offered by SNU.

As briefly mentioned in the introduction to this chapter, there are several English proficiency tests other than the TEPS and SNULT English test that were developed or are currently being administered jointly by the TEPS

TEPS and Its Family of Tests **45**

Center and TEPS Council (see Table 3.1). These tests include *i*-TEPS, TEPS-Speaking and Writing, and TSW-MOFA. First, *i*-TEPS stands for "integrated TEPS" and is a computer-based English proficiency test that was first administered in 2009. The test is made up of not only multiple-choice item sections (i.e., listening comprehension, grammar/vocabulary, and reading comprehension) but also constructed-response sections (i.e., speaking and writing). Simply put, the multiple-choice sections of the test can be regarded as a shortened version of the original, paper-based TEPS, and the speaking and writing sections are newly added portions consisting of eight performance-based constructed-response tasks (five speaking and three writing tasks).

Second, TEPS-Speaking and TEPS-Writing (TSW) are stand-alone computer-based speaking and writing tests that are very similar to the speaking and writing sections of *i*-TEPS. Early in 1999, the LEI developed a computerized speaking test called the Test of Oral Proficiency (TOP) together with a paper-based writing test called the Test of Written Proficiency (TWP). These two performance-based tests were initially used by some universities and government organizations and also in English language competitions/contests. TOP became a regular test in 2002, and years later in August 2008, the TOP and the computerized TWP were renamed to TEPS-Speaking and TEPS-Writing, respectively. Since then these two computer-based performance tests have been

TABLE 3.1 The TEPS and Its Family of Tests

Major features	*TEPS*		*i-TEPS*	*TEPS-Speaking & Writing(TSW)*	*TSW-MOFA*	*SNULT****
	Original	*Revised*				
Languages	English	English	English	English	English	Chinese, (English), French, German, Japanese, Russian, Spanish
Sections*	L, G, V, R	L, V, G, R	L, G, V, R, S, W	S, W	S, W	L, R
No. of items**	200 MC	135 MC	135 MC, 8 CR (5S+3W)	10 CR (6S+4W)	11 CR (8S+3W)	100 MC
Mode	PBT	PBT	CBT	CBT	CBT	PBT
Score scale	10–990	0–600	0–400	0–100	0–100	0–100

Note. L=Listening comprehension; G=Grammar; V=Vocabulary; R=Reading comprehension; S=Speaking; W=Writing

** MC=multiple-choice; CR=constructed-response
*** The SNULT test for English was discontinued in 2017.

administered together as a test battery, although TEPS-Speaking is occasionally administered alone. For this reason, we often use the label TEPS-Speaking & Writing and its abbreviation TSW to refer to the two tests together as a single package. TSW consists of six speaking tasks and four writing tasks. Included among the six speaking tasks are warm-up questions, reading aloud a dialogue, answering questions in everyday situations, telling a story based on a picture sequence, giving a presentation based on a graph, and expressing an opinion on an issue. The writing tasks include dictation, writing an email, writing a summary, and expressing an opinion on an issue.

Third, another related stand-alone test of speaking and writing is TSW-MOFA, which is a customized version of the TEPS-Speaking and TEPS-Writing tests assembled for the Ministry of Foreign Affairs (MOFA). This special version of the TSW is taken by diplomats and embassy/consulate officers to be dispatched by, and other government officials working in, the MOFA of South Korea. In TSW-MOFA, prompt topics for speaking and writing tasks tend to address issues relevant for Korean diplomats. The speaking test, for instance, contains a presentation task in which a test-taker is asked to give a presentation on a Korean tradition described in a series of pictures (e.g., traditional games and sports, art, holiday celebrations). One unique feature of the writing test is the inclusion of Korean-to-English translation and translated summarization tasks. The readers should note, however, that the focus of discussion in this chapter is on the TEPS because it is the core (English) testing program for SNU LEI with the largest testing volume among the various tests in the TEPS family. From time to time, nevertheless, these other related tests of the TEPS family are also brought into discussion when deemed necessary in describing and explaining relevant issues for the TEPS.

The Localized Nature of the Tests

TEPS is designed to be a general English proficiency test for Korean EFL test-takers, and the development of TEPS partially coincided with the Korean government's globalization (or internationalization) efforts. Thus, the implicit, underlying norms of English use were possibly built on the dominant ideology of English for international communication, with American English conceptualized as the standard of language usage. At the same time, TEPS was designed and developed, from the beginning, with an intention to create an English proficiency test that is sensitive to the needs of EFL/ESL learners, particularly Korean learners of English. It has several characteristics that reflect the unique Korean context and problems Korean EFL learners struggle with and thus the TEPS item writers and test editors pay special attention to when they not only create, review, and edit items but also assemble test forms for each test administration. These localized features of TEPS can be discussed at various levels of test design and administration.

Structure of TEPS

The overall structure of a language test can be reflective of not only a theoretical/operational definition of the intended test construct adopted for the test (i.e., a model or a theory of language proficiency) but also a variety of practical compromises to suit the local needs of assessment. Both the original and revised TEPS have similar structures for the total test and individual sections, although the number of items for each section is somewhat different in the two tests. Both tests are divided into four distinct sections of listening comprehension, grammar, vocabulary, and reading comprehension. The reason that the TEPS tests came to have the current structure is reflective of local concerns.

In this regard, one noteworthy localized feature of TEPS is that both the original and revised TEPS have separate grammar and vocabulary sections, which to some extent reflects a reality that grammar and vocabulary have traditionally been very important components of English language learning and teaching in the Korean EFL context. Even when a CBT version of TEPS, which is called *i*-TEPS, was developed and administered, a shortened, combined version of the grammar and vocabulary sections was retained, although the speaking and writing sections had to be newly added to the test. As a matter of fact, due to the strong influence of the communicative language teaching and testing paradigms and increasing concerns for washback on English learning and teaching, the grammar and vocabulary sections have been removed from, or absorbed by other sections in, several international English language proficiency tests (e.g., internet-based TOEFL).

Second, the original TEPS has a total of 60 listening comprehension items which is larger than the number of reading comprehension items (40 items), although it was drastically reduced to 40 items in the revised TEPS. Nevertheless, the number of items in the listening section is still greater than that in the reading section (40 vs. 35 items). There are a number of practical reasons for this difference. One is that the listening items and listening section as a whole tend to have a higher discriminating power for Korean EFL test-takers than the reading items and the reading section. It is partly due to the fact that English language teaching in schools has traditionally been focused more on written English, more specifically vocabulary, grammar, and reading comprehension. Another important, more practical consideration is that much less testing time is needed for the listening section due to the inherent nature of listening activities. In real-life communication situations, listening (and speaking) is carried out at real-time speed, and thus the recorded text, instructions, and response

48 Yong-Won Lee, Heesung Jun, and Ja Young Kim

options can be played at a speed similar to real-life situations. For these reasons, it would be much more cost-efficient and cost-effective to increase the number of the listening items than the reading ones in terms of maintaining a high score reliability for the total test.

Item Format and Item Writing Procedures

In order to enable the idea of assessment localization to be realized in the actual process of test creation, the TEPS team of assessment development consists of not only Koreans with very high English proficiency but also native speakers of English with EFL teaching experience who understand the typical errors made by Korean learners of English and the difficulties that Korean speakers experience in the process of learning English as a foreign language. Although the test is not directly tied to the national and local curricula of English, the Korean-English bilingual item writers and editors are very well aware of the phonological, lexical, collocational, morphological, and grammatical errors committed frequently by Korean EFL learners. Also, such knowledge and awareness can play a very important role in assessing and predicting the difficulty of test items, which is also a fundamental basis of creating or assembling equivalent (or parallel) test forms for TEPS.

One area where this is particularly relevant is the grammar and vocabulary sections, as item writers and editors consider L1 (first language) influence when writing and reviewing test items in these sections. Grammar points that Koreans often have trouble with are tested in the grammar section, for example, determiners, prepositions, tense, and subject-verb agreement. Also, loanwords from English and vocabulary that Korean students learn at school are considered when predicting the difficulty of vocabulary items. Consider the following item that tests phrasal verbs:

A: Ian should take the job offer in Seoul.
B: I know. He shouldn't _____ such a good opportunity.

    (a)   kick off
*(b)   pass up
    (c)   let down
    (d)   drop out

This item's difficulty was 0.146, and distractor (a) was chosen by 61% of the test-takers. The Korean expression that best fits the blank can be directly translated to "kick" in English, and this L1 interference appears to have been the reason behind the attractive distractor (a). Because many TEPS item writers and editors are familiar with the Korean language, it is possible to add distractors like these to the vocabulary items. At the moment, there is not a fixed ratio of items with localized and globalized focuses. Basically, each test form is assembled in accordance with the TEPS specification document, which provides general guidelines for determining the ratio of different item formats, genre/topical areas of passages, gender/occupation/social role distribution of interlocutors, and other important variables.

It is worthwhile to mention here that the local context can present some challenges to the creation of equivalent test forms that share a common set of anchor items across forms. Like in other East Asian countries, many Korean test-takers take test-taking very seriously and do everything possible to obtain high scores (e.g., taking test prep courses; sharing test item and score information on online bulletin boards; seeking help from private tutors). In addition, as Korean people today are so well connected with each other on the internet through online test preparation communities and forums, instructors at test preparation institutes and test-takers are able to collaborate to reconstruct the test form shortly after every administration, which means that there is a high risk in reusing the items already used in a previous form. Such situations make it almost impossible either to pretest items for item calibration purposes or to use a common set of items across test forms for test equating purposes. Therefore, a new test form has to be created for every test administration, and test-equating methods that do not require common items across test forms are used, such as some variations of the IRT true score equating and the equipercentile equating methods (TEPS Center, 2017). Some of the used test forms from regular administrations of original TEPS were provided periodically to a select group of private English language teaching institutes (or *hakwons*), so that they could create, and make available, commercial test preparation materials for their students and other prospective TEPS test-takers.

Quality Control and Fairness

This section summarizes a series of qualitative and psychometric procedures adopted by the TEPS Center for the purposes of quality control and fairness assurance for TEPS and its family of tests. The TEPS Center of SNU LEI has test specification documents for these tests that define the test construct and structure and stipulate the time limits and desired distributions of different item types and passage topics. Internal documents, such as the *TEPS Item Writer's Guide*, *TEPS Reviewer's Guide*, and *TEPS Technical Report*, provide useful guidelines for item writing and review and for statistical analysis of test data for these tests (TEPS Center, 2016a, 2016b, 2017). These documents and standards have been developed and updated based on a series of internal research studies (e.g., Ahn, 2002, 2003; Cho, Byun, Ryu, & Ryu, 2009; Choi, 2008c; Kim, Park, Lee, & Leaper, 2001; Lee, 2009; Lee, Anderson, & Ahn, 2009) and on other publicly available standards of educational and psychological testing (AERA, APA, & NCME, 1999, 2014). The TEPS Center goes through several stages of formal systematic review to ensure that the standards for quality and fairness are applied consistently in the process of reviewing/revising items, constructing test forms, and investigating evidence of validity, reliability, and comparability of scores that are the essential aspects of quality and fairness review at the TEPS Center of SNU LEI.

Item Writing and Review

The TEPS Center of SNU LEI holds periodic meetings for review of items before and after each administration. TEPS items are written by both external item writers and internal researchers of SNU LEI who have gone through item writing training and certification procedures offered by the TEPS Center. The minimum degree requirement for both English native speaker and Korean-English bilingual item writers is a master's degree in English or other related fields. Most of the external item writers are professors and lecturers of English at the tertiary level in Korea and abroad. Once the items are written and submitted to the Center through a web-based system maintained by the Center, they are reviewed and recommended to be (a) accepted for inclusion in the item database of the Center if the items are satisfactory, (b) returned to the original writer with suggestions for revision, or (c) rejected.

The *TEPS Item Writer's Guide* and *TEPS Reviewer's Guide* mentioned earlier (TEPS Center, 2016a, 2016b) provide very useful instructions and guidelines for both item writers and reviewers. Item writers create items, and then the TEPS development unit reviews the items to check whether test materials are created in accordance with specifications and guidelines provided by the Center and whether any stereotypes of persons or roles in terms of gender, age, religion, and physical condition are present in the materials. If the items pass the item review for fairness and content appropriateness, they are classified according to various item features and placed in a large item database (or pool) to be selected and used for the construction of new test forms. Since these TEPS items are not piloted (or pretested) before administrations, one important job of item writers and reviewers is to judge and confirm the difficulty level of each item according to the 5-point TEPS item difficulty scale.

Some of these items are selected and retrieved on screen from the item pool by a test assembler to construct a test form for each administration. When a set of items is selected and assembled for each section of a particular test form, this is done in accordance with the TEPS test specification document, which stipulates how each section is structured and balanced in terms of various passage and item features (e.g., topics, discourse genres/domains, situations, participant relationship, text complexity, item types, subskills being assessed by items, difficulty levels). Once the initial version of a test form is completed, this draft version of the test form is reviewed, edited, and revised through multiple stages of test form review by test editing specialists, English professors, and professional staff.

Psychometric and Statistical Item Analysis

After the finalized test form is administered as a live test, the TEPS psychometric/statistical unit conducts a preliminary item/test analysis to compute and review various psychometric indices for the test form, which include items difficulty, item discrimination, reliability coefficients, and distractor statistics for each item. If any suspicious or aberrant statistical behavior of items is detected (e.g., when more test-takers with high ability choose an incorrect option rather than the key), the TEPS item review committee meeting is convened to discuss whether the test item contains a potential mis-key or whether there is an error with the test item. After all of the issues raised during the process of the preliminary item analysis and review are resolved, the TEPS statistical analysis unit finally proceeds to the remaining process of scoring, scaling, and test equating. The results of the final item/test analyses are discussed and communicated periodically to the TEPS test development unit, so that the valuable information obtained from this process can be utilized to create better test items, create test forms more effectively, and revise (or refine) TEPS item construction standards and guidelines. In particular, the results of item difficulty analyses in terms of predicted-actual difficulty differences are shared through regular workshops with the TEPS development unit staff. The accuracy of item difficulty prediction by item writers/reviewers and test form assemblers is evaluated after each test administration in comparison with the empirical item difficulty values obtained from the actual live test data.

It is also worthwhile to mention here that item response theory (IRT) is used to conduct the item and test analysis for each administration of TEPS. The statistical information obtained through the classical test theory (CTT) analysis is used as a primary means to evaluate the quality of the items and the test, partly because it is intuitively easier to talk about the CTT-based statistical information with the TEPS development unit staff. Nevertheless, IRT is also used as a very important tool for item analysis, scaling, and test equating by the TEPS psychometric/statistical unit staff. For each test administration, unidimensional IRT models (mostly the two-parameter logistic model) are run on the scored item response data to evaluate the model-data fit, calibrate items, and obtain the test-taker ability measures for each section of the TEPS. An IRT-based true score equating method is also used to adjust the form to form difficulty differences for the TEPS and ensure the score comparability across different administrations of the TEPS, no matter which test form the test-takers take.

Reliability

The TEPS Center provides statistical evidence of reliability to judge how consistently a test of interest measures the intended construct(s) across items, test forms, and testing occasions (or time) and estimate the proportions of true

52 Yong-Won Lee, Heesung Jun, and Ja Young Kim

score and error variances in the observed score variance for the test. We use Cronbach's alpha, which is the most popular index for internal consistency. In addition, the standard error of measurement (SEM) is provided. Cronbach's alpha and SEM are computed for the four sections in all test forms before test data are subjected to confirmatory factor analysis. For example, for all sections across eight administrations in 2015–2016, the alpha values ranged from 0.84 to 0.93 with their SEM varying from 2.58 to 3.34. Overall, these alpha and SEM values indicate good reliability, given the raw score scales of the listening (0–60), grammar (0–50), vocabulary (0–50), and reading sections (0–40) of TEPS. In the case of the speaking and writing sections of *i*-TEPS or the stand-alone TEPS-Speaking and Writing (TSW) tests, inter-rater correlations and inter-rater reliability coefficients are computed along with the agreement rates (exact and adjacent agreement rates) for each task on each of the rating dimensions. When there is a score difference of 2 or greater on a scale of 0 to 5, a third rater is asked to adjudicate the case. The inter-rater reliability coefficients and agreement rates tend to be very high, ranging from 0.8 to over 0.9 even before adjudication, and they become slightly higher after the score discrepancies are resolved. Although the implicit language norms of the TEPS family of tests are based on American English, the raters of the speaking and writing tests consist of both English native speakers from North America (the U.S. and Canada) and Europe (the UK) and Korean-English bilingual speakers, and there are no penalties imposed on unique accents and features of various local/international English varieties.

Score Comparability

In order to assure the quality of test results, scores on different forms of the test should be comparable in a group of test-takers, no matter which test form the test-takers receive (Kolen & Brennan, 2004). As new TEPS forms are developed and administered many times each year, maintaining score comparability is crucial. TEPS scores across different administrations are connected through a test equating procedure based on item response theory (IRT), which examines the relationship between examinees' ability and true scores on the two test forms to be equated. The IRT equating is conducted by specifying a true score on Form X, finding the examinee's ability to that true score, and finding the true score on Form Y corresponding to that ability. For each administration of TEPS, there are at least 5,000 examinees, and therefore, the randomly equivalent groups design for equating is mostly used. The TEPS Center keeps track of any changes in group characteristics across administrations in terms of career, educational background, and purpose of taking the TEPS. Figure 3.1 shows the stability of the original TEPS total scale score across multiple administrations. It should, however, be noted that such a test equating procedure is currently used only for the TEPS that consists only of multiple-choice items. For the

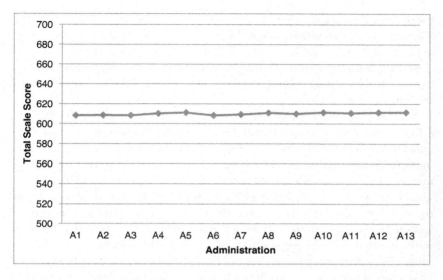

FIGURE 3.1 Pattern of Total Scale Scores

speaking and writing tests, an attempt is made to create equivalent forms in the test assembly stage by ensuring that items are written and edited while strictly adhering to the *TEPS-Speaking & Writing Item Writing Guidelines* (TEPS Center, 2015). After the speaking and writing tests are administered and scored, the average scores of the two test forms taken by homogeneous test groups are also compared in order to examine form equivalence.

Validity

Validity is one of the most important attributes of test quality, and thus, appropriate evidence to support intended inferences from test results needs to be collected and evaluated on a continuous basis (Chapelle, Enright, & Jamieson, 2008). The TEPS Center examines and evaluates regularly validity evidence collected and accumulated through psychometric and test content analyses, which demonstrates the relationships among different sections of the test, their relationships with the total test, the relationships between the total test score and other criterion measures available for the test of interest, and the factor structure of the total test.

First, the correlations between the four sections tend to be high, and those between the section scores and the total test scores are even higher. For one recent form of the original TEPS, the correlational coefficients among the four sections ranged from 0.74 to 0.85, while those between the section and total scores varied from 0.86 to 0.95. This pattern of correlations seems to be very consistent with the findings of previous studies and recent theories of language proficiency (Sawaki, Stricker, & Oranje, 2009; Stricker, Rock, & Lee, 2005). The prevailing hypothesis is that different knowledge and skill components are expected to be highly correlated due to the interrelated nature of these components that constitute communicative competence but distinct enough to warrant the existing common practice of reporting separate scores for these sections in addition to the total score.

Second, since the multiple-choice sections of both the original TEPS and *i*-TEPS have similar test structures, the correlational coefficients can be computed between the section scores of the original TEPS and those of *i*-TEPS. The multiple-choice portion of *i*-TEPS, including listening comprehension, grammar, vocabulary, and reading comprehension, can be regarded as a shortened version of the original, paper-based TEPS. Such a paralleled test structure between the two tests enables us to examine the patterns of correlations between the section scores and examine construct validity evidence in a framework similar to the multi-trait-multi-method framework (MTMM) (Bachman, 1990; Henning, 1987). According to the logic of MTMM, the correlations between the same trait/construct measured through different methods (convergent validity) should be higher than those between different traits measured through the same method (discriminant validity).

Analyses of the correlational patterns obtained for selected recent test forms of TEPS and *i*-TEPS revealed that the correlations computed between the same traits (or sections) between the paper-based and computer-based tests (i.e., TEPS and *i*-TEPS) tend to be higher than the rest of the correlations. The correlation values computed between the same sections across recent forms of TEPS and *i*-TEPS ranged from 0.53 to 0.79, while those between the four different sections across the two tests ranged from 0.31 to 0.68. This shows that the TEPS listening comprehension score, for instance, is correlated more highly with the *i*-TEPS listening comprehension score (0.79) than with any other section scores of *i*-TEPS (0.47, 0.31, 0.68), which also suggests that the listening comprehension sections of the two tests are measuring the same construct or very closely related constructs. Similar patterns were observed for the other three sections (grammar, vocabulary, and reading comprehension).

Third, for the sake of demonstrating the construct validity of the original TEPS, confirmatory factor analysis is conducted with the TEPS section score data on a regular basis. Both the communality indices and factor loadings are obtained for each of the test sections under a single latent factor (general English proficiency) model. Within such a simple factor structure model, the communality value for each section shows how much of the section score variance is accounted for by the single latent factor, whereas the factor loading means the correlations between the section score and the latent factor (McDonald, 1985; Stevens, 2002). The range of communality (R^2) for the four sections obtained for eight test forms from the years of 2015–2016 ranged approximately from 0.69 to 0.85, implying that the four section scores reasonably explain the single latent construct underlying all of the four sections—Korean test-takers' general

English proficiency. The factor loadings of the sections on the underlying latent trait also ranged from 0.84 to 0.92 across the eight test forms, suggesting reasonable relationships in the factor structure. Similar results were consistently observed across forms over many years (TEPS Center, 2017).

Test Use and Impact

This section discusses the uses of TEPS scores and the impact of test score use. The focus is on the TEPS because it has the largest test-taker volume. Since TEPS is a general English proficiency test rather than an English for specific purposes (ESP) test, TEPS tries to cover the topics, content, and contexts representing a broad range of knowledge domains, discourse genres, and social sectors in accordance with the TEPS test specification. Broadly speaking, TEPS test forms are assembled with two loosely defined target test-taker populations (or score use groups) in mind. These groups are (a) academic (e.g., universities, high schools, and other educational institutions) and (b) non-academic (e.g., governments, companies, and other governmental/non-governmental public institutions).

First of all, many academic institutions in Korea accept TEPS scores as a useful indicator of students' English language proficiency (Choi, 2008a; Hwang et al., 2013; Song & Park, 2002; Stevens, Jin, & Song, 2006). Approximately 80 universities in Korea use the scores for the following purposes:

- graduate school entrance;
- college English level test (placement test);
- selection of gifted language students;
- qualification exam for thesis writing in graduate school;
- selection of scholarship recipients;
- graduation requirement; and
- admission of transfer students.

TEPS scores seem to have been accepted by these universities because the test content covers academic English in addition to business/occupational English in a balanced way. The TEPS is also known to discriminate well among high-proficiency test-takers because the test includes difficult items to assess advanced English proficiency. Such a test appears to have been useful in the contexts listed earlier that draw highly competitive applicants.

On the other hand, non-academic institutions, such as companies, government organizations, and the military, accept TEPS scores for the following purposes (Choi, 2008a; Stevens et al., 2006):

- selection of employees and personnel, such as military personnel for the Korean Augmentation to the United States Army (KATUSA) and professional research agents in lieu of military service;
- evaluation of employees for promotion;

- selection of employees for study abroad; and
- evaluation of effectiveness of language training programs, such as pre- and post-training evaluation in teacher training programs for in-service English teachers.

The non-academic institutions seem to accept TEPS scores because the TEPS is a general purpose test that includes everyday English and business English as well. In some cases, as in the selection of professional research agents in lieu of military service, only TEPS scores are accepted because it discriminates well among high-proficiency test-takers. As applicants in these contexts tend to be uniform in their English proficiency (all being students at top-tier research universities in Korea), TEPS scores appear to have been useful for discriminating among these applicants.

In addition, TEPS scores can be submitted to meet the minimum English requirement to take national exams, including the civil service exams and judicial exams, as well as certification exams to be certified as appraisers, public accountants, tax accountants, actuaries, public labor attorneys, and patent attorneys, for example (Kim, 2000; Stevens et al., 2006). By accepting TEPS scores (or scores from other English proficiency tests), the administrators of these national exams and certification exams are absolved from having to develop their own English tests for the purpose of screening candidates.

As of yet, the impact of TEPS score use and the washback effects of the TEPS have not been extensively researched, but they have been partially described in an article by Choi (2008a) in terms of the general impact of EFL testing on EFL education in Korea. Choi (2008a) points out that Korean college students spend much of their time and energy on English test preparation for employment or further study after graduation. Although for the majority of these students, the test that they are studying for is the TOEIC, some study for the TEPS to apply to certain organizations or graduate schools that only accept TEPS scores. Since many of the English tests that companies and graduate schools accept are multiple-choice, Korean test-takers tend to work on improving their test-taking strategies rather than English proficiency. This can be seen through the publication of dozens of English test preparation books every year and the proliferation of test preparation institutes offering both online and offline courses (Senior, 2009). As a result, the discrepancy between test scores and actual English proficiency has continued to be an issue.

Recently, there has been a shift among Korean test-takers and test score users towards tests of productive English skills (Kim, 2014), particularly as Samsung decided to accept only the Oral Proficiency Interview-computer (OPIc) scores from applicants as evidence of their English proficiency. Other major companies in Korea have followed suit, and now many job applicants take the OPIc or the TOEIC Speaking Test. Even so, test-takers continue to focus on improving their test scores on these productive skill tests. Therefore, many test-takers, who have to retake these tests multiple times to obtain the scores they want or need, complain about the financial burden placed on them (Choi, 2008a) because the test fee for productive skill tests is much higher than that for receptive skill tests. Although TSW does not have as large a test-taker pool as the OPIc or the TOEIC Speaking Test, it still has a considerable retest rate, sometimes even up to 35%. More research is definitely needed to further investigate the issues of washback and impact.

Research and Innovation

This section summarizes the major validation efforts for TEPS score use. Several journal articles have been published to disseminate validity evidence for the TEPS (e.g., Choi, 1993a, 1994a, 1997b, 1999; Choi & Lee, 2001). Nevertheless, one should note that most of the research conducted for the TEPS and its family of tests over the last three decades or so is of an internal nature. Over 50 research projects have been conducted since 1991 within the LEI to develop the TEPS family of tests, validate their use, and explore possible revisions.

The first group of studies was conducted in the development stages of the TEPS. In this phase, which was from 1991 to 1998, the research projects were concerned with needs analysis, test development, construct validation, and test method facets. During this period, the researchers at the LEI were actively investigating the need for a general English proficiency test developed in Korea and were invested in developing the actual test as well as validating the use of scores from the test. These efforts culminated in the development of the TEPS, TOP, and TWP. The major research projects from this first phase are summarized in Table 3.2.

During the initial test development stages, Choi (1993a, 1994a) were the first published articles to discuss the content and construct validity of a prototype of TEPS, then called SNUCREPT. Along with a description of the test structure, test content, and test method facets, the results from a pilot test were presented to show that the score reliability for the test was acceptable, with alpha coefficients for all four subtests being above 0.80. Choi (1995) also conducted a comparability study on SNUCREPT and TOEIC and concluded that the two tests are not comparable in terms of the content and test methods.

These studies were followed by two external reviews of SNUCREPT. Oller (1995) supported the speededness of the test because it reflects "the fact that language processing normally occurs under certain highly restrictive temporal constraints" (p. 161). SNUCREPT was evaluated to have "performed rather well on the whole" (p. 164), but it was suggested that "the isolated sentence-based items" in certain parts of the test be reworked to incorporate the items into a "meaningful and episodically organized context" (p. 166). This suggestion appears not to have been incorporated into the TEPS by the initial developers in order to retain the one-passage-one-item test feature whose purpose

58 Yong-Won Lee, Heesung Jun, and Ja Young Kim

TABLE 3.2 Research on the Development of TEPS

Study	Work done/Findings	Implication/Action Taken
Park, Lee, Hong, Shin, and Choi (1992)	A survey of 794 people showed the need for a proficiency test to assess practical English used in the workplace.	Development of a practical and general English proficiency test began.
Choi (1993b, 1994b)	The first and second pilot tests were developed and administered to 738 and 314 college students, respectively, in Korea. Results were analyzed.	Revisions were made and a second pilot test was developed; further research was undertaken to investigate the feasibility of operating an item bank.
Choi (1997a)	The feasibility of operating an item bank for large-scale administration operation of the test was investigated by administering a pilot test to Korean university students (n=408).	Revisions were made to the test based on item and test statistics.
Baek and Shim (1997)	For an existing oral interview exam at the SNU LRI, instructions for the interviewers and evaluation guidelines were revised.	A need to either further improve on the existing oral interview exam or develop a new oral proficiency test was identified.
Choi (1998)	The Test of Oral Proficiency (TOP) was developed and piloted with 74 test-takers and 8 raters.	Revisions to the number and types of tasks were proposed; follow-up research was recommended to validate the slightly revised test methods of the TOP.

was to avoid local dependence among items. Bachman (1996) also gave a positive review of SNUCREPT, saying that it is "a well-designed and carefully researched EFL proficiency test" that is "soundly grounded in both applied linguistic and psychometric theory" (p. 381). However, it was suggested that to improve the authenticity of the test, the inclusion of the grammar and vocabulary subtests should be reconsidered and item types such as short-answer completion tasks that require test-takers to produce language could be included. Again, the initial developers of the test appear not to have taken these suggestions. The TEPS remained a completely multiple-choice test, and the grammar and vocabulary sections have come to be known as being unique to TEPS compared to other English proficiency tests.

Choi (1997b) then investigated the test-takers' perception of the test method facets of the SNUCREPT. The characteristics discussed in the paper were

(a) formality-specific assessment of vocabulary and grammar, (b) presentation of test content in aural mode only in the listening comprehension section, (c) presenting the passage and question twice in certain parts of the listening comprehension section to allow for a two-step process of macro-listening and micro-listening, (d) the one passage-one item principle in the listening and reading comprehension sections to minimize the local item dependence effect, and (e) speededness through the presentation of a large number of items in a limited amount of time. The 314 test-takers who took a pilot SNUCREPT generally perceived these test method facets as valid and desirable, and the results added support for the features being retained in the TEPS.

The second group of studies was conducted after the TEPS became operational in January 1999. From 1999 to 2003, the research projects were focused on item writing (Kim & Lee, 2003; Kim et al., 2001; Lee, 1999), sensitivity of dialogue and passage content (Ahn, 2002, 2003), predicting the difficulty of items (Lee, Kim, & Park, 2002; Park, 2003), item analysis (Choi, 2003), and various measurement issues (Choi & Lee, 2002; Choi & Park, 2001). In this phase, the purpose was to stabilize the TEPS and continue to improve its quality. The major research projects in the second phase are summarized in Table 3.3.

TABLE 3.3 Research on the Stabilization of TEPS

Study	Work Done/Findings	Implication/Action Taken
Lee (1999)	The grammar and vocabulary items in the first six TEPS forms were analyzed in terms of the proportions of different grammatical and lexical features.	The number of colloquial and idiomatic expressions tested needs to be controlled, as they affect test-takers' perceived difficulty of the TEPS.
Kim et al. (2001)	A comprehensive manual for writing TEPS test items was written.	Item writers wrote items based on the manual.
Choi and Lee (2002), Choi and Park (2001)	Psychometric issues in scoring were investigated.	Improvements continued to be made in the scoring procedure. The test times were retained.
Lee et al. (2002)	The correlation between researchers' predicted difficulty of reading items and the actual item difficulty was higher than that between readability indices and the actual item difficulty.	Readability indices cannot be the only predictor of the difficulty of reading comprehension items.

(Continued)

60 Yong-Won Lee, Heesung Jun, and Ja Young Kim

TABLE 3.3 (Continued)

Study	Work Done/Findings	Implication/Action Taken
Ahn (2002, 2003)	Guidelines were made on what sensitive topics and issues should be avoided in dialogues and passages.	These guidelines were added to the *TEPS Item Writer's Guide* and *TEPS Item Reviewer's Guide*.
Choi (2003)	Items that can be potentially problematic based on items statistics were analyzed.	Item reviewers were trained to consider difficulty of vocabulary and expressions used in options when predicting the difficulty of items.
Kim and Lee (2003)	The grammar items in seven TEPS forms were analyzed, and suggestions were made on which grammatical features should be grouped together.	The item writing manual was revised to reflect the suggestions on categorizing grammatical features in grammar items.
Park (2003)	The predicted and actual item difficulty of two hundred vocabulary items were compared and analyzed. The difficulty of distractors was found to affect the difficulty of a vocabulary item.	Item reviewers were trained to consider the relatedness of the options as well as collocations in predicting the difficulty of vocabulary items.

Choi (1999) followed up on the pre-operational validation studies of TEPS with an investigation of test-takers' perceptions of the fairness of the TEPS as they took the first operational test. From a phone survey of 1,043 test-takers, it was found that overall, "the majority of the test-takers consider TEPS a valid test of desirable test methods and a potential candidate to substitute for other conventional EFL tests" (p. 594). Also presented were the descriptive statistics and IRT-based test results of the first TEPS as well as evidence for criterion validity by comparing test-takers' scores on the TEPS to those on the TOP. Regarding the issue of speededness for TEPS, Choi and Lee (2002) conducted a study to investigate the effects of speededness of TEPS on test performance. The participants were administered TEPS with a shorter test time and regular test time. They compared two test scores for one administered with a shorter test time against the other which was administered with a regular test time. There was no difference in scores for the extremely high ability test-takers, while scores for the test-takers in the middle rank decreased, and the scores for the low ability test-takers increased. The conclusion of this study is that speededness increased discrimination among the students in the middle and low ranks.

In the third phase, from 2005 to 2010, there continued to be projects on maintaining the quality of the TEPS, including revision of the existing item writing process (Cho et al., 2009), test review process (Kim & Kim, 2009; Lee, 2009; Lee et al., 2009), and item database (Son et al., 2010). At the same time, however, many other research projects were conducted to revise the TOP and TWP to TSW, a computer-based test of the two productive skills (Lee, Bong, Hirch, & Anderson, 2008; Ryu et al., 2006b, 2006c), and eventually to develop a new test called *i*-TEPS, a computer-based test of the four skills/components tested in the TEPS plus the two productive skills (Choi, 2008b, 2008c; Lee, Kim, & Moon, 2008; Song, Park, Shin, & Jin, 2007; Ryu et al., 2006a). An online rating program was also developed to facilitate the rating of the spoken and written responses from productive skill tests (Son, Park, Choi, Bant, & Kim, 2005). The major research projects from this third phase are summarized in Table 3.4.

TABLE 3.4 Research on the Maintenance of TEPS and Development of New Tests

Study	Work Done/Findings	Implication/Action Taken
Son et al. (2005)	An online rating program was developed to allow raters to rate spoken and written responses online.	Facilitated the rating of the spoken and written responses from the TOP and TWP and eventually the TSW and *i*-TEPS
Lee, Bong et al. (2008), Ryu et al. (2006b, 2006c)	The TOP and TWP were revised into TEPS-Speaking & Writing (TSW).	The TSW became a regular test in 2008.
Choi (2008b, 2008c), Lee, Kim, and Moon (2008), Song et al. (2007), Ryu et al. (2006a)	A computer-based test that integrates TEPS and TSW, called *i*-TEPS, was developed to test the four language skills as well as grammar and vocabulary.	The number of items in MC sections was reduced from 200 to 135 for the *i*-TEPS, with that of the speaking and writing sections of the *i*-TEPS being reduced from 10 to 8. Almost all item types of TEPS and TSW were retained in the *i*-TEPS.
Cho et al. (2009)	The item writing process was analyzed and suggestions were made to make it more efficient.	Facilitated the management of new items at the TEPS Center.
Kim and Kim (2009)	The online test review system was revised by updating menus and features.	Facilitated the test review process at the TEPS Center.

(Continued)

TABLE 3.4 (Continued)

Study	Work Done/Findings	Implication/Action Taken
Lee (2009), Lee et al. (2009)	The test review process was analyzed and suggestions were made to make it more efficient.	The item writing manual and test review manual were revised and updated, facilitating the test review process.
Son et al. (2010)	The item database program was updated, and the test form production process was streamlined into three steps—item writing, item reviewing, and test form production.	Facilitated the production of test forms at the TEPS Center.

One notable study in the development of the *i*-TEPS was Lee, Kim, and Moon (2008) which investigated psychometric properties of the optimal scenario of section structure restructuring for New TEPS (which became *i*-TEPS). They examined the effect of decreasing the number of items in TEPS on the reliability of the four sections—listening comprehension, grammar, vocabulary, and reading comprehension—and on the reliability of a composite score using multivariate generalizability. The reliability of listening comprehension was higher than those of the other three sections, and the reliability of reading comprehension part 3 was relatively high, although there were only three items. Decreasing the number of items from 200 to 100 or 120 did not significantly affect the reliability of the composite score. Based on these findings, the number of items in *i*-TEPS was decided on to be 135.

In the fourth phase, from 2010 to present, numerous research projects have been conducted in an effort to revise the TEPS family of tests, particularly the TEPS and, to a lesser extent, the TSW. Projects included a series of expert meetings (Jun et al., 2014; Kim et al., 2012), needs analyses (Lee et al., 2015), feasibility studies (Lee et al., 2016), prototyping studies, pilot studies, and field studies (Kwon et al., 2018) to revise the TEPS. A series of studies done to develop a new (or revised) TEPS confirmed that many test-takers found the original TEPS to be overly long and difficult for them. Since all of the 40 reading items took a one-item-per-passage format in the original TEPS, it meant the test-takers had to read a total of 40 passages, and the same was true for the listening section made up of 60 items. There were also test-takers' concerns about the difficulty level of some vocabulary items intended to discriminate high proficiency test-takers. In response to such findings, the TEPS Center investigated the feasibility of reducing the number of items for all four sections, introducing a two–items-per-passage format to the listening and reading sections, and adding to the reading section some new text formats (e.g., emails, online news articles, mobile phone messages) representing a wider range of communication contexts through pilot studies and finally decided to incorporate these new features into the revised TEPS. The revised TEPS became operational in May 2018. For the TSW, content expert meetings have been held and revisions have been proposed for the two sections (Chung et al., 2013; Son, Choi, Jung, Kim, & Son, 2010), but pilot testing and further research are still needed before the actual implementation of the revised TSW can take place. The major research projects in this fourth phase are summarized in Table 3.5.

TABLE 3.5 Research on the Revision of the TEPS and Its Family of Tests

Study	Work Done/Findings	Implication/Action Taken
Chung et al. (2013), Son, Choi et al. (2010)	Revisions were proposed for the TSW, including the deletion of tasks and addition of new tasks.	More research, including prototyping and pilot testing, is required before implementing a revised TSW.
Jun et al. (2014), Kim et al. (2012)	Experts agreed that the TEPS should be revised to better reflect recent changes in theories of second language learning and assessment and in the English use environment.	Specific changes need to be proposed and their feasibility should be investigated.
Lee et al. (2015)	A needs analysis showed that English language learners in Korea perceive the TEPS to be difficult but would respond positively to introducing new item types in the listening and reading sections.	The feasibility of implementing a revised TEPS should be investigated.
Lee et al. (2016)	The feasibility of implementing a revised TEPS was investigated.	A revised TEPS form should be developed and pilot tested.
Kwon et al. (2018)	Four large-scale pilot tests of the revised TEPS produced acceptable item and test statistics. Test-takers showed a favorable response to the changed features in the revised TEPS.	The TEPS Center should continue to actively conduct research to stabilize the revised TEPS and collect validity evidence for the revised test.
Lee et al. (2019)	The first ten administrations of the revised TEPS produced stable and reliable scores. A standard setting study was conducted and the reporting of subskill scores on score reports was investigated for the revised TEPS.	The TEPS Center should conduct further standard setting and test comparison studies to enhance score interpretation and use.

In addition to research studies conducted for the TEPS and its family of tests for many years, there have been various technological and psychometric innovations either attempted or successfully adopted for these tests. First, from the beginning stage, the TEPS attempted to use one of the powerful modern psychometric theories called IRT as its basis for item/test analysis, test-taker proficiency estimation, and score reporting. This tradition continued to be embraced and further developed by the TEPS Center. It is amazing that the TEPS has been using IRT-based test equating methods to ensure score comparability across test forms, given that even the most popular domestic testing program, KCSAT, has not been using equating methods. Second, the TEPS Center has tried to utilize computer-based test delivery and scoring for the i-TEPS. This was made possible because the TEPS Center decided to develop and use an item database for creating, editing, and storing items in a systematic way. The CBT test delivery system was also developed and used for TSW and TSW-MOFA, which also necessitated the development of online rating systems for these tests. Raters can log in to the online rating systems to get additional training before being allowed to score the spoken and written responses. Third, more recently, corpus analyses are being used to assess frequency and difficulty levels for a target word and distractor words for vocabulary items and to analyze the textual characteristics of listening and reading passages. Finally, graph-based distractor analysis is being used in identifying and flagging items that need further review by TEPS development unit staff in the preliminary item analysis stage. This particular method of analysis allows us to monitor the functioning and behavior of response options at different proficiency levels and gain valuable insights about how to improve the quality of a key and distractors and thereby improve item discriminability and overall test quality.

The Way Forward

As of 2019, TEPS is currently at a very critical juncture in many ways. First, TEPS is set to celebrate its 20th anniversary in 2019. Although TEPS enjoyed huge success during the first 14 years, it has been met with many new challenges since then. Test-taker surveys of the original TEPS repeatedly revealed that the test-takers in general found the test to be too difficult and challenging for them (Kwon et al., 2018). In response to such feedback from the major stakeholder groups of TEPS, the original TEPS was revised, and the revised TEPS was successfully launched in May 2018 after a series of research studies was carried out to inform revision of the original TEPS. It is our hope that the new test features would be appealing to Korean test-takers and bring back many of them to the revised TEPS.

Since the revised TEPS is currently going through an initial period of stabilization and refinement, there are a number of research and operational issues that need to be addressed in the years to come. The following are some of the major areas of further research and investigation for the revised TEPS and its family of tests.

First, a series of validation studies should be conducted to stabilize the revised TEPS and collect and accumulate validity evidence for the newly launched test. On the psychometric front, studies have been already completed to create a new scale for the test, to devise, validate, and implement appropriate procedures for test equating and test data analysis, and to provide score conversion tables between the original TEPS and the revised TEPS (KELTA, 2018). Nevertheless, additional studies still need to be urgently done in order to establish the score conversion relationships directly between the revised TEPS and other major international and domestic English proficiency tests. In addition, various modern psychometric analyses, such as differential item functioning (DIF) analysis and generalizability (G) theory analysis, need to be added to the regular quality-control procedures for the revised TEPS and its family of tests.

In conjunction with this, a new series of studies also needs to be done to establish the meanings of different score bands (e.g., standard setting or score anchoring studies) for the revised TEPS as part of a larger effort to increase the interpretability and usability of the scores from the revised TEPS and its family of tests. As discussed previously, standard setting studies were conducted to establish important cut scores and performance descriptors for different score levels for the listening and reading sections of the revised TEPS using the CEFR as a reference scheme. The CEFR was used in these studies to help the score users interpret TEPS scores not only in terms of its own locally defined scale but also in reference to an international proficiency scale. It is necessary to conduct similar studies for the remaining sections of the test and find ways to revise the cut scores and score band descriptors for the total score as well.

Second, another important direction for future research and development is to develop and validate a computer-based (or internet-based) version of the new test. One of the TEPS family of tests, *i*-TEPS, is a computer-based test of vocabulary, grammar, and four different skills of English. Similarly, a CBT or iBT version of the revised TEPS can be developed. A number of basic studies need to be conducted to make it possible to create an item bank and computer- (or internet-) delivery system to support such technology-enhanced tests. In parallel with such efforts, it would be worthwhile to consider developing and deploying automated scoring of writing and speaking technology for TSW as well.

Third, another important thread of research for TEPS has to do with investigating the social consequences of the TEPS family of tests in Korean society and the potential washback effects of the revised TEPS on English language learning and teaching in Korea. Despite the increasing call for investigating the socio-political dimension of language tests in the field of language assessment, there has been a dearth of research on the social, political, and educational dimensions of TEPS and its related tests. There should be a more active program of research in this area inside and outside SNU LEI.

In relation to this, it also seems necessary to investigate ways to enable the TEPS and its family of tests to generate and provide useful diagnostic feedback for Korean English language learners in addition to section and total scores. A study is currently being done to revise the score report for the revised TEPS in such a way that the score report can provide more enhanced information to inform future learning activities, such as the test-takers' patterns of strengths and weaknesses in a particular section of the test, and preferably some recommendations and advice for remedial learning. Ideally, such efforts should be accompanied by the effective use of new frameworks, methodologies, and tools in assessment design (e.g., innovative construct/skill definition), item/test content analysis (e.g., discourse analysis using tools such as Coh-Metrix and LexTutor), and psychometric analysis (e.g., cognitive diagnostic psychometric models).

References

Ahn, J. (2002). *Seeking a balance in TEPS passages: A study in sensitivity issues* (Research Report No. 35). Seoul: SNU Language Education Institute.

Ahn, J. (2003). *Seeking a balance in TEPS listening conversation: A study in sensitivity issues* (Research Report No. 38). Seoul: SNU Language Education Institute.

American Educational Research Association (AERA), American Psychological Association (APA), & National Council on Measurement in Education (NCME). (1999). *Standards for educational and psychological testing*. Washington, DC: AERA.

American Educational Research Association (AERA), American Psychological Association (APA), & National Council on Measurement in Education (NCME). (2014). *Standards for educational and psychological testing*. Washington, DC: AERA.

Bachman, L. F. (1990). *Fundamental considerations in language testing*. Oxford: Oxford University Press.

Bachman, L. F. (1996). Review of Seoul National University Criterion-Referenced English Proficiency Test (SNUCREPT). *Language Research, 32*(2), 373–383.

Baek, J., & Shim, J. (1997). *Seouldaehakgyo eohakyeonguso eohakgeomjeongsiheom gusulneungnyeokcheukjeong* [Oral proficiency examination of the Language Research Institute at Seoul National University] (Research Report No. 8). Seoul: SNU Language Education Institute.

Chapelle, C. A., Enright, M. K., & Jamieson, J. (Eds.). (2008). *Building a validity argument for the Test of English as a Foreign Language^TM*. New York, NY: Routledge.

Cho, C., Byun, C.-K., Ryu, M.-S., & Ryu, D.-S. (2009). *Plans for improving the item-writing system of TEPS* (Research Report No. 61). Seoul: SNU Language Education Institute.

Choi, I.-C. (1993a). Construct validation study on SNUCREPT (Seoul National University Criterion-Referenced English Proficiency Test). *Language Research, 29*(2), 243–275.

Choi, I.-C. (1993b). *Language proficiency test gaebal yeongu* [Research on the development of a language proficiency test] (Research Report No. 2). Seoul: SNU Language Education Institute.

Choi, I.-C. (1994a). Content and construct validation of a criterion-referenced English proficiency test. *English Teaching, 48*, 311–348.

TEPS and Its Family of Tests **67**

Choi, I.-C. (1994b). *Seouldae yeongeoneungnyeok geomjeongsiheom gaebal* [Development of Seoul National University Criterion-Referenced English Proficiency Test] (Research Report No. 3). Seoul: SNU Language Education Institute.

Choi, I.-C. (1995). A comparability study on SNUCREPT and TOEIC. *Language Research, 31*(2), 357–386.

Choi, I.-C. (1997a). *SNUCALTS (Seoul National University Computer-Administered Language Testing Service) tadangseong geomjeung* [Construct validation on SNUCALTS (Seoul National University Computer-Administered Language Testing Service)] (Research Report No. 6). Seoul: SNU Language Education Institute.

Choi, I.-C. (1997b). Essential test method facets of a general English proficiency test and their validity as perceived by test-takers. *Language Research, 33*(4), 773–799.

Choi, I.-C. (1998). *Yeongeo moeui gusul myeonjeop siheomeui gaebal mit tadangseong gumjeung yeongu* [Development and validation of a simulated oral interview] (Research Report No. 17). Seoul: SNU Language Education Institute.

Choi, I.-C. (1999). Test fairness and validity of the TEPS. *Language Research, 35*(4), 571–603.

Choi, I.-C. (2003). *TEPS naeyong tadangdo geomjeung* [Content validation of TEPS] (Research Report No. 39). Seoul: SNU Language Education Institute.

Choi, I.-C. (2008a). The impact of EFL testing on EFL education in Korea. *Language Testing, 25*(1), 39–62.

Choi, I.-C. (2008b). *New TEPS gaebal banghyang geomto* [Review of new TEPS development] (Research Report No. 52). Seoul: SNU Language Education Institute.

Choi, I.-C. (2008c). *New TEPS munje yuhyeonge daehan yeongu* [Development of table of specifications for the new TEPS] (Research Report No. 55). Seoul: SNU Language Education Institute.

Choi, I.-C., & Lee, H. (2001). A trend analysis of individual TEPS scores. *Language Research, 37*(3), 675–710.

Choi, I.-C., & Lee, H. (2002). *TEPSui sokdohwa bangsigi suheomgyeolgwae michineun yeonghyang* [The effect of speededness of the TEPS on test performance] (Research Report No. 33). Seoul: SNU Language Education Institute.

Choi, I.-C., & Park, C. (2001). *TEPSui tadanghan chaejeom bangsigeul wihan neungnyeok mosuui chujeongbangbeop tadangdo* [Validation of ability parameter estimation methods for TEPS scoring schemes] (Research Report No. 29). Seoul: SNU Language Education Institute.

Chung, S., Lee, Y. S., Lee, B., Lee, Y.-W., Kim, J., Lee, J.-W., . . . Byun, J. (2013). *TEPS malhagi sseugi siheom gaejeong bangan yeongu* [Research for the revision of TEPS-Speaking & Writing] (Research Report No. 76). Seoul: SNU Language Education Institute.

Henning, G. (1987). *A guide to language testing.* Boston, MA: Heinle & Heinle.

Hwang, J., Lee, S.-H., Kim, S. J., Shin, J.-S., Yoon, H. B., Kim, D.-H., & Kim, E. J. (2013). A study on premedical curriculum reform of one medical school. *Korean Journal of Medical Education, 25*(4), 299–308.

Jun, Y. C., Ryu, D.-S., Park, Y. J., Lee, Y., Shin, S.-H., . . . Byun, J. (2014). *TEPS 2.0 gaebareul wihan gicho yeongu* [Research for the development of TEPS 2.0] (Research Report No. 77). Seoul: SNU Language Education Institute.

Kim, M.-W., Jeong, S., Kim, J.-W., Lee, Y.-W., Lee, Y., Shin, S.-H., . . . Lee, G. (2012). *Jeonggi TEPS jeonmyeon gaejeongeul wihan gicho yeongu* [Basic research for a complete revision of the regular TEPS] (Research Report No. 73). Seoul: SNU Language Education Institute.

Kim, P. S. (2000). Human resource management reform in the Korean civil service. *Administrative Theory & Praxis, 22*(2), 326–344.

Kim, S. (2014). *Teaching TOEFL listening to Korean college students using MALL (mobile-assisted language learning)* (Unpublished master's thesis). University of Oregon.

Kim, S., & Kim, Y. (2009). *Inteuranet munhang geomto peurogeuraem gae seoneul wihan yeongu* [Research on improving the Intranet program for item review] (Research Report No. 56). Seoul: SNU Language Education Institute.

Kim, S., & Lee, K. (2003). *TEPS munbbeop munhang gaebal—gibon gumun munhangeul jungsimeuro* [Developing TEPS grammar items—Focusing on the basic sentence structure items] (Research Report No. 41). Seoul: SNU Language Education Institute.

Kim, S., Park, Y., Lee, K., & Leaper, D. (2001). *Jonghapjjeogin TEPS chulje jichimseo jejak* [Making a comprehensive manual for test writing] (Research Report No. 32). Seoul: SNU Language Education Institute.

Kolen, M. J., & Brennan, R. L. (2004). *Test equating, scaling, and linking: Methods and practices.* New York, NY: Springer.

Korea English Language Testing Association. (2018). *Gaejeong TEPSwa Gongineohaksiheomgan howanganeungdo mit jeomsu whansan yeongu* [A study on the compatibility and score conversion between the revised TEPS and other certified language proficiency tests]. Seoul: Author.

Kwon, H., Lee, Y.-W., Lee, Y., Park, Y.-J., Kim, J., Jun, H., . . . Park, H. (2018). *Gaejeong TEPS yebisiheom gaebalgwa tadangdo geomjeung yeongu* [Development and validation of a pilot test form for the revised TEPS] (Research Report No. 80). Seoul: SNU Language Education Institute.

Lee, B., Kim, C., Park, Y. J., So, Y.-S., Lee, Y., & Jun, H. (2016). *2016nyeondo sinTEPS ihaeng yebi tadangseong geomjeung saeop* [Verification of preparation for New TEPS] (Research Report No. 79). Seoul: SNU Language Education Institute.

Lee, B., Park, Y. J., So, Y.-S., Lee, Y.-J., Kim, C., Jun, H., . . . Yeom, S. (2015). *2015nyeondo sinTEPS gaepyeon saeop* [The development of New TEPS] (Research Report No. 78). Seoul: SNU Language Education Institute.

Lee, D., Bong, J.-S., Hirch, R., & Anderson, P. (2008). *TEPS-Writing siheomui gaeseone daehan yeongu* [A study on redesigning the TEPS—Writing test] (Research Report).

Lee, K. (1999). *TEPS munbbeopgwa eohwiui naeyong guseonge gwanhan yeongu* [A study on content organization of TEPS grammar and vocabulary section] (Research Report No. 26). Seoul: SNU Language Education Institute.

Lee, K., Kim, S., Park, Y. J. (2002). *TEPS dokhae nanido sanjeong* [Assessing the difficulty levels of TEPS reading comprehension items] (Research Report No. 36). Seoul: SNU Language Education Institute.

Lee, S. (2009). *TEPS geomto chegye gaeseonan* [Evaluation and proposal for reforms on the current TEPS reviewing process] (Research Report No. 60). Seoul: SNU Language Education Institute.

Lee, S., Anderson, P., & Ahn, J. (2009). *Geomto/chulje jichim gaejeong mit yeonguwon gyoyukgwajeong gaeseon* [Revising the review/writing manuals and improving the training process of researchers] (Research Report No. 62). Seoul: SNU Language Education Institute.

Lee, Y.-W., Kim, S., & Moon, Y. (2008). *TEPS yeongyeok jaeguseongeul wihan simricheukjeonghakjeok gicho yeongu* [A preliminary psychometric investigation into optimal scenarios of section structure restructuring for New TEPS] (Research Report No. 49). Seoul: SNU Language Education Institute.

Lee, Y.-W., Kwon, H., Lee, Y., Lim, E., Jun, H., Song, M., . . . Min, S. (2019). *New TEPS anjeonghwa bangan mit tadangdo geomjeung yeongu* [Research for the stabilization and validation of the New TEPS] (Research Report No. 81). Seoul: SNU Language Education Institute.

McDonald, R. P. (1985). *Factor analysis and related methods.* Hillsdale, NJ: Lawrence Erlbaum Associates.

Oller, J. W. Jr. (1995). Review of content and construct validation of a criterion-referenced English proficiency test. *English Teaching, 50*(3), 161–168.

Park, N., Lee, S., Hong, J., Shin, J., & Choi, I.-C. (1992). *Oegugeosiheom gaeseoneul wihan seolmunjosa kyeolgwabunseok bogoseoh* [Report on the analysis of results from a survey to improve the foreign language proficiency test] (Research Report No. 1). Seoul: SNU Language Education Institute.

Park, Y.-Y. (2003). *Eohwiui yecheuk nanidowa silje nanido bigyo yeongu* [A comparative study of difficulty levels between prediction and student response] (Research Report No. 43). Seoul: SNU Language Education Institute.

Ryu, D.-S., Park, Y.-Y., Kwon, H.-S., Song, M.-J., Min, E.-K., Ahn, J., . . . Jin, D. (2006a). *TEPS gaeseonbangan yeongu* [Reforming TEPS] (Research Repot No. 45). Seoul: SNU Language Education Institute.

Ryu, D.-S., Park, Y.-Y., Kwon, H.-S., Song, M.-J., Ryu, E. J., Shin, S.-K., . . . Jin, D. (2006b). *TOP/TWP sian whakjeongeul wihan yeongu* [Research for the development of a new form of TOP & TWP] (Research Repot No. 47). Seoul: SNU Language Education Institute.

Ryu, D.-S., Park, Y.-Y., Son, Y., Son, C., Ahn, J., Hong, K.-S., & Jin, D. (2006c). *TOP gaeseonsian yeongu* [Reforming TOP] (Research Report No. 46). Seoul: SNU Language Education Institute.

Sawaki, Y., Stricker, L., & Oranje, A. (2009). Factor structure of the TOEFL internet-Based Test (iBT). *Language Testing, 26*(1), 5–30.

Senior, R. (2009, January 15). Korean students silenced by exams. *The Guardian.* Retrieved from www.theguardian.com/world/2009/jan/15/south-korea-students

Son, C. Y., Choi, H. C., Hwang, J.-J., Jung, H., Park, J. Y., Kim, S. H., . . . Lee, S. Y. (2010). *TEPS munjae-eunhaeng system mit chaejeom system yeongu* [Design and development research for TEPS item bank and IRT scoring system] (Research Report No. 66). Seoul: SNU Language Education Institute.

Son, C. Y., Choi, H. C., Jung, H., Kim, Y., & Son, J. (2010). *TEPS-Writing chaejeom-chegye gaeseoneul wihan yeongu* [Research for improving the scoring system of TEPS-Writing] (Research Report No. 69). Seoul: SNU Language Education Institute.

Son, C. Y., Park, Y.-Y., Choi, I.-C, Bant, S., & Kim, S. (2005). *Malhagi/sseugi eungsi mit chaejeom peurogeuraem gaebal* [TOP/TWP testing & evaluation programs development] (Research Report No. 44). Seoul: SNU Language Education Institute.

Song, M.-J., & Park, Y.-Y. (2002). Assessment of task validity for two proficiency tests at an English contest. *Language Research, 38*(1), 443–464.

Song, M.-J., Park, Y.-Y., Shin, S.-K., & Jin, D. (2007). *Saeroun TEPS gaebaleul wihan yeongu* [Research for the development of a new TEPS] (Research Report No. 48). Seoul: SNU Language Education Institute.

Stevens, G., Jin, K., & Song, H. J. (2006). Short-term migration and the acquisition of a world language. *International Migration, 44*(1), 167–180.

Stevens, J. P. (2002). *Applied multivariate statistics for the social sciences.* Hillsdale, NJ: Lawrence Erlbaum Associates.

Stricker, L. J., Rock, D. A., & Lee, Y.-W. (2005). *Factor structure of the LanguEdge test across language groups* (TOEFL Research Monograph No. MS-32; ETS RR-05-12). Princeton, NJ: Educational Testing Service.

TEPS Center. (2015). *TEPS-Speaking & Writing item writing guidelines* (internal document). Seoul: SNU Language Education Institute.

TEPS Center. (2016a). *TEPS item writer's guide* (internal document). Seoul: SNU Language Education Institute.

TEPS Center. (2016b). *TEPS reviewer's guide* (internal document). Seoul: SNU Language Education Institute.

TEPS Center. (2017). *TEPS technical report* (internal document). Seoul: SNU Language Education Institute.

4

VIETNAMESE STANDARDIZED TEST OF ENGLISH PROFICIENCY

A Panorama

Nguyen Thi Ngoc Quynh

The Introduction of VSTEP in the Context of Education Reform in Vietnam

Vietnam is going through a rapid demographic transition from what was once a young population feeding into the workforce during the last three decades towards an aging society (World Bank, 2013). This means that Vietnam can no longer rely on the size of its workforce to advance its profound socio-economic reforms. Instead, from now on this nation needs to focus on making its workforce more productive by equipping them with adequate and necessary skills and competencies (World Bank, 2013). According to the World Bank's (2013) survey on workforce skills in 2011–2012, competence in a foreign language was identified as one of the ten most important job-related skills in Vietnam (p. 16).

In addition, in the context of rigorous globalization and regionalization, English language ability is believed to be an indispensable tool to bring Vietnam into the modern world (Dudzik & Nguyen, 2015). Particularly, now that the ASEAN Economic Community (AEC), of which Vietnam is a member, has been officially effective since 2015, the labor force of one ASEAN country can look for jobs in another. Employment becomes more competitive across borders. The Vietnamese workforce, therefore, needs to be trained adequately to ensure their competitiveness. In this regard, the national Human Resource Development Strategy for 2011–2020 set a goal "to have about 30.5 million personnel trained by 2015, accounting for approximately 55% of the 55 million working people and 44 million personnel by 2020 (accounting for a total 63 million working people)" (MOET, 2013, p. 22). However, limitations in English capacity are among the nation's "biggest limitations" (Dudzik & Nguyen, 2015).

In this nation where virtuous and talented people are considered the key factors for sustaining State development, and knowledge the greatest asset of the nation (as stated in the symbolic Memoir on the Stele of Doctors at its Temple of Literature in Hanoi), education has always been the top priority and the major key to developing national human resources. Therefore, in response to growing demand for foreign languages to address the socio-economic reform as well as the rapid regional and international integration, the government of Vietnam is committed to large-scale reform in foreign language education. In 2008, they issued a government decision to renovate thoroughly the tasks of teaching and learning foreign languages within the national education system in order to produce graduates who gain the capacity to use a foreign language independently before joining the national workforce (MOET, 2008, p. 1). This decision, entitled Teaching and Learning Foreign Languages in the National Education System, Period 2008–2020 (MOET, 2008), gave birth to the National Foreign Language 2020 Project, which was renamed the National Foreign Language Project (hereafter as the NFL Project) when it was revised in 2017. This project is expected to bring about comprehensive reform of teaching, learning, and assessment of foreign languages at all education levels.

The first significant achievement of the NFL Project has been the issuing of a six-level foreign language competency framework (which is called as the CEFR-VN in this chapter for short) aligned to the Common European Framework of Reference for Languages in 2012 (Nguyen, T. N. Q., 2016a, 2016b). This framework consists of Levels 1 to 6, which are equivalent to the six levels A1, A2, B1, B2, C1, and C2 of the CEFR. The issuing of this framework put an end to the persistent ambiguity in identifying foreign language proficiency levels in Vietnam. The common practice before its arrival was that education institutions adopted the scales assumed by whatever sets of textbooks or materials they chose for their courses. When one institution or teacher uses multiple materials in their course, multiple frameworks may be used at the same time. Although the most common evaluation scales were elementary, pre-intermediate, intermediate, upper-intermediate, or advanced levels, the interpretations of these levels may differ from one institution to another. Therefore, the CEFR-VN is an essential step towards the standardization of foreign language education and assessment in Vietnam (Nguyen, T. N. Q., 2016b). Its alignment to the widely used global CEFR makes it possible for Vietnamese language learners and educators to claim their proficiency levels are compatible with international standards (Nguyen, T. N. Q., 2016b). Meanwhile, on the part of administrators and managers, this framework serves as the basis for their management and setting of foreign language capacity standards. In fact, soon after the introduction of the CEFR-VN, the education sector issued a series of policies on foreign language proficiency standards for learners and teachers: primary and lower secondary teachers are now required to be at Level 4 (B2 level on the CEFR) while upper secondary and university English teachers are required to reach Level 5 (C1 level); graduates from English-major tertiary programs are required at Level 5 (C1), while those from non-English major programs need to be at Level 3 (B1), effective from the school-year 2012–2013 (MOET, October 31, 2013).

Once the standards had been set, there was a pressing need for a national tool to measure the Vietnamese people's English capacity against these standards. However, at that time, the common practice in Vietnam was that tests were mostly cut-and-paste versions of available tests or resources from printed or online teaching and testing materials, or resembled international tests such as IELTS, TOEFL, TOEIC, or Cambridge English Qualifications. There was little validation research to assure the validity and reliability of these tests. Therefore, tests were mostly used for domestic or institutional purposes. There was a lack of a national foreign language test.

The changes and reforms at the national scale, education-sector scale, and specifically in English education and assessment that are described in this chapter resulted in a widespread and immense demand for standardization in assessment. Vu (2016) names the stage from the outset of the NFL Project till 2016 as the "Standardization-as-validation stage." Soon after the NFL Project officially started in 2012, the leading agency in English education in the country, the University of Languages and International Studies, Vietnam National University, Hanoi (ULIS) was commissioned and funded to develop the first-ever made-in-Vietnam standardized EFL test, called the Vietnamese Standardized Test of English Proficiency (widely called as VSTEP for short) targeting levels 3 to 5 according to the CEFR-VN (or levels B1 to C1 according to the CEFR). This multi-level test, which is now referred to as *VSTEP.3–5*, is the first variant of the VSTEP.

There was a debate over whether to develop one multi-level test or two level-based tests (i.e., Level 3 and Level 5) at the start of the NFL Project. The former was then adopted because it was believed that it would take less time and cost less to develop one test than two different level-based tests. This single first test was therefore intended to be a quickest solution to address the pressing demand for standardized assessment at that time, because this multi-level test can at the same time cater to the needs of a wide range of target assessment groups (Nguyen, H., 2014). Specifically, the three levels of English proficiency that it targets include the most common and important language standards required by the government for multiple groups of learners and laborers, who take up the majority proportion of the number of English learners and users in Vietnam: the B1 level is the exit standard of non-English major undergraduate students and master students, and at the same time it is the professional standard of primary English teachers and the English capacity requirement for the tenure of Level 2 official and lecturer positions; the B2 level is required for graduation by doctoral students of all majors and for the appointment of lower-secondary English teachers; and the C1 level is the graduation standard for English-major students, as well as the professional standard for upper-secondary and tertiary English teachers.

The VSTEP.3–5 development was treated as one of the top priorities of the first phase of the NFL Project in order to obtain a standardized assessment tool. It was therefore carried out intensively with utmost effort and energy.[1] The process consisted of four phases, following the guidelines provided by ALTE (2011).

The major tasks are as follows (Tran et al., 2015):

- Phase 1—Planning: Analyzing TLUs by means of survey questionnaires on 450 English users; identifying the test constructs, target test takers and members of four teams of test designers; and reviewing the literature and identifying theoretical models for each section;
- Phase 2—Designing: Designing two full tests based on the initial test specifications and speaking and writing rating scales; piloting these tests on 50 test takers; and reviewing the test format and test specifications;
- Phase 3—Trying out: Piloting one VSTEP sample test and one IELTS test on 210 test takers across Vietnam; validating the VSTEP sample test; setting the cut-scores of VSTEP using Rasch modelling, Angoff Method and expert paneling; and revising the test format and test specification; and
- Phase 4—Informing concerned stakeholders: Reporting the VSTEP development result to the MOET, the NFL Project, and linguists from around Vietnam. As a result, the MOET of Vietnam stipulated Decision No. 729/QD-BGDDT dated March 11, 2015 to publish the VSTEP format in the whole of Vietnam.

With the direction of the NFL Project, the ULIS test development team gained support and collaboration from several other big English education universities including Hue University and the University of Da Nang for the test piloting and review. In addition, the project team received technical support from and exchanged with some international language test developers and testing and assessment institutions.

The project outcomes, the first VSTEP test format and specification, were appraised by the Ministry of Education and Training (MOET), who officially issued it as a national standardized test for use and recognition in the whole national system on March 11, 2015 (MOET, 2015).

After the completion of the first VSTEP test design project, the ULIS team was commissioned by the NFL Project to develop the format and specification of three level-based VSTEP variants, following similar procedures to the development of the VSTEP.3–5. To date, the following three level-based tests have been designed: VSTEP.2 (level 2- or A2-based) (officially released by the MOET in May 2016), VSTEP.1 (level 1- or A1-based) and VSTEP.3 (level 3- or B1-based) (Nguyen, H., 2015, 2017a, 2017b). As a result, there is now a full range of standardized language tests targeting at all levels in the CEFR-VN, with the exception of Level 6 (or C2), which is believed to be beyond the capacity of most Vietnamese people. These tests are intended to be good national tools to measure the English ability of Vietnamese adult learners against the standards set for different professions and levels of qualification. As of the time this chapter is being written, all the VSTEP test variants are paper-based with speaking tests conducted as one-to-one face-to-face interviews. Table 4.1 summarizes the descriptions of these VSTEP variants.

The Localization of VSTEP

The previous section does not provide enough information on why Vietnamese educational policy makers and managers chose to develop Vietnamese standardized EFL tests rather than importing ready-made tests developed by well-established international test developers such as Cambridge Assessment English, Educational Testing Service (ETS), or others for use as national assessment tools, although importing tests was proposed by a considerable number of educational leaders and supported by some education firms and enterprises at that time. The central concerns arising out of the development of new Vietnamese EFL tests are formulated in two key questions: *Can we do it?* and *Should we do it?*

Despite these concerns, advocates of a national testing system succeeded in gaining the approval and funding for their test development projects and have brought about the development and production of the first-ever made-in-Vietnam standardized EFL tests. What played a decisive factor for this "innovative" policy is the Vietnamese educational think-tank's vision and awareness of the growing trend in English assessment in the region and the world towards locally produced EFL tests. During the first decade of the twenty first century, together with the expansion of the use of the CEFR globally, it was brought to the attention of English educators in Vietnam that there was an increasing number of EFL tests being developed by different institutions in Asia: the General English Proficiency Test (GEPT) developed by the Language Training & Testing (LTTC); the National English Ability Test (NEAT) developed by the Korea Institute for Curriculum and Evaluation (KICE); the Test of English for Academic Purposes (TEAP) developed by the Eiken foundation; and the College English Test (CET). All these tests aimed to provide learners a localized alternative test of English proficiency to IELTS, TOEFL or other imported tests. Learning about the development and use of these tests in these contexts gradually built up the confidence among members of the Vietnamese think-tank regarding the necessity and feasibility for non-native speakers in a specific educational and cultural context to develop their own English assessment tools that are not only valid and reliable, but also more affordable, culturally appropriate and suitable for the English learners in their contexts. In addition, the

TABLE 4.1 Test Formats of the VSTEP

VSTEP Level	Module	Test format	Test Time	Max. Score	Passing Standard
VSTEP.1	Listening	Short announcements (True/False) Short conversations (sentence completion with one word only) Short conversations (Matching) Longer conversations (multiple-choice 3 options) Short talks (multiple-choice 3 options)	Approx. 25 minutes	25	The total score is equal to or above 65.
	Reading	Map reading (sentence completion with one word only) Matching signs and explanations Short text (multiple-choice 3 options) Short news extracts or memos (multiple-choice 3 options)	30 minutes	25	
	Speaking	Greetings and social interaction Information exchanging Picture description	7 minutes	25	
	Writing	Form completion Picture description	20 minutes	25	
VSTEP.2	Listening	Instructions/announcements (multiple-choice 3 options) Table completions (short answers with no more than three words each) Conversations (multiple-choice 3 options) Answering questions (multiple-choice 3 options)	Approx. 25 minutes	25	The total score is equal to or above 65.
	Reading	Cloze (multiple-choice 3 options) Matching signs and explanations Note/form completion (short answers with no more than three words each) Reading comprehension (multiple-choice 3 options)	40 minutes	25	
	Speaking	Greetings and social interaction Description Discussion	8 minutes	25	
	Writing	Sentence building Writing a note Writing a postcard/letter	35 minutes	25	

VSTEP.3	Listening	Short instructions or announcements (multiple-choice 4 options)	Approx. 35 minutes	25	The total score is equal to or above 65.
		Short conversations (multiple-choice 4 options)			
		Long conversations (short answers with no more than 3 words)			
		Longer conversations (multiple-choice 4 options)			
		Short talk (short answers with no more than 3 words)			
	Reading	Cloze (multiple-choice 4 options)	40 minutes	25	
		Matching			
		Reading comprehension (multiple-choice 4 options)			
		Reading comprehension (multiple-choice 4 options)			
	Speaking	Social interaction	10 minutes	25	
		Description			
		Discussion			
	Writing	Rewriting	45 minutes	25	
		Description			
		Letter writing			
VSTEP.3–5	Listening	Short conversations & talks (multiple-choice 4 options)	Approx. 45 minutes	10	4.0–5.5: Level 3
		Long conversations (multiple-choice 4 options)			6.0–8.0: Level 4
		Long talks (multiple-choice 4 options)			8.5–10: Level 5
	Reading	Reading comprehension (4 passages—multiple-choice 4 options)	60 minutes	10	
	Speaking	Social interaction	12 minutes	10	
		Solution discussion			
		Topic development			
	Writing	Letter writing	60 minutes	10	
		Essay writing			

ULIS task force, who took influential roles in the think-tank on assessment reform for the NFL Project, visited KICE and LTTC in 2012–2013 to learn more about their test development and production experience. The exchange and collaboration with these institutions and several renowned researchers in language testing and assessment from Taiwan, Australia and the United States have shaped a strong belief among those involved in the assessment reform project in the *Can* and the *Should* for a local standardized EFL test in Vietnam.

In what follows, I discuss different aspects of localization of VSTEP tests by analyzing different implications of the ways these tests (and indeed other tests mentioned too—GEPT, NEAT, TEAP, and CET) have been referred to in the literature as—"locally produced," "localized," or simply "local" tests—in the context of Vietnam. In fact, there have not been straightforward statements of what these terms mean for these tests; and researchers seem to expect a common sense interpretation of these terms. However, the chapters in this book clearly show that this is not the case. In fact, not only do these terms refer to different aspects of difference between these tests and the existing renowned international tests, but each of them is also interpreted differently in different contexts. This is in fact one of the major messages of the current book. In this regard, the following sections provide the operationalizations of these terms in the context of Vietnam from the viewpoints of VSTEP test developers.

"Locally Produced"

The literal meaning of "locally produced" refers to the limited geographical scope of the production of the tests. In practice, this term has been mainly interpreted in two major ways in the literature: first, it implies that the tests are developed or produced by institutions within certain nations, states, or territories and normally widely used by people there (for example, in Wu, 2014, 2016); and the second interpretation is that these tests are produced by non-native speakers, who as defined in the Cambridge Dictionary are those who do not speak a particular language (English in this case) since they were infants, but have learned in childhood or as adults in some specific and local educational settings (an example of this view is presented in Dunlea, 2013). These two views are not mutually exclusive; however, the implications of these views are very different in different contexts. The following sections further clarify these views and their operationalizations in the case of VSTEP.

VSTEP Is a Made-in-Vietnam Test

For years, in order to obtain proof of English proficiency at international standards for employment or education purposes, Vietnamese learners of English have had no other choice but to take tests provided by international testing organizations such as IELTS by the British Council, Cambridge, and IDP, TOEFL and TOEIC by ETS and its authorized provider in Vietnam, or English Qualifications by Cambridge ESOL (known now as Cambridge Assessment English). If we take an economic view and consider testing and assessment to be a type of service, these tests are in fact imported goods, while VSTEP is produced locally within Vietnam and thus a made-in-Vietnam product. The cost to take the imported international tests is often higher than the average income of Vietnamese people and beyond the affordability of many ordinary learners, whereas the fee for VSTEP is kept at a lower cost that is more reasonable for Vietnamese learners. In addition, while the money spent on international tests mostly benefits foreign agencies, VSTEP fees go to national institutions, and therefore contribute to the domestic economy.

In this regard, the development of VSTEP and efforts to promote the use of this locally produced test over other international tests is in line with the national campaign "Vietnamese people use Vietnamese products" launched by the Communist Party in 2009, which has rapidly attracted consumers throughout the country and has quickly become a symbol of patriotism for the Vietnamese people. Thus, there is a certain nationalistic connotation embedded in the term "locally produced" for VSTEP. This is intended to protect the (political) economy of English language proficiency testing in Vietnam. Dendrinos (2013) provided a thorough discussion of the fact that language tests are in fact "national products" and suggests the importance of gaining the market for locally produced language tests over international tests. Further discussion of the impact of this nationalism in English education and testing in Vietnam is given in a later section of this chapter.

VSTEP Is Made by the Vietnamese

As described earlier in the chapter, VSTEP is the result of joint work by the ULIS task force, headed by the then ULIS President, and other leading national experts in English education, with financial and policy support from the NFL Project. In the context of persistent common cut-and-paste practice in English assessment and little validation or standardization in testing and assessment, this innovation requires great commitment and courage from the test development team, as well as strong will and support from the leaders and managers. From a small group of test developers who were new graduates from overseas doctoral and master programs in 2010 (Le, 2017), the VSTEP test format and specification development project and the production of the tests have built up national capacity in foreign language testing and assessment. Both the number of capable test developers and their capacity through hands-on experience from the VSTEP format and specification development project and subsequent test production has increased. Therefore, in the case of VSTEP, test developers are striving to transform the challenge of non-native speakers producing English

80 Nguyen Thi Ngoc Quynh

language tests into an opportunity of building up professionalism and technical capacity for human resources.

"Localized"

There are also two main views of the "localized" nature of these EFL tests. The first is based on the assumption that there are "international standards" for language tests and these localized tests adopted some operationalization or modification of these common standards. The distinction between localization and internationalization is central to this view. As for localized EFL tests, advocates of this view focus on the differences between these tests and the current well-established international tests such as IELTS, TOEFL, Cambridge English Qualifications, and so on. Meanwhile, the second view of "localized" focuses more on the context-specific peculiarities or uniqueness of the tests. The localization of VSTEP tests reflects both these views.

Localization Versus Internationalization

The goal of VSTEP developers is to make the tests suitable and appropriate for Vietnamese people while being aligned to international standards. As suggested by Fulcher & Davidson (2007), it is necessary to make adjustments of international standards to suit the language use context in test development. Dunlea (2013) notes that this localization occurred as the test development projects began by referring to well-known or international "benchmarks." In the case of Vietnam, the alignment started from the stage of developing the CEFR-VN. The project adopted the same common ground theoretical framework—Bachman's Communicative Language Ability as that of the CEFR. Based on the available resources of the CEFR including the descriptors, matrix of themes, situations, and topics and the English Profile resources, the team added more descriptors and revised the matrix of topics and situations to suit adults' contextual use of English in Vietnam. Specifically, during this project, a series of methods were used to ensure alignment, including continuous training and peer-review of level-specific key features among the development team, surveys, in-depth interviews of EFL teachers' evaluation of the relevance of the extended descriptors, and expert reviews by world-class researchers who are specialists of the CEFR. As a result, 75 skill-specific descriptors were added (20 listening, 18 reading, 12 speaking, and 25 writing) (Nguyen, H., 2014; Nguyen, T. M. H. et al., 2017).

One example of the extension of the CEFR is the descriptor on writing skill at Level 2 (A2) as follows: "*Can produce simple written transaction records.*" This reflects the fact that working people in Vietnam need to use English for this purpose very often, and the average English proficiency level of the workforce is around A2 level; therefore, this descriptor is explicitly stated and added in the CEFR-VN.

VSTEP: A Panorama **81**

Based on the adopted version of the international framework of language proficiency (i.e., the CEFR-VN), the ULIS task force developed the format and specification of VSTEP.3–5 aligned to these scales. As discussed earlier, the team conducted a validation study to compare the VSTEP test scores of 210 pilot test takers across Vietnam with their IELTS scores. The correlations were all significant and from moderate to strong (Tran et al., 2015; Nguyen, H., 2014). This empirical research provides evidence of the endeavor to assure equivalence of VSTEP test results with those from renowned international "benchmarks."

Context-Specific Peculiarities

The main value of the localization of VSTEP does not stem from how different it is from the international standardized tests. It lies instead in the appropriateness and fairness the test brings about for its target test takers. The test development supports the view by Shohamy (2001) that "tests are not neutral but rather embedded in political, social and educational, ideological and economic contexts." The discussions earlier in this chapter of VSTEP being "made-in-Vietnam" and "made by the Vietnamese" reflect this view. The following paragraphs provide detailed analyses of the localization that makes VSTEP a test "made *for* the Vietnamese."

VSTEP tests are made to address the demand for English proficiency assessment of Vietnamese people, as discussed earlier in further detail, against the standards for their levels of qualification and professions. This supports O'Sullivan's (2014) assertion that localization is required when we are testing a well-defined population within a well-defined context in order to make decisions that will apply only to that context. All VSTEP variants are designed for adult Vietnamese learners and users of English 18 years old and above. However, each VSTEP variant targets a certain level group and therefore a certain pool of test takers who can be identified in relation to the standards set by the government. For example, VSTEP.3–5 targets at Levels 3 to 5 (B1 to C1). According to the current policies on English ability standards, these levels are required for English teachers, tertiary students, senior officials, and lecturers. Meanwhile, levels 1 and 2 (A1 and A2) are required standards for laborers of various professions. Therefore, VSTEP.3–5 is designed to assess more academic skills than VSTEP.1 and VSTEP.2. This can be seen not only in their test tasks. For example, for the writing section, VSTEP.3–5 has an essay writing task, while VSTEP.2 has a note writing task and a postcard writing task, and VSTEP.1 has a form-filling task. In terms of content, it can be expected that VSTEP.3–5 covers a greater proportion of educational domain than the other two, while VSTEP.1 and VSTEP.2 show greater coverage of social and occupational domains. These distinctions among variants of the same test are specific to the context of English assessment in Vietnam, in line with the current government policies and standards. This reflects the view that locally produced tests are well placed to assess which test features could be modified while still maintaining acceptable levels of validity (Dunlea, 2013).

The second tenet of VSTEP localization is its appropriateness to the education system of Vietnam. Unlike GEPT in Taiwan which is a curriculum-related test (Wu, 2016, 2017), VSTEP is a non-curriculum related test and is intended to assess general English proficiency. However, during the conceptualization stage to design the test format and specification, the team conducted a comprehensive survey of English target language use (TLU) in Vietnam, of which the use at school and higher education institutions plays an important role. A set of the themes, situations, and topics were then developed and are regularly updated now to suit what Vietnamese learners learn at upper-secondary schools, colleges and universities. In addition, the test tasks were proposed based on a survey of tasks and activities that Vietnamese learners are used to at school. To start with, a compilation of tasks, activities, and situations that English learners at ULIS and other member universities are exposed to in their curricula[2] was developed by a group of five senior English teacher trainers. Based on this collection, a survey was developed to collect teachers and learners of English for their review. This is how VSTEP creates its relation to the English education system in Vietnam.

VSTEP is also localized to suit Vietnamese culture and language use. This localization is built up through the process of contextual mediation in test design and development (Saville, 2009, 2010; Wu, 2016). The outcomes of the localization include suitable topics, content, situations, as well as task types, and so on as discussed earlier. Although the current chapter is not a comprehensive account of all localized features of VSTEP tests, a few examples are discussed in the following paragraphs.

First, in terms of content, for each VSTEP variant, the test specification clearly requires one reading text to be about Vietnam or an Asian country. This assures the interest as well as familiarity of the content to the target test takers.

As for listening papers, item writer guidelines explicitly recommend the use of Vietnamese names to a certain degree in the texts, specifically with consideration of using these names for items that test the ability to comprehend implication or inferred information.

In addition, the 10-point scale of VSTEP tests is also another localized feature. This is intentional to suit the scoring system of Vietnam's education system. This is intended to make it easier for VSTEP scores to be used in various education contexts and purposes.

Finally, the localization of VSTEP can be seen from the use made of their results. As these test formats are issued by the Ministry of Education and Training, they automatically gain the recognition and usage nationwide. Many education institutions replace their own tests or even some international tests by VSTEP during 2016 and 2017 for their entry or exit language exams. Like many other locally produced EFL tests in Asia, as can be seen in other chapters of this book, the support from government and sector, and the status of being a national test endow VSTEP with an advantage in expanding its use and recognition in the education sector in Vietnam.

"Local" (or the Dilemmas of Local Tests)

The third term that VSTEP tests and other EFL tests developed in Asia are often associated with in the literature is "local." In terms of literal meaning, the term denotes the distinction between "local" and "international" or "global" tests in the scope of use and recognition. This term therefore presents dichotomous implications for test developers in that it suggests both challenges and directions. First, it reflects the challenge that all locally produced tests with no exception have to face. That is, the challenge to expand their test use and to gain recognition outside their "locality." In terms of test use, Wu (2016) shared the results of the survey on the use of English language tests in Taiwan. It was found that Taiwanese students at the tertiary level continue to prefer international tests such as TOEFL, TOEIC, and IELTS to GEPT, despite the fact that high school students prefer the GEPT. Similar reactions can be found for VSTEP, as the test developers are trying to promote its use by English users in other sectors than education, and perhaps in the future by Vietnamese people working and living outside the borders.

More importantly, all developers of local tests strive for greater recognition both nationally and internationally. This is a constant mission and challenge. One goal of VSTEP development is to show the world proof of Vietnamese people's English capacity for opportunity in regional and global integration. Therefore, international recognition is crucial for it to reach its goal.

In this regard, the term "local" implies the universal direction of these test developers—to strive to improve their quality to attract more test users and to gain more recognition (ILTA Code of Ethics, 2000/2018; Dunlea, 2013). The following section summarizes the procedures and methods ULIS have been employing to enhance VSTEP test quality.

VSTEP Quality Assurance and Quality Control

As asserted by Dendrinos (2013), language tests such as VSTEP and most, if not to say all, other locally produced English proficiency tests introduced in this book are in fact "glocal" (global + local) tests. According to Dendrinos's view, "glocalization involves locally operated schemes, set up to serve domestic social conditions and needs, which are informed by international research and assessment practices" (Dendrinos, 2013, p. 8). In other words, besides localization, these tests follow salient global or international norms or standards in test development and design to assure their quality. In this regard, this section describes the procedures employed by ULIS to assure and control the quality of their VSTEP tests.

As noted by Green and Jay (2005), a distinction should be made between quality assurance and quality control. While the former is concerned with processes and involves the management of activities and resources to improve benefits to stakeholders, the latter is concerned with outcomes and involves checking that products (i.e., tests) meet intended standards (p. 5). Both of these are highlighted by VSTEP developers at ULIS, as discussed further in subsequent sections.

Particularly, ULIS is committed to pursuing the goal of becoming a center of excellence in language testing and assessment. Therefore, the visions adopted for VSTEP at this leading English education and assessment institution in Vietnam are Validity, Sustainability, Transparency, Equity, and Practicality. The initials of these make up the abbreviation of the test's name. Four of them are associated with ULIS's visions of the quality assurance and quality control of their VSTEP tests: validity, transparency, practicality, and equity (which means fairness in test results). They are discussed in detail in this section, while sustainability and equity (which means fairness in test accessibility) will be touched upon in the following section on VSTEP impact.

Validity

ULIS supports the view that assuring the validity of tests is not only the responsibility of the test developing organization (ILTA Code of Ethics, 2000/2018), but in fact it provides them with a strategy to grow. This is why validation research was given priority as soon as the VSTEP tests were introduced. Following the distinction between quality assurance and quality control, in ULIS's view, validation research, on the one hand, will provide evidence to stakeholders of the validity of the tests and test scores, as well as of the consequences that the test scores bring about (i.e., quality assurance); on the other hand, this work helps to establish and develop the validity of the tests, or in other words, bringing them up to the expected standards (i.e., quality control).

A research agenda to conduct systematic quality assurance and control research was introduced in late 2016 (Carr et al., 2016) using an assessment-based approach to validation (Bachman & Palmer, 1996, 2010; Chapelle, Enright, & Jamieson, 2008; Kane, 1992). Following Bachman and Palmer's (2010) approach of constructing an assessment use argument (AUA), four main claims were specified: intended consequences, decision made on the basis of VSTEP scores, interpretations, and assessment records. For each claim, one or more essential qualities were specified. Consideration of these essential qualities would prompt test developers to design assessment to optimize them, and guide VSTEP validation researchers in collecting qualitative and quantitative evidence in relation to each of these qualities to evaluate the claims regarding intended interpretations.

VSTEP: A Panorama **85**

As a result, a validation project framework for VSTEP researchers at ULIS was developed that identified the types of qualitative and quantitative evidence being collected to support the following four claims made about the test: that VSTEP test scores and descriptions of examinee performance consistently and properly represent test takers' performance on the test; that interpretations of test scores are appropriate; that decisions made on the basis of test scores are equitable and values-sensitive; and that the consequences of using the VSTEP are beneficial to stakeholders.

Some work in relation to the framework has been in progress; but there have been few technical reports and research findings ready for publication. Two most recent publications by ULIS research team are Nguyen, T. N. Q. (2018) and Nguyen, T. P. T. (2018). Both are in support of Claim 4. The former presented the results of a study on the consistency of scoring in the VSTEP.3–5 Writing Test. It examined three forms of the VSTEP.3–5 writing tests administered in 2015 and 2016, and adopted the triangulation approach in the analysis by combining many-facet Rasch measurement with generalizability theory, while adding consideration of inter-rater score correlations as an additive source of information on scoring consistency. It was found that the dependability and reliability results of all three test forms were sufficient (Φ and $E\rho^2$ values were all around 0.8 and above) to support important decisions if need be.

The publication by Nguyen, T. P. T. (2018) reported the results of the investigation of content validity of VSTEP.3–5 Reading Test, or its relevance and coverage of the content compared with the description in test specification and the actual performance of examinees. Three testing experts conducted the analysis using Bachman and Palmer's (1996) framework and test score analysis. The results showed that there was a relatively high consistency of the test content with the test design framework and the test takers' performance.

The findings have so far provided positive evidence to support the validity claims of VSTEP tests. However, much more is expected to come in the upcoming times.

Transparency

Convinced by the view that communication with different stakeholders is essential for advancement (Fulcher, 2015; O'Sullivan, 2014), ULIS aims at public communication of their VSTEP validation results whenever available. On the one hand, such transparency will keep the whole test development team at ULIS constantly alert of their conformity to good ethics and practices and continually striving for better performance to improve their tests. On the other hand, this is a strategy for the new VSTEP tests to get known by the regional and international public and professional arena more quickly.

There are two major strategies for ULIS to maintain the transparency of VSTEP tests. First, the ULIS team regularly presented their work-in-progress or completed reports on VSTEP development and validation at regional and international conferences: to name a few, Nguyen, T. N. Q. (2013), Tran et al. (2015), Nguyen, T. N. Q. and Do (2015), Nguyen, T. N. Q. (2016a, 2016b), Dunlea, Nguyen, Nguyen, Thai, and Nguyen (2016), Carr et al. (2016), Dunlea, Spiby, Nguyen, T. N. Q., Nguyen, T. Q. Y., Thai, H. L. T., & Nguyen, T. P. T. (2017), Nguyen, T. N .Q., Nguyen, T. Q. Y., Nguyen, T. P. T., Thai, H. L. T., & Carr (2017), Nguyen, T. N. Q., Nguyen, T. Q. Y., Thai, H. L. T., Nguyen, T. P. T., Dunlea, & Spiby (2017), Nguyen, T. N. Q., Thai, H. L. T., Bui, T. S., & Carr, T. N. (2017), Nguyen, T. M. H. et al. (2017), and Dunlea et al. (2018a & 2018b). ULIS is an active institutional member of the Academic Forum on English Language Testing in Asia (AFELTA). This is a forum where ULIS team can learn from and exchange the experience with other developers of locally produced EFL tests to both draw good lessons and practices for VSTEP improvement, and to gain the other member organizations' recognition of VSTEP. In addition, many ULIS researchers are active members of the Asian Association for Language Assessment (AALA) which attracts both mid-career talented and dedicated researchers in Asia and world-class researchers from leading language testing organizations such as the British Council, Cambridge Assessment English, ETS, and Pearson.

In addition, ULIS team are pursuing a goal to increase their publications in professional journals and books on VSTEP in particular, and English testing and assessment in the context of Vietnam in general in the years to come with priorities on the topics to address the four claims in the AUA validation framework.

The second strategy for ULIS to enhance their transparency as well as the accountability of VSTEP tests is to invite well-known international testing experts or firms to conduct validation studies either separately or collaboratively with ULIS researchers. This strategy is not new but has been applied to good effect by some other local EFL test developing organizations in Asia (for example, LTTC in Taiwan for GEPT, or EIKEN for TEAP). What should be noted here is that such a strategy was applied very early in the process of developing VSTEP; in fact, as soon as it was first introduced. In 2016–2017, the ULIS VSTEP research and development team conducted a collaborative research project with the Assessment Research Group at the British Council and the British Council Vietnam exams team to undertake a comprehensive test comparability study to investigate the similarities and differences between Aptis and VSTEP in the context of Vietnam. The study builds on a framework for investigating test comparability piloted in Taiwan and reported by Wu, Yeh, Dunlea, and Spiby (2016) following Weir's (2005) socio-cognitive approach. Dunlea et al. (2018b) provides a detailed report on this study.

Also soon after VSTEP was officially introduced, another major collaborative research project on VSTEP as a strategy to promote the transparency of VSTEP was conducted by the ULIS team and a world-leading specialist sponsored by the Regional English Language Office at the U.S. Embassy in Vietnam. The outcome of this project is the AUA framework described in the previous section that provides guidance for the entire research and development work by the ULIS team.

More joint research with international experts is expected to occur in the years to come. Not only are the research results themselves valuable for ULIS teams as these are professional and subjective evaluations of their work in many aspects, which can be reported to the world, but the procedures and experience in working with these experts are highly beneficial for the team. The quality assurance and control protocols are then strengthened to better the validity of the tests, which will benefit all stakeholders in Vietnam.

Practicality

Practicality is one expected quality of tests in Bachman and Palmer's (1996) view of test usefulness. In their view, the practicality of the test is the degree to which there are enough resources to develop and use the test. In this regard, ULIS has been pursuing two important missions. First, they are developing an extensive repertoire of copyrighted input materials for VSTEP development including an increasing number of texts, scripts, and audio recordings. In the meantime, ULIS has focused on training VSTEP item writers and raters (speaking and writing) following a solid training curriculum[3] to build up human resources for the development and delivery of VSTEP tests.[4]

In another view of practicality, Hughes (2003) defines it as follows: "other things being equal, it is good that a test should be easy and cheap to construct, administer, score and interpret" (p. 56). With the aim to make VSTEP more practical, easier and cheaper to administer and score, ULIS is developing a computer-based version of the tests. The project was piloted in 2017 and is being finalized at the time this chapter is being developed. A report on this project was presented at the AALA Conference in Shanghai in October 2018.

Equity = Fairness in Tests

Following Wu's (2016) view, equity has two different meanings for VSTEP developers at ULIS: fairness in tests and fairness in accessibility. The former is discussed here as a required quality of VSTEP tests and test scores, while the latter will be analyzed later in the next section on the impact of VSTEP.

Fairness in tests has been emphasized at ULIS. It is considered to be a function of multiple factors: test development, administration, and rating.

First, in terms of test development, Weir (2005) asserts that in order to assure fairness (or equity) of tests, test developers are obliged to address how different characteristics of candidates, including experiential characteristics, are catered for by their tests. O'Sullivan (2000) defines experiential features as those that are related to the test taker's educational and cultural background, experience in preparing and taking exams, as well as knowledge of the demands of a particular exam. Understanding the test taker's experiential characteristics helps test developers in creating tests that are appropriate to the targeted candidature. In support of these views, VSTEP developers set out to develop their own made-in-Vietnam tests, as discussed in the first section of this chapter, with an aim to provide fairer and more appropriate EFL tests for Vietnamese learners of English, which are suitable for the educational, cultural, and English language use contexts of Vietnam.

In addition, ULIS maintains a strict policy of test and item writer training, with careful selection of writers with regular monitoring and evaluation of their performance. From 2016, all VSTEP writers are obliged to attend an intensive 300-hour training and meet the requirements of this training to be entitled to enter the roster. In order to avoid bias, which is one of the major risks to fairness, ULIS applies two rounds of expert reviews against a checklist developed by the team.

Moreover, in order to make sure that test takers know the test formats and are familiar with test demands (O'Sullivan, 2000) before taking VSTEP tests, a number of procedures have been applied: first, all registered test takers are provided with an information brochure and a link to the information webpage of VSTEP tests. Second, one information session is conducted before every test when test takers are invited to directly listen to a talk on VSTEP test format, test tasks, test procedures on test day, and scoring procedure. There are chances for one-to-one consultation either at this information session or at the information booth at the ULIS Center for Language Testing and Assessment. In addition, there is a hotline telephone number, email, and Facebook account for test takers to contact ULIS staff for any query about the tests.

Another administrative aspect to assure fairness is the strict measures employed to prevent cheating. A Code of Conduct at test events has been developed and strictly applied including the requirements of test taker seating, security, and audio and video recording of test administration. All staff involved in test administration have to attend formal training by the university offered every two years and are required to attend a briefing session either the day before or an hour before the actual test delivery. University inspectors are commissioned to monitor the performance of all test administrators. In addition, from mid-2016, local police officers are invited to be at the test site to collaborate with ULIS staff in preventing and dealing with cheating cases.

Finally, in terms of rating, in order to assure fairness, all VSTEP raters have to meet the requirements of English proficiency (C1 level and above) and fulfill the requirements of a formal training. As for the speaking test, all interviews are audio-taped; and 2%–5% of those interviewed are re-rated for quality assurance. When the re-rating of this portion shows error, more or all interviews will be re-rated, depending on the causes detected. As for VSTEP writing tests, there is a norming session at the beginning of the rating session of every test in which all raters are asked to rate five same test taker papers in order to assure the consensus among raters. Moreover, the ULIS Center for Language Testing and Assessment also conducts regular inter-rater and intra-rater reliability research for monitoring and evaluation of rating practices[5] (e.g., Nguyen, T. N. Q. et al., 2017). Specifically, to check the inter-rater reliability, the traditional Cronbach's alpha and correlations are used for regular quality control. All the indices must be above 0.88 for acceptable reliability. The papers will be re-marked if the results are poor.

In addition, G-theory is also used to analyze the variance components or the dependability of speaking and writing scores. The results of the studies reported in Nguyen, T. N. Q. et al., 2017 and Nguyen, T. N. Q., 2018 using mGENOVA showed that the score variance by ULIS speaking and writing raters were mostly due to individual factors (i.e., test takers).

To investigate intra-rater reliability, Rasch analyses on rater severity, misfit, and bias are calculated. The Infit and Outfit Mean-square indexes must be within 0.5–1.5. All misfitting raters will be asked to go through norming and training sessions again. Nguyen, T. N. Q. et al. (2017, 2018) reported the results of FACETS (many-facet Rasch) on the inter-relation between task-type, test date and subscale. They found that all measurement results were close to zero, which showed the adequate reliability and consistency, and the equity or fairness of the rating.

VSTEP Impact

Equity = Fairness in Accessibility

While the previous section describes what is done at ULIS to assure the equity or fairness of VSTEP in test results, what follows discusses the impact of VSTEP in assuring equity or fairness in test accessibility for learners of English in Vietnam.[6] In this view, equity does not only mean a goal of test quality, but it also refers to the changes that ULIS as the flagship institution in English education and assessment in Vietnam is committed to bringing about through VSTEP test development and delivery.

As a made-in-Vietnam test, the VSTEP fee is kept at a much lower price than that of currently available international English proficiency tests. At this time, the full fee for ordinary VSTEP test takers is about 40% of that for TOEFL iBT or IELTS tests. In addition, ULIS offers special discount policies for its own students.[7] As a result, VSTEP is more affordable and therefore more accessible for most of Vietnamese learners of English. This is the equity that ULIS wishes to create with their VSTEP tests since there is now a fairer chance of being assessed in English capacity by a quality tool for more people of different sectors, incomes, and purposes. This has been particularly evident in the education sector with a sharp increase in the number of teachers and learners to be assessed since the arrival of VSTEP. According to a report by the NFL Project in early 2017, within three years since VSTEP was introduced, about 13,000 Vietnamese teachers and students were assessed. Particularly, by the end of the first phase of the NFL Project in 2016, the majority of English teachers have been assessed, which enables the government to capture an overall picture of the current capacity of English teachers for their policy making in terms of teacher development. In the meantime, it is hoped that VSTEP will be used more and more by people from other sectors for other purposes rather than educational. In fact, the number of officials in Hanoi, Hai Phong, and several other cities who have taken VSTEP tests to provide proof of their English proficiency at A2 and B1 levels for promotion in their working tenure has grown significantly over the years. In addition, from an institutional perspective, VSTEP is intended to become an affordable standardized tool for educational institutions to assess the entry and exit levels of their students, which makes it easier for them to manage their English courses and control the quality of their service. VSTEP therefore helps to ensure equity among English educational institutions, especially between private and public sectors, across the national education system. In the past, only "elite" institutions used international tests such as Cambridge English Qualifications, TOEFL, TOEIC, or IELTS as "take away" credits for their graduates. Today, most institutions can afford VSTEP national standardized tests as part of their graduation certification protocols.

Sustainability

The most important impact that ULIS is striving to bring about through the development of VSTEP tests is the sustainability of English education and assessment in Vietnam. This can be created in several ways. First, as VSTEP tests are made by the Vietnamese, the development of these tests leads to the development of an increasing number of testing professionals, from test writers, raters, invigilators to managers. Together with adequate policies and regulations in quality control and assurance, the capacity of these human resources is being improved through carefully designed training and frequent hands-on practice. As a result, this helps to build up the national capacity in standardized English testing and assessment.

Second, VSTEP is meant to reduce the use and therefore the dependence on imported international English teaching and testing materials in Vietnam. This is because, as noted by Dendrinos (2013), international English proficiency testing is a "self-serving" project (pp. 2–7), which means that these tests are tools for publishers from the inner circle nations (i.e., where English is the native language, such as the UK and the U.S.) to maintain and expand their markets in other nations around the world. As we all know the close reciprocal linkage[8] between testing and teaching and learning, means that the market for tests also entails there is one created for language teaching, and learning, which involves the creation of accompanying goods, such as textbook sets, testing paraphernalia, ELT multimedia and fee-paying services such as training or exam preparation courses (cf. Dendrinos, 1999, 2013; Pennycook, 1994). To date, international testing organizations have been enjoying the natural and widely taken-for-granted advantage of linking being "native" with being standard and set the model or norms for English testing in other countries. They have in fact been using many strategies to maintain this, including putting their ideology in the content of tests and promoting the construct of monolingual competence in all their tests (Dendrinos, 2013). These "self-serving" strategies have helped to maintain the long-lasting presence and influence of international English proficiency testing and education in non-English speaking countries including Vietnam. In this regard, it is hoped that once VSTEP tests are used by more learners and institutions in Vietnam in place of international tests, especially as entry and/or exit assessments in educational programs in the educational system, the use of imported materials will also be reduced and locally produced materials will be produced and used alternatively. Studying or teaching to the test is always an unwanted but inevitable washback effect of any test, especially for high-stakes and standardized tests like VSTEP. This is the negative side of this washback effect of VSTEP tests. However, for VSTEP developers, "the other side of the coin," which is the chance for the whole education and assessment of English in Vietnam to escape from the persistent dependence on imported English testing and education materials means much more. It is the responsibility of VSTEP testing institutions, including ULIS, to constantly work on research and quality control and assurance to minimize the negative side of the washback effect. In their view, sustainability in English education and assessment is a combination of the availability of capable testing professionals and the increased market for localized tests and teaching and learning materials. The development of a glocal EFL test, VSTEP, is meant to bring about such sustainability.

Other Impacts

Besides equity and sustainability in English education and assessment, VSTEP has in fact had several other impacts on education as a whole in Vietnam. The first and most important impact is that it has provided English educators and especially education policy makers in Vietnam with not only the evidence of the feasibility of a made-in-Vietnam and made-by-the Vietnamese English proficiency test but also the knowledge of the what and how things have to be done to develop such a test. It is this full package of professional and practical lessons and reflections that is building up the increasing confidence among national education managers and policy makers of Vietnam's rights and capacity to autonomy in English education and assessment. Such confidence is of grave importance at this stage of education reform, because it can then be translated into practical policies and strategies to promote such localization or glocalization. Without such, these initiatives would soon become just vain attempts. For decades, serial attempts and reform initiatives in English education in Vietnam have been proposed and trialed,[9] some of which were meant to increase the national autonomy and self-reliance, but little evidence can be seen of the development of Vietnam's autonomy and independence in English education and assessment. Schools and teachers continue to rely on imported English syllabuses and materials, and learners still have to take international English proficiency tests for their international academic and employment purposes. What has been done and achieved from VSTEP design and development has helped to initiate and build up the will and confidence of such autonomy for Vietnam's English education and assessment. However, much more concrete and timely actions and strategies are needed to foster this reform.

In addition, experience and lessons learned from the development of VSTEP tests have set models and norms for standardization of assessment of other foreign languages taught in Vietnam's education system. At national level, the NFL Project has funded projects started in 2016 on the design and development of proficiency tests and curriculum of Korean and Japanese for Vietnamese learners. At institutional level, specifically at ULIS, glocalized proficiency tests of all foreign languages taught at the university including French, Russian, Chinese, German, Japanese, Korean, and Arabic are being developed for use as the required exit assessment of their bachelor degree courses.

Overall, VSTEP has brought about or contributed to multiple changes in education and the assessment of English and other foreign languages. These impacts are significant in the context of the ongoing education reform in Vietnam.

Research and Contribution

VSTEP research and development can contribute to the language testing literature in several ways.

First, the account of the development of the CEFR-VN, its adoption of the CEFR with additive thematic features, situations, and activities and extended level descriptors and the VSTEP tests based on this operationalized framework may be useful for developers of other CEFR-aligned language tests, and possibly to some extent to the general language testing researchers. The work on the development of national frameworks for English teaching, learning and assessment such as the CEFR-J in Japan (Negishi & Tono, 2014) or the once so-called Common Chinese Framework of Reference for English (CCFR-E) and recently the China's Standards of English (CSE) (Jin, Wu, Alderson, & Song, 2017) have attracted a lot of attention from the field and relevant stakeholders.

In this regard, the operationalization of the national CEFR-VN in combination with VSTEP tests in Vietnam may also be of interest to these audiences.

Second, in pursuit of its visions of validity, sustainability, transparency, equity, and practicality, ULIS's empirical studies on VSTEP reflect the operationalized localization and glocalization (cf. Dendrinos, 2013) of their tests. The approach adopted for the development of VSTEP is a high-stakes, non-curriculum related test, which is made suitable for the educational and cultural features and the use of English in Vietnam. What and how to make these tests localized may be worthwhile topics for VSTEP researchers and other interested language test researchers.

In addition, one common concern among developers and users of most locally produced EFL tests has been the tension between localization and globalization. Each test developing institution has its own strategies to maintain salient global features and qualities of their locally made tests. The glocalization as a combined process of operationalizing local features in tests while adhering to essential global requirements has been a priority research area at ULIS. Studies on glocalization may include a wide range including benchmarking studies. Examples include the study on VSTEP benchmarked with IELTS scales (Tran et al., 2015), comparability studies such as the joint study on VSTEP and Aptis in alignment with the CEFR by ULIS and the British Council (cf. Dunlea et al., 2016, 2017, 2018a, 2018b), standard setting studies (e.g., Nguyen, T. Q. Y., 2018), inter-rater reliability and intra-rater reliability studies (e.g., Carr et al., 2016), and item analysis (e.g., Nguyen, T. N. Q. et al., 2017). The view of triangulation and combining multiple analysis approaches in compiling support for validity claims (such as the combination of descriptive statistics, Cronbach's alpha and correlations through SPSS, and mGENOVA, FACETS presented in Nguyen et al., 2017; Nguyen, T. N. Q., 2018) also reflects the methodological operationalization of glocalization for VSTEP. In these regards, besides the empirical findings, VSTEP researchers at ULIS also contribute their views on the worthwhile research agenda (see the discussion of the AUA validation framework in the previous sections) and research priorities to meet their goals. Providing that constraints and limitations are common for all new test designers and developers, these may be more or less useful lessons to be exchanged with colleagues in other contexts.

Moreover, one peculiar feature of VSTEP is the role of government in test development, management, and quality control. Some locally produced English proficiency tests in Asia that are introduced in this book also involve governmental support. However, accounts of the value of this vary across these tests. The case of VSTEP shows both advantages and disadvantages to governmental participation in language test development and delivery. On the positive side, besides funding support, the government helped to ensure several other favorable conditions for VSTEP development, especially at the early stage of the project. These included a timely synergy of experts and staff from other institutions with ULIS task force when needed, low-cost mobilization of target test takers for test pilot and trial, and especially large-scale national official recognition and use of the test since its arrival. On the negative side, VSTEP practice has suggested several disadvantages and challenges in harmonizing the government factor in test development. Examples of these include the sensitivity in test ownership, the accountability among different commissioned test delivery institutions, and particularly the risk of changes in macro policies on teaching, learning, and assessment when there is a change in management or leadership of the sector.

Finally, another peculiarity of VSTEP is its struggle towards standardization, both at national level and at institutional level (i.e., ULIS). Although ULIS is the institution commissioned to design the test specification, real VSTEP tests are developed and administered by several English education universities and agencies appointed by the Ministry.[10] This is a source of variation. In order to assure standardization, at national level, MOET issues several documents to regulate test development and administration. The most important to date has been the Circular 23/2017 issued on September 29, 2017 by MOET, which describes the minimum requirements of a language test center. In addition, the government also set the requirements of quality control and assurance including rater training, test development, and validation procedures. Under their policy papers, the government does not claim any limitation on the number of national language test administration and certification centers, but the strategy to control and assure quality and standardization is that they maintain high demands on the appointment of any candidate institution and strict, and regular supervision of the performance of the appointed and strict punishment on all wrong doing. At institutional level, ULIS is adopting strictly designed administration procedures to assure quality. The partnership between the government and the VSTEP testing agency in test quality control may be a useful case for further research investigation.

Future Directions as Conclusion

With the successful arrival of VSTEP, ULIS has proven its continued flagship role in foreign language education and assessment in its country. However, in order to meet their own goals set out from the start of this endeavor, which are validity, transparency, equity, and practicality in testing so as to build up sustainability and equity in English education and assessment for the nation, much more has to be done in the future. In particular, because VSTEP is still a new test and ULIS itself is a junior player in the world testing community, and inevitably faces a series of constraints and challenges in various aspects of its work, it makes sense to carefully identify priorities for each of their future development stages. As a conclusion to this chapter, the following paragraphs discuss ULIS's priorities for the coming years to strengthen their VSTEP tests.

Making VSTEP Better

Three priorities have been set by ULIS to make VSTEP tests better. First, it aims at improving the glocalization of the tests, which means on the one hand, the test task content will be made more relevant to the local context, while on the other hand there will be more studies to generate evidence of their validity, and alignment to the CEFR. Improving localization involves the development of a large corpus of English use in Vietnam, which can be used as the input resources for test writers. More item writer training will also be implemented to guide them to increase the localized features in the tests while maintaining salient global features and alignment to the global CEFR levels. The latter involves a number of validation studies on the alignment of VSTEP tests to the CEFR.

The second priority in making VSTEP better is to ensure its scoring validity through improving the quality of VSTEP speaking and writing raters. It is required by MOET that all raters be trained and only those who complete the requirements of the training can be authorized to rate VSTEP tests.[11] In the meantime, ULIS conducts regular inter-rater reliability and intra-rater reliability studies so as to monitor the performance of raters over multiple administrations.

The third priority focuses on the standardization and quality control across test centers in Vietnam. This involves ULIS's advocacy to the sectoral leaders and relevant agencies to provide guidelines and supervision to control quality of VSTEP delivery across the nation. It also requires joint work between ULIS and other English education universities and institutions in conducting trainings on VSTEP test writing and VSTEP speaking and writing rating for staff from these institutions.[12] More needs to be done to make sure that all writers and raters are trained and monitored.

Making VSTEP Stronger

By making VSTEP stronger, it means that VSTEP becomes more competitive and used or taken by more Vietnamese people (i.e., "made for the Vietnamese"). Two priorities are identified to address this. First, ULIS is developing a computer-based version of the test as a strategy to lower the administrative cost of the tests and thus to enhance the accessibility and competitiveness of the tests over other tests.

In addition, in order to increase the number of VSTEP test takers, not only within the education sector as they are now but also from other sectors in Vietnam, ULIS is focusing on communication and promotion of the tests and the research base that underpins them. In particular, they are focusing on the development of printed test materials including test guidelines and practice tests, as well as an online VSTEP practice test bank.

Making VSTEP More Recognized

The ultimate goal of VSTEP developers, like that of all other developers of locally produced EFL tests, is to make their tests recognized more and more, not only domestically, but also internationally. In fact, such recognition is conditional to the strength and growth of VSTEP, and consequently to the sustainability of English education and assessment for which VSTEP developers strive.

To gain more recognition for VSTEP tests and test results within Vietnam, ULIS adopts a combination of three strategies: (1) assuring quality service in test administration; (2) a communication campaign on the role and benefits of VSTEP tests; and (3) policy advocacy to authorities and sectoral leaders on VSTEP validity and usefulness (Bachman & Palmer, 1996).

Meanwhile, in order to gain international recognition, ULIS sets top priority in publishing and presenting their empirical research reports to get VSTEP known regionally and internationally. A comprehensive research agenda has been planned out and implemented ever since VSTEP's official introduction. In addition, ULIS proactively collaborates with and invites international experts to conduct joint research on VSTEP to increase the accountability and transparency of their research findings.

ULIS has prioritized the activities listed in this section for VSTEP developers in the coming years. In the long run, ULIS's goal is to become a center of excellence in language testing and assessment and to make their VSTEP tests useful and well recognized. Although the plan is ambitious, there is a collective belief at ULIS that as long as they have the will, there is a way for them to reach their goals.

Notes

1. The first public release of this test development project was at the Academic Forum on English Language Testing in Asia (AFELTA) Conference in September 2013 in Taiwan (Nguyen, 2013) when the project was just kick-started. It was completed at the end of 2014.
2. ULIS delivers English programs for not only English-major students within ULIS but also non-English major programs for students in other member universities of the Vietnam National University, Hanoi (VNU). The compilation was done based on the existing curricula.
3. There are strict entry requirements for the training curriculum including a master's degree in a relevant major, C1-level English proficiency, and at least three years' teaching experience. The trainees need to meet all training requirements to be awarded the license to work as VSTEP writers or raters.
4. By June 2018, 155 raters and 60 item writers had been trained. Their performance is recorded and regularly checked for quality assurance purposes.
5. The formulas and protocols for checking inter- and intra-rater reliability were developed for ULIS by Prof. Nathan Carr (California State University, Fullerton). A report on this study was presented at the AALA Conference in 2017.
6. It is intentional to structure the chapter in this way so as to go through all the visions adopted for VSTEP by ULIS (Validity, Sustainability, Transparency, Equity,

and Practicality) whose initials make up the abbreviation of the test's name. In the previous section, the V (Validity), T (Transparency), and P (Practicality) have been discussed in sequence. The E (Equity) is meant to be the transition between the two consecutive sections.

7. As of the time this chapter was written, ULIS students are entitled to one free VSTEP test and 70% discount for following tests until the end of their degree; while all students at other university members of VNU are entitled to 50% discount.
8. Or what has been viewed as the washback effect of testing on teaching and learning.
9. There have been a lot of projects funded by the government or non-governmental organizations on developing English teachers' capacity in English curriculum design, material, and test development during the last few decades.
10. To date, four institutions have been appointed by the government to administer VSTEP tests and to award national certificates of English proficiency. These centers are under the strict and regular supervision of the Ministry of Education and Training.
11. This is regulated by Decision number 2913 dated August 23, 2016, by Vietnam's Ministry of Education and Training.
12. ULIS developed the training curriculum framework, which was approved by MOET and regulated in a decision in late 2016.

References

Association of Language Testers in Europe. (2011). *Manual for language test development and examining—for use with the CEFR*. Strasbourg: Council of Europe.

Bachman, L. F., & Palmer, A. S. (1996). *Language testing in practice*. Oxford: Oxford University Press.

Bachman, L. F., & Palmer, A. S. (2010). *Language assessment in practice*. Oxford: Oxford University Press.

Carr, N., Nguyen, T. N. Q., Nguyen, M. H., Nguyen, T. Q. Y., Thai, H. L. T., & Nguyen, T. P. T. (2016). *Systematic support for a communicative standardized proficiency test in Vietnam*. Paper presented at the 4th British Council New Directions in English Language Assessment: Standardised Testing and Proficiency Scales, Hanoi, Vietnam.

Chapelle, C. A., Enright, M. K., & Jamieson, J. M. (Eds.). (2008). *Building a validity argument for the Test of English as a Foreign Language*. New York, NY: Routledge.

Dendrinos, B. (1999). The conflictual subjectivity of the EFL practitioner. In A. F. Christidis (Ed.), *"Strong" and "weak" languages in the European Union: Aspects of hegemony* (Vol. 2, pp. 711–727). Thessaloniki, Greece: Centre for the Greek Language.

Dendrinos, B. (2013). Social meanings in global-glocal language proficiency exams. In D. Tsagari, S. Papadima-Sophocleous, & S. Ioannou-Georgiou (Eds.), *International experiences in language testing and assessment*. Frankfurt am Main: Peter Lang.

Dudzik, L. D., & Nguyen, T. N. Q. (2015). Vietnam: Building English competency in preparation for ASEAN 2015. In R. Stroup & K. Kimura (Eds.), *ASEAN integration and the role of English language teaching*. Phnompenh: IDP Education (Cambodia).

Dunlea, J. (2013). *Recognition for locally developed tests: An overview of regional approaches*. Plenary presentation at the 1st British Council New Directions in English Language Assessment conference, Beijing, China.

Dunlea, J., Nguyen, T. N. Q., Nguyen, T. Q. Y., Thai, H. L. T., & Nguyen, T. P. T. (2016). *Reporting on the pilot phase of a test comparability project*. Paper presented at the 4th British Council New Directions in English Language Assessment conference, Hanoi, Vietnam.

Dunlea, J., Spiby, R., Nguyen, T. N. Q., & Nguyen, T. Q. Y. (2017, December). *A closer look at two tests aligned with the CEFR*. Paper presented at the 5th British Council New Directions in English Language Assessment conference, Shanghai, China.

Dunlea, J., Spiby, R., Nguyen, T. N. Q., Nguyen, T. Q. Y., Nguyen, T. M. H., Nguyen, T. P. T., & Thai, H. L. T. (2018a). Aptis–VSTEP comparability study: Investigating the usage of two EFL tests in the context of higher education in Vietnam. *Technical Report*. University of Languages and International Studies, Vietnam National University, Hanoi.

Dunlea, J., Spiby, R., Nguyen, T. N. Q., Nguyen, T. Q. Y., Nguyen, T. M. H., Nguyen, T. P. T., . . . Bui, T. S. (2018b). *Aptis–VSTEP comparability study: Investigating the usage of two EFL tests in the context of higher education in Vietnam*. Retrieved from www.britishcouncil.org/aptis-vstep-comparability-study

Dunlea, J., Spiby, R., Nguyen, T. N. Q., Nguyen, T. Q. Y., Thai, H. L. T., & Nguyen, T. P. T. (2017, June). *Developing a multi-method design for carrying out comparability studies of tests aligned with the CEFR*. Paper presented at the 14th European Association for Language Testing and Assessment conference, Sèvres, France.

Fulcher, G. (2015). *Re-examining language testing: A philosophical and social inquiry*. London and New York, NY: Routledge.

Fulcher, G., & Davidson, F. (2007). *Language testing and assessment: An advanced resource book*. London: Routledge.

Green, T., & Jay, D. (2005). Quality assurance and quality control: Reviewing and pre-testing examination material at Cambridge ESOL. *Research Notes, 21*, 5–7.

Hughes, A. (2003). *Testing for language teachers*. Cambridge, UK: Cambridge University Press.

International Language Testing Association. (2000/2018). *Code of ethics*. Retrieved from https://cdn.ymaws.com/www.iltaonline.com/resource/resmgr/docs/ILTA_2018_CodeOfEthics_Engli.pdf

Jin, Y., Wu, Z., Alderson, C., & Song, W. (2017). Developing the China Standards of English: Challenges at macropolitical and micropolitical levels. *Language Testing in Asia, 7*, 1.

Kane, M. T. (1992). An argument-based approach to validity. *Psychological Bulletin, 112*(3), 527–535.

Le, V. C. (2017). English language education in Vietnamese universities: National benchmarking in practice. In E. S. Park & B. Spolsky (Eds.), *English education at the tertiary level in Asia: From policy to practice*. Abingdon and New York, NY: Routledge.

Ministry of Education and Training. (2008). *Government decision 1400: Teaching and learning foreign languages in the national educational system, period 2008–2020*. Hanoi, VN: Author.

Ministry of Education and Training. (2013). *Education in Vietnam in the early years of the 21st century*. Hanoi, VN: Viet Nam Education Publishing House.

Ministry of Education and Training. (2013, October 31). *Official Dispatch 7274 /BGDĐT-GDĐH on guidelines for the implementation of the National Foreign Language 2020 in tertiary institutions*. Retrieved from www.moet.gov.vn/?page=1.19&view=4559

Ministry of Education and Training. (2015, March 11). *Government decision 729: Issuance of the test of English proficiency levels 3–5 in the Vietnam's six-level framework of foreign language competency*. Hanoi, VN: Author.

Negishi, M., & Tono, Y. (2014). *An update on the CEFR-J project and its impact on English language education in Japan*. Paper presented at the 5th ALTE International Conference, Paris, France.

Nguyen, H. (Ed.). (2014). *Technical report on the development of test format and specification of Vietnamese Standardized Test of English Proficiency levels 3 to 5 for post-secondary English learners.* Retrieved from www.vstep.vn/sites/default/files/17.4.2015_vstep_report.pdf

Nguyen, H. (Ed.). (2015). *Technical report on the development of test format and specification of Vietnamese Standardized Test of English Proficiency level 2 for adult learners.* Unpublished internal report.

Nguyen, H. (Ed.). (2017a). *Technical report on the development of test format and specification of Vietnamese Standardized Test of English Proficiency level 1 for adult learners.* Unpublished internal report.

Nguyen, H. (Ed.). (2017b). *Technical report on the development of test format and specification of Vietnamese Standardized Test of English Proficiency level 3 for adult learners.* Unpublished internal report.

Nguyen, T. M. H., Nguyen, H., Do, T. T. H., Tran, T. H. P., Huynh, A. T., Dang, T., . . . Davidson, F. (2017, May). *Developing the Vietnamese Standardized Test of English Proficiency.* Paper presented at the 3rd International Conference on Language Testing and Assessment, Shanghai, China.

Nguyen, T. N. Q. (2013, September). *Language testing and assessment in Vietnam: The status quo and future development.* Paper presented at the Academic Forum on English Language Testing in Asia (AFELTA) Conference in Taiwan.

Nguyen, T. N. Q. (2016a, October). *Reform in English education and assessment in Vietnam: Lessons learned and future directions.* Plenary presentation at the 5th International Symposium on Foreign Language and Literature Teaching—Feng Chia and Southeast Asia, Taichung, Taiwan.

Nguyen, T. N. Q. (2016b, October). *Aligning to the CEFR: from assessment to curriculum design.* Paper presented at the 4th British Council New Directions in English Language Assessment conference, Hanoi, Vietnam.

Nguyen, T. N. Q. (2018). A study on the validity of VSTEP writing tests for the sake of regional and international integration. *VNU Journal of Foreign Studies, 34*(4), 115–128.

Nguyen, T. N. Q., & Do, T. M. (2015, July). *Developing a made-in-Vietnam standardised test of English proficiency for adults—The status quo and future development.* Plenary presentation at the TESOL Symposium, Da Nang, Vietnam.

Nguyen, T. N .Q., Nguyen, T. Q. Y., Nguyen, T. P. T., Thai, H. L. T., & Carr, N. T. (2017, June). *Using multiple approaches to examine the dependability of VSTEP speaking and writing assessments.* Paper presented at the 4th Asian Association for Language Assessment conference, Taipei, Taiwan.

Nguyen, T. N. Q., Nguyen, T. Q. Y., Thai, H. L. T., Nguyen, T. P. T., Dunlea, J., & Spiby, R. (2017, June). *A multi-method study to investigate the constructs measured by two EFL tests and their comparability in the context of Vietnam.* Paper presented at the 4th Asian Association for Language Assessment conference, Taipei, Taiwan.

Nguyen, T. N. Q., Thai, H. L. T., Bui, T. S., & Carr, T. N. (2017, June). *Analysing items, improving tests, and enhancing guidance for test writers on the Vietnamese Standardized Test of English Proficiency (VSTEP).* Paper presented at the 4th Asian Association for Language Assessment conference, Taipei, Taiwan.

Nguyen, T. P. T. (2018). An investigation into the content validity of a Vietnamese Standardized Test of English Proficiency (VSTEP.3–5) reading test. *VNU Journal of Foreign Studies, 34*(4), 129–142.

Nguyen, T. Q. Y. (2018). *An investigation into the validity of the cut-scores of VSTEP.3–5 listening test* (Unpublished doctoral dissertation). University of Languages and International Studies, Vietnam National University, Hanoi.

O'Sullivan, B. (2000). Exploring gender and oral proficiency interview performance. *System, 28*, 373–386.

O'Sullivan, B. (2014, September). *Adapting tests to the local context*. Plenary presentation at the 2nd British Council New Directions in English Language Assessment conference, Tokyo, Japan.

Pennycook, A. (1994). *The cultural politics of English as an international language*. London: Longman.

Saville, N. (2009). *Developing a model for investigating the impact of language assessment within educational contexts by a public examination provider* (Unpublished doctoral dissertation). University of Bedfordshire, UK.

Saville, N. (2010). Developing a model for investigating the impact of language assessment. *Research Notes, 42*, 2–8.

Shohamy, E. (2001). *The power of tests: A critical perspective of the uses of language tests*. Harlow: Longman.

Tran, T. H. P., Nguyen, H., Do, H., Dang, T., Nguyen, H., Huynh, A. T., . . . Davidson, F. (2015, March). *A validation study on the newly-developed Vietnamese Standardized Test of English Proficiency (VSTEP)*. Poster presented at the 2015 Language Testing Research Colloquium, Toronto, Canada.

Vu, T. P. A. (2016, October). *25 years of language assessment in Vietnam: Looking back and looking forward*. Plenary presentation at the 4th British Council New Directions in English Language Assessment conference, Hanoi, Vietnam.

Weir, C. J. (2005). *Language test validation: An evidence-based approach*. Oxford: Palgrave.

World Bank. (2013). *Skilling up Vietnam: Preparing the workforce for a modern market economy—Vietnam development report 2014*. Retrieved from http://documents.world bank.org/curated/en/610301468176937722/pdf/829400AR0P13040Box0379879B C0PUBLIC0.pdf

Wu, J. (2014, April). *Ensuring quality and fairness in the Asian EFL context: Challenges and opportunities*. Plenary presentation at the 5th ALTE International Conference, Paris, France.

Wu, J. (2016, October). *Locally appropriate English language test—locality, globality & validity*. Plenary presentation at the 4th British Council New Directions in English Language Assessment conference, Hanoi, Vietnam.

Wu, J. (2017, November). *Choosing an international exam or a locally-produced exam: attitudes and perceptions among stakeholders*. Paper presented at the Assessing World Languages Conference, Macau, China.

Wu, R., Yeh, H., Dunlea, J., & Spiby, R. (2016). *Aptis–GEPT comparison study: Looking at two tests from multiple perspectives using the socio-cognitive model* (British Council Validations Series, VS/2016/002). London: British Council.

5

TESTING TERTIARY-LEVEL ENGLISH LANGUAGE LEARNERS

The College English Test in China

Yan Jin

Introduction

In 2017, a total of 18.25 million tertiary-level English language learners registered to take the College English Test (CET), a national English language testing system in China (see its official website: http://cet.neea.edu.cn/). These students were primarily motivated to take the test to fulfil the requirements of their institutions: College English is a compulsory course required of students in higher education institutions in China, and the CET is an exit test to assess the English language proficiency of tertiary-level learners upon their completion of the College English program. The sheer volume of the CET indicates that the development and delivery of the test is a daunting challenge and its impact on individuals, institutions, and the educational and social systems is deep and wide-ranging. In this chapter, I will present an account of the development of the CET in the past three decades. The purpose of the chapter is to demonstrate the value and challenges of developing and using a contextualized local test to promote English language education at the tertiary level in China.

Milestones of the College English Test

For historical reasons, Russian, instead of English, was taught as a foreign language in schools and universities after the People's Republic of China was founded in 1949. The first national syllabus for teaching English as a foreign language in tertiary institutions was developed and implemented by the State Education Commission in 1962. Textbooks of English were published around the same period, but no national assessment was developed. After the publication of the teaching syllabus, an increasing number of college students began

102 Yan Jin

to learn English, instead of Russian, as their first foreign language. The trend, however, was interrupted by the "cultural revolution" during the 1960s and 1970s. The implementation of the open-door policy in the late 1970s gave rise to the need for university graduates with a higher level of English proficiency. English was again given due attention and became one of the three compulsory subjects assessed in the university entrance examination. In the early 1980s, a new national teaching syllabus for English language education at the tertiary level was developed and published for trial implementation. The syllabus was revised in the mid-1980s (State Education Commission, 1985, 1986; see Dai & Hu, 2009, for more details).

Following the revision of the national syllabus, a group of professors recognized the need for a national assessment to promote the implementation of the national syllabus. The idea was supported and endorsed by the State Education Commission. A working group consisting of 12 professors from different universities in different parts of the country was set up to develop the College English Test (CET). Led by Professor Yang Huizhong from Shanghai Jiao Tong University, the group of professors designed the first versions of the CET Band 4 (CET-4) and CET Band 6 (CET-6), which assessed the proficiency of listening, reading, and writing in English as a foreign language (Jin, 2010; Yang, 2003).

Test Development and Management

The group of professors, who were named the College English Test Working Group, designed the testing system from scratch. The group took charge of all the work of test development and management, including test registration, item writing, test delivery, scoring, equating, and score reporting. With the support of the State Education Commission (Ministry of Education after March 1998), the working group was in close contact with the British Council, which organized training programs for item writing and reviewing in Shanghai Jiao Tong University, and funded CET researchers to visit the Centre for Applied Language Studies, University of Reading, UK. The British Council also sent language testing expert Professor Cyril Weir and educational measurement specialist Dr. Tony Wood, both from University of Reading, as consultants to the CET program, to provide guidance on test validation (Weir & O'Sullivan, 2017). Significant outcomes resulted from the Sino-British cooperative validation study 1990–1995 (Yang & Weir, 1998), the first of its kind in modern language testing history in China (see *Research and Innovation*).

The National College English Testing Committee (NCETC) was formally set up by the Higher Education Department of the State Education Commission in 1994 (State Education Commission, 1994). Professor Yang Huizhong from Shanghai Jiao Tong University was appointed as chair of the committee. In the mid-1990s, the committee revised the test content and format of the

CET-4 and CET-6 and launched the CET Spoken English Test (CET–SET) in 1999.

The year 2005 witnessed a major transition of the CET management system. Before 2005, the Higher Education Department of the State Education Commission (Ministry of Education after March 1998) was the governmental institute managing the CET test operation and making test-related policies. The strength of this government institute lay in its attention to the impact of testing on teaching and learning and its delicate handling of the relationship between teaching, learning, and testing. The Higher Education Department was also in charge of the development and implementation of the national curriculum of college English education, or College English Teaching Syllabus (State Education Commission, 1985, 1986). The curriculum providers viewed an external assessment of college students' English proficiency as an indispensable component of English language education. With the increasing number of test takers and increasingly higher stakes of the CET in the early 2000s, the Ministry of Education considered the National Education Examinations Authority (NEEA), a ministerial institute in charge of national education examinations, more suitable for managing the CET program. In June 2005, the NEEA replaced the Higher Education Department to play the managerial role in the CET. As a professional testing organization, the NEEA has rich experience in managing large-scale assessments. The transition ensured successful implementation of the CET when the test population soared to 18 million a year. The three stages of the CET managerial system are presented in Table 5.1.

Revision of Test Content and Format

A major strength and distinguishing local feature of the CET lies in the fact that it is an exit test specifically designed for the College English program, and as a result, the assessment criteria of the CET are closely aligned to the national curriculum (also see *The Interface between Teaching, Learning, and Testing*). Following

TABLE 5.1 The Three Stages of the CET Managerial System

Stages	The test developer	The test manager
1987–1993: Test design and development	The College English Test Working Group	Higher Education Department, State Education Commission
1994–2004: Test validation and revision	The National College English Testing Committee	Higher Education Department, State Education Commission (Ministry of Education)
2005–now: Continuing reform and validation	The National College English Testing Committee	National Education Examinations Authority, Ministry of Education

the revision of the College English curriculum requirements, and to address the issues identified in CET washback studies (see *Washback on Teaching and Learning*), the content and format of the CET have accordingly undergone several major revisions. For example, changes in the input materials used in the CET at various stages of its development are described in Table 5.2.

Basically, the CET has adopted a componential view of the construct of language proficiency, assessing language skills independently (See Appendix 1 for subskills assessed in the CET). Listening and reading skills have always been given considerable attention, accounting for 60%–70%. The listening input materials used to be short dialogues and short passages. In the later versions, long conversations, news, lectures, and reports have been included to enrich the types of input materials. The growing exposure to a variety of text types over the decades reflects similar developments in communicative approaches to language teaching. In the reading part, long texts were added to assess expeditious reading skills in the early 2000s. Over the years, apart from multiple-choice questions, the assessment of the two receptive skills have used a variety of formats, including dictation, short answer questions, sentence translation (from English into Chinese), banked cloze, true or false or information not given, sentence completion, matching, and so on. Discrete-point items assessing vocabulary and grammar were abandoned in the late 1990s. Integrative tasks (cloze and error correction) were replaced by paragraph translation from Chinese into English in 2013. The tendency to adopt innovative tasks such as sentence translation and matching is reflected in similar developments in other major exams such as Cambridge English language examinations (see Weir, Vidaković, & Galaczi, 2013).

In terms of productive skills, unlike many English examinations around the world, from the start there has been a productive writing task in the CET, which has become an individually timed task (30 minutes) since the early 1990s. The decision on the relatively lower weight of this task (15%) was made in accordance with the requirement set in the national teaching syllabus, which

TABLE 5.2 The Input Materials Used in the CET in the Past Three Decades

	The first two decades	*The third decade*	*The latest version*
Listening	Short dialogues, passages	Short dialogues, long conversations, passages	Long conversations, passages, news, lectures, reports
Reading	Short passages	Short and long passages	Short and long passages
Writing	Outline in Chinese or English	Outline in Chinese or English, table, chart	Outline in English, picture, table, chart, quotation
Translation	/	Sentences in Chinese	Paragraph in Chinese

TABLE 5.3 The Latest Version of the CET (Since 2016)

Part	Test content	Test format	Time
Writing (15%)	Writing	Essay writing	30 mins
Listening (35%)	News (CET-4); lecture/ report (CET-6) Long conversation Passage	Multiple-choice	25–30 mins
Reading (35%)	Lexical comprehension Comprehension of long text In-depth comprehension	Banked cloze Matching Multiple-choice	40 mins
Translation (15%)	Translation from Chinese into English	Paragraph translation	30 mins
Speaking	A separate computer-based test, reporting graded scores of A+, A, B+, B, C+, C, and D (for further detail see *A Comparison of the Speaking Tests of CET, TOEFL iBT and IELTS*)		

laid emphases on reading and listening (see also *Linking Assessment Criteria to Curriculum Requirements*). A title and an outline (in Chinese) had been provided as writing prompts until recently. In the latest version of writing, various types of input materials are used as prompts: pictures, tables, charts, or quotations. Titles are not provided; instead, test takers are encouraged to find an appropriate perspective as the focus of their argument. The translation task was recently added to the CET in 2013 to answer the Chinese government's call for attention to "giving a good Chinese narrative, and better communicating China's message to the world." The topics of the source text in the task are about Chinese culture, customs, history, geography, social and economic development. Similar to writing, translation from Chinese into English involves cognitive processes such as macro-planning, organization, translation (execution), monitoring, and revision. Therefore, scores of the two tasks are merged into one sub-score (Writing and Translation) in the CET score report. Speaking was not assessed till 1999, when the CET Spoken English Test (CET–SET) was inaugurated, using the format of face-to-face interview. The current version of the speaking test adopts a computer-based paired format. Table 5.3 presents the content and format of the latest version of the CET.

Features Unique to the Local English Language Test

Zheng and Cheng (2008) conducted a review of the CET for the journal *Language Testing*, in which the CET is described as "a large-scale language test with distinctive Chinese characteristics" (p. 416). In this section, I will identify the features unique to the context of English language assessment in China.

106 Yan Jin

I will first describe the intended purposes of the CET and the way in which the test serves its purposes. I will discuss the banded system of English language teaching and testing and the interface between the CET and College English teaching and learning, focusing on the alignment of assessment criteria and curriculum requirements. As a case study, I will compare the CET speaking test (CET–SET) with two well-known international tests, TOEFL iBT developed by the Educational Testing Service in the U.S. and IELTS by Cambridge Assessment English in the UK.

The Interface Between Teaching, Learning, and Testing

The Banded System of the CET

The most frequently asked question about the CET is why it has two bands, Band 4 and Band 6, and what the bands mean. The banded system of the CET has its roots in College English curriculum requirements. In the College English Teaching Syllabus or Curriculum Requirements (State Education Commission, 1985, 1986; Higher Education Department of the Ministry of Education, 1999, 2007), college students are required to take English courses during the first two years, called the foundation stage. As there are two semesters each year in the Chinese higher education system, college students learn English during the first four semesters. In each semester, students are expected to attain learning objectives specified in band descriptions, Band 1 through Band 4. Upon entering colleges, students take a placement test, the result of which is used for assigning students to classes at an appropriate level, typically Bands 1 or 2. Students who begin with Band 1 will finish Band 4 in two years and take the CET-4 at the end of the fourth semester. Students who begin with a lower (pre-Band 1) or a higher Band (Bands 2, 3, or 4) will take a shorter or longer period of time to reach Band 4. Band 5 and Band 6 are the higher requirements for those learners who have finished the foundation stage. That is, after completing Band 4, students are encouraged to continue English language education by attending various optional courses provided to further improve their level of English as well as specific skills such as listening to news or reports, reading academic journal articles, debating, and academic writing. Upon completing the post-foundation stage, students can take the CET-6, which places more emphasis on academic English.

To put it simply, the CET-4 is aligned to the basic-level curriculum requirements and targeted at college students who have completed their English learning at the foundation stage, whereas the CET-6 is aligned to the higher-level curriculum requirements and targeted at those who have completed post-foundation studies. This outcome-based evaluative practice divides teaching and learning objectives into bands and measures the exit level of English proficiency, Band 4 or Band 6, greatly improving the coherence as well as the efficiency of

English language teaching, learning, and assessment at the tertiary level. No external international test currently available is capable of this level of appropriateness or delicacy required in matching assessment with the local curriculum.

Linking Assessment Criteria to Curriculum Requirements

The College English Curriculum Requirements (Higher Educational Department of the Ministry of Education, 2007) were developed by the National College Foreign Languages Teaching Advisory Committee under the auspices of the Higher Education Department of the Ministry of Education. The document specifies course objectives, teaching requirements, course design, teaching model, curriculum evaluation, and teaching administration. The College English Test Syllabus was developed by the NCETC under the auspices of the same governmental department before 2005 and the NEEA in the recent decade (for the latest version see National College English Testing Committee, 2016). With the intention of assessing the level of students' English proficiency upon completing College English courses, the NCETC links the assessment criteria closely to the curriculum requirements. That is, the assessment criteria are specified with explicit and direct reference to the national curriculum, making the CET a curriculum-based achievement test.

Micro-Level Features of the Local English Test

As a test specifically designed for tertiary-level English language learners in China, the CET has distinctive Chinese characteristics, both at the macro level as presented earlier and at the micro level, as reflected in its choices of lexis, language functions, and topics. Vocabulary requirements for college English learners, for example, are set out in the College English curriculum. The latest version requires a vocabulary size of 4,500 words for learners at the basic level (i.e., CET-4) and 5,400 words for learners the intermediate level (i.e., CET-6). Wordlists are provided in the CET test syllabus (National College English Testing Committee, 2016). Language functions specified in the curriculum provide guidance on CET item writing, especially the speaking and writing tasks. Topic and test takers' background knowledge are the most important contextual factors in a local language test. The basic requirement is that topics are relevant to college students' campus life and their future work. Social issues such as e-shopping, shared use of bikes, public transportation, and air pollution are popular topics for the CET speaking and writing tasks. These topics are familiar and relevant to test takers and have some degree of controversy, which are expected to engage CET test takers in critical thinking about the social values and cultural meanings associated with the things happening around them. Special care is taken to ensure that topics will not bring about construct-irrelevant easiness or difficulty due to test takers' background knowledge.

The Development and Implementation of the CSE

Educational policies constitute yet another important contextual variable that may impact on language assessment. A recent development in English language education in China is the release of a national framework of reference for English language education, titled China's Standards of English Language Ability (CSE), by the NEEA in June 2018. Following the approach of the Common European Framework of Reference for Languages (Council of Europe, 2001), the CSE uses calibrated and categorized can-do descriptors to exemplify what a Chinese learner of English can do from level 1 through to level 9. Given the close and long-standing relationship between curriculum requirements and English language tests, the CSE is perceived as the new kid on the block. The implementation of the CSE therefore may experience macro-political challenges that arise in coordinating and negotiating views of different stakeholders as well as micro-political challenges from practitioners who may pay lip service to the new framework (Jin, Wu, Alderson, & Song, 2017). As noted in Jin (2017), the multiple groups of stakeholders and their different roles in the CSE indicate "the complexity of the endeavour and the scale and depth of change which the new standards will effect on the English language education in China" (p. 7). Changes are also envisaged in the task design, scoring criteria, and score reporting of the CET, but it remains to be seen how the curriculum, assessment, and proficiency standards interweave to form a coherent system of English language education.

A Comparison of the Speaking Tests of CET, TOEFL iBT, and IELTS

To further illustrate the uniqueness of the local English test, I will compare the features of the CET Spoken English Test (CET–SET) with those of international English language tests targeted at learners of a similar proficiency level. The reason for choosing the speaking tests for comparative purposes is mainly due to the striking contrasts among the contextual variables incorporated in their design and delivery. I will first briefly describe the purposes and targeted test takers of the speaking components of TOEFL iBT, IELTS and CET, and then compare in some detail the tests with respect to item specifications, presentation model, assembly model, and delivery model. Through the analysis in this part, I will make the case that local contexts play an important role in conceptualizing and operationalizing the construct of English language proficiency.

Test Purposes and Targeted Test Takers

The test purposes and test taker profiles will be looked at first. Both TOEFL iBT and IELTS are intended to evaluate the speaking proficiency of students whose native language is not English and check their readiness for pursuing undergraduate or graduate study in higher education institutions in an English-speaking context (Educational Testing Service, 2009; Cullen, French, & Jakeman, 2013). Unlike the two admission tests, the CET–SET is designed as an exit test for evaluating the speaking proficiency of college students who have completed College English courses in China. Students are required to take the CET written tests before they are eligible to register for the CET–SET.

Test Specifications

A test's specifications provide "the official statement about what the test tests and how it tests it. The specifications are the blueprint to be followed by test and item writers, and they are also essential in the establishment of the test's construct validity" (Alderson, Clapham, & Wall, 1995, p. 9). In Fulcher and Davidson (2009), specifications are also referred to as "blueprints," for they are literally "architectural drawings for test construction" (p. 128). The three speaking tests will be compared in this section following the four sub-layers of architectural documentation for language test construction specified in Fulcher and Davidson (2009, p. 129): item specifications, assembly models, presentation models, and delivery models.

Item specifications describe the items or tasks and any materials upon which they depend. For speaking tests, task format, preparation and response time, and topics are important contextual variables for constructing items. An assembly model depicts how the items/tasks should be combined to produce a test form. In simpler terms, item specifications determine the content of the test and an assembly model shapes the way various components of a test are structured to form a test. Table 5.4 presents the task format, preparation, and response time of each task, and how the tasks are combined in each test.

A presentation model specifies how items/tasks are presented to test takers. In a speaking test, the presentation model defines the way test tasks are presented to test takers and the way examiners interact with test takers. The most important variable of presentation in a speaking test is therefore the role of examiners. A delivery model tells us how the test is administered. In a computer-based test, there may be computer simulated examiners or videos of human examiners. In an oral interview test, examiners can play the role of interlocutor, or assessor, or both. The speaking test of TOEFL iBT uses a computer-based format, which involves one-way communication. There are no interlocutors. Assessors, who are native speakers of English, listen to recordings and score performances. IELTS speaking, in contrast, is conducted face to face, involving interaction between the examiner and the test taker. Examiners are recruited, trained, and certified by Cambridge Assessment English and play the dual role of interlocutor and assessor. The CET–SET adopts a computer-based paired format, engaging test takers in both monologic tasks and a discussion task between the two test takers. Videos of human examiners, who are native speakers, are employed

110 Yan Jin

TABLE 5.4 Item Specifications and Assembly Models of the Three Speaking Tests

Test	Part	Task format	Preparation/ response time	Length
TOEFL iBT	Tasks 1 & 2	Question and answer	15/45 seconds	About 8
	Tasks 3 & 4	Read, listen and speak	30/60 seconds	minutes
	Tasks 5 & 6	Listen and speak	20/60 seconds	
IELTS	Part 1	Introduction and interview	0/4–5 minutes	About 11–13 minutes
	Part 2	Individual long turn	1/2 minutes	
	Part 3	Two-way discussion	0/4–5 minutes	
CET-SET Band 4	Task 1	Reading aloud	45/60 seconds	About 8
	Task 2	Question and answer	0/40 seconds	minutes
	Task 3	Individual presentation	45/60 seconds	
	Task 4	Paired discussion	1/3 minutes	
CET-SET Band 6	Task 1	Warm-up questions	0/30 seconds	About 7
	Task 2	Individual presentation	1/1.5 minutes	minutes
	Task 3	Paired discussion	0/3 minutes	
	Task 4	Further-check questions	0/45 seconds	

to play the role of interlocutors. Assessors, who are English language teachers at the tertiary level with an advanced level of proficiency in English, listen to recordings and score performances.

Comments on the Three Speaking Tests

Comparisons between international language tests such as TOEFL and IELTS have attracted much attention in the field of language testing (e.g., Bachman, Davidson, Ryan, & Choi, 1995; Spolsky, 1995). Weir et al. (2013) highlighted the substantive differences "between the United Kingdom and the United States in their approaches to language testing from 1913–1966" (p. 422). One explanation for the predominant focus on the psychometric qualities of a test in the U.S. was the need to produce tests on an industrial scale in the early 20th century. Language testers in the UK, in contrast, "identified a greater concern with context validity and relating examinations to what was going on in the language classroom" (Weir et al., 2013). The difference was characterized as "a concern with the *how* in the United States as against the *what* in the United Kingdom" (Weir et al., 2013).

The same explanation would seem to apply to the differences between the current speaking assessments of TOEFL iBT and IELTS. The computer-based delivery of TOEFL iBT speaking improves its assessment efficiency. In the test, a total of six tasks are used to guarantee the internal reliability. An automated scoring engine SpeechRater plays the role of the second rater to further improve scoring validity. The limitation of the format is that test takers can only talk to the computer, not to human examiners or other test takers. That is, the construct being assessed is oral production, not interaction. The IELTS, on the other hand, prioritizes the construct to be assessed: the interactive nature of speaking activities. Therefore, IELTS speaking adopts the most direct assessment format: face-to-face oral interview. To ensure scoring validity, only authorized IELTS examiners are eligible to score IELTS speaking tests.

When the CET–SET was inaugurated in 1999, it adopted a group interview format, in which three test takers and two examiners formed a test group. Each test taker answered the examiner's questions, made presentations, and participated in a group discussion among the three test takers. The format sought to maximize assessment efficiency by assessing three test takers at the same time. Talking to their peers in the group could also avoid the issue of imbalanced power relationship between the examiner and the test taker in the oral interview of IELTS and increase reciprocity from candidates. While the topics of the two international speaking tests are mainly about campus life and study in an English-medium context, those of the CET are about social issues, campus life and study in higher education institutions in China. Until 2012, a total of 58 CET–SET test centers had been established and over a thousand examiners had been trained. The volume of the test, however, was seriously constrained by the number of quality examiners as well as the availability of test venues. A different solution was necessary.

Since 2013, the computer-based CET–SET has been developed and implemented. One unique feature of the computer-based speaking test is its paired format. The test developer views interactional competence as an important component of the speaking construct: test takers not only talk to the computer, but also talk to each other in the discussion task. This is the first time for a paired format to be used in large-scale, high-stakes computer-based speaking assessments. The task, in fact, simulates an increasingly popular mode of oral communication in real life, that is, non-face-to-face oral interaction (e.g., talking via Skype or WeChat) (cf. Nakatsuhara, Inoue, Berry, & Galaczi, 2017).

International tests, useful as they are, cannot cater to the degree of localization required in the Chinese context. They are very broad spectrum, general types of proficiency-oriented tests designed for test takers from a variety of cultural and educational backgrounds. It is therefore difficult for international tests to contextualize their construct definition and operationalize the constructs in a specific context. In pursuit of test fairness, for example, international tests resolve to take a neutral stance on topics for speaking and writing, reducing the degree of topic relevance and interestingness to test takers. International tests are by their very nature trying to be all things to all people and cannot meet the requirements of one country as against many.

Quality Control and Test Fairness

Quality Control of Test Items

"A well-constructed test is an instrument that provides an accurate measure of the test-taker's ability within a particular domain. . . . However, constructing a good test is a complex task involving both science and art" (Brown, 2004, p. 4). The most important but difficult requirement in constructing a good test is to ensure the quality of its items. Items of good quality, by definition, should assess important and meaningful information detailed in the tests' specifications, and items should be at an appropriate difficulty level with satisfactory discrimination power. Only with items of good quality, will it be possible for a test to be fair and unbiased, reliable and valid, and appropriate for its purposes.

Over the years, the NCETC has been following a systematic procedure of item writing, reviewing, piloting, and moderation (see Figure 5.1). Instead of relying solely on item writers to produce high-quality items, the committee breaks the procedure of item writing into several major steps: Stage 1 preparing texts, Stage 2 writing raw items and piloting, Stage 3 data analysis and item review, and finally Stage 4 final review of each test form and version by the committee before putting them into operational use. The truncated procedure has the advantage of maximally ensuring the quality of test items at each phase of item construction and avoiding unnecessary waste of time and effort. In traditional procedures, items submitted by an item writer are likely to be rejected for one or several of the following reasons: inappropriate texts, unsuitable question areas, or poor item quality. In the current model of item production, it is not possible for items to be rejected because of inappropriate source texts. The quality of the texts has already been controlled before items are produced. Nor is it likely that an item is rejected because it assesses a trivial, unimportant detail. The question areas of each text are determined through text mapping (Sarig, 1989). Piloting is also essential for quality control. Each selected-response item is subject to piloting with over one thousand students,

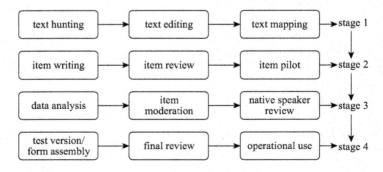

FIGURE 5.1 The Procedure of CET Item Writing

Testing Tertiary-Level Learners **113**

who will take the operational CET two weeks later. The motivation of these students is ensured by reporting a higher score of the pilot and the operational test. Post-pilot items are revised, first by local reviewers, to improve their difficulty level, discrimination power, and fairness, and then by native speakers, to further improve the language quality of input materials and items.

The experience of CET item construction over the three decades has shown that the prerequisites of achieving high-quality items are qualified and dedicated item writers, appropriate and motivated candidates for pilot tests, professional statisticians for data analysis, and experienced reviewers for item moderation. Close collaboration between local item writers and native speakers in the processes of text hunting, item writing and reviewing has also proved to be an effective measure to control the quality of test items.

Data analyses are conducted after each test at the item level, the task level, and the test level, and the results are reported at each bi-annual committee meeting. Following a recent revision of the test content and format in 2013, the quality of the revised CET-4 items was evaluated using both classical test theory and the Rasch model (Zhang & Chen, 2015). The results of the analyses indicated that the revised items satisfied the measurement quality requirements, providing some empirical evidence in support of the validity of the revised CET-4.

Rating of Constructed-Response Items

In the CET there are both restricted-choice and constructed-response questions. Proportions of the former are always much larger than the latter, due mainly to the practicality issue with the scoring of constructed-response tasks. In the current version, 70% of the paper-based CET are multiple-choice or matching questions assessing listening and reading comprehension, and the remaining 30% are constructed-response items (CRI) assessing essay writing and paragraph translation from Chinese into English. While multiple-choice questions can target a variety of higher-level processes: discriminating between ideas, identifying main points, inferring points left unexpressed, interpreting speaker attitude, reporting logical connections, identifying a conclusion reached, there is some concern about their appropriateness for "activating the higher-level processing required in constructing an organized representation of the text" (Weir et al., 2013, p. 157). Weir et al. (2013) also argue that in short answer questions the answer has to be sought rather than being provided for the student as in multiple-choice, therefore, "if a student gets the answer right, one can be more certain that this has not occurred for reasons other than comprehension of the text" (p. 150). In the multiple-choice format we do not have this guarantee as the option itself rather than the text may have suggested the answer or appeared superior to the other available alternatives. The benefits of CRIs, however, come at a price. Livingston (2009) noted that "(O)ne of

114 Yan Jin

the greatest problems in constructed response testing is the time and expense involved in scoring. The process often includes elaborate systems for monitoring the consistency and accuracy of the scores" (p. 5).

Since the mid-1990s, various types of constructed-response questions have been introduced to the CET, including dictation, short answer questions, sentence translation, paragraph translation, and so on. After each test, around 3,000 raters in twelve marking centers in different parts of the country are invited to rate millions of scripts. The scoring process is time-consuming, expensive, and subjective. Qualified raters are difficult to find, and rating consistency is hard to ensure. In this part, the quality control measures taken by the NCETC in rating the CRIs, particularly essays and paragraph translation, will be described.

In each CET marking center, there is one director and several chief supervisors. The director is either an NCETC member or Dean of an English language department in universities. Supervisors are chosen from experienced raters and appointed by the director. For each operational marking event, a highly experienced and dedicated pool of raters are invited and trained. The raters are all tertiary-level English language teachers who have a good knowledge of test takers' strengths and weaknesses. Before each marking session, a meeting is organized by the NCETC, in which the director and two supervisors of each marking center meet in Shanghai (where the NCETC office is located) to select one set of benchmark scripts and two sets of sample scripts to be used for rater training. Take essay writing as an example. Scripts of essay writing are assigned a score of 0–15 based on band descriptions: Band 1 (0–3), Band 2 (4–6), Band 3 (7–9), Band 4 (10–12), Band 5 (13–15). Benchmark scripts with a mid-point score of each band (i.e., 2, 5, 8, 11, and 14) are selected and used in rater training. Sample scripts are also selected for performances of various types and at different levels, including some borderline cases. The discussion among the participants during the process of selecting the scripts serves as a standardization procedure to improve inter-center consistencies, that is, the twelve marking centers are expected to apply the same criteria in rating the scripts assigned to their centers.

To further improve the consistency, reliability and efficiency of CRI rating, the NCETC, in collaboration with an information and technology company, developed an online marking system in 2003 for all constructed-response items, including dictation, short answer questions, and essays. After three years' trial implementation, the marking system was put into operational use in 2006. Double rating is mission impossible given the time, human resources, and budget available: for each administration, a total of 12 marking centers, each having 200–300 authorized CET markers, work for about two weeks to complete the scoring of 9 million tests. The online CRI marking system, therefore, adopts the approach of single holistic rating plus random quality checking of no less than 20% of the scripts. Furthermore, to ensure inter- and intra-rater consistencies, an online training module is built into the marking system, which enables real-time monitoring of raters' performance and provision of immediate feedback to raters.

Ensuring the Fairness of the CET

Test takers of the CET, to a large extent, constitute a homogenous group in terms of their first language background, English language education background, motivation for learning English, and so on. Potential bias of test content may not be a serious issue, although attention needs to be paid to the different levels of social and economic development in various parts of the country. Topics of listening and reading materials as well as writing and translation tasks are carefully chosen to avoid possible impact of social and economic development on learners' background knowledge. To avoid subject matter bias, the test developer strives to achieve a balance of test materials in the areas of humanities and social sciences, science and technology, business and economics, as well as medical and life sciences.

The other concern with test fairness is the provision of accommodations to test takers with disabilities. In the early years of the CET, few students with disabilities registered to take the CET. With the rising stakes of the CET, there have been an increasing number of requests for test accommodations in recent years. Up till 2017, the CET has been able to provide three types of accommodation: lip-reading for test takers with hearing problems, enlarged fonts for test takers with weak eyesight, and papers in Braille for blind test takers. In each case, adjustments are also made to test takers' response time.

In a testing-oriented educational culture, cheating has always been a pressing fairness concern for test developers, especially in those responsible for a large-scale, high-stakes test such as the CET. In the first two decades of the CET test operation, the late 1980s to the early 2000s, test takers cheated by the traditional means of copying from their neighbors' scripts. On top of strict invigilation, raters of CET constructed-response items were given the scripts in batches of five test takers who had sat closest to each other during the test. This was to help raters identify the scripts bearing too close a resemblance. Suspicious scripts would be reported to the supervisor for further investigation, including for example, checking these test takers' responses to selected-response items. The other means of cheating during the period was impersonation, that is, hiring someone to act as ghost examinee in the test. This was largely prevented by comparing the photo on an admission ticket, which would also be printed on the score report, with the person taking the test. The other preventative measure was to rely on test takers checking each other's identity, because test takers from the same department were arranged in the same or nearby test rooms. Named and anonymous reports of impersonation cases had been received by the NCETC after test administration.

In the recent decade, technology has been used, paradoxically, for cheating on exams, especially high-stakes tests, leading to the so-called high-tech cheating. When taking the CET, test takers who have pre-paid for cheating "services" would get answers to selected-response items through mini-earphones that are difficult for invigilators to detect (Garner & Huang, 2014; Huang & Garner, 2009). To combat this type of cheating, the NEEA and the NCETC developed an innovative measure, which employs multiple versions and multiple forms (MVMF) in the paper-based CET (Jin & Wu, 2017). Test versions share the same test content, but the orders of texts and options differ from one version to another. Test forms contain different source texts and different questions. By using MVMF, test takers cannot identify the version and the form of their papers, and service providers cannot work out answers to a number of versions and forms during the test time. Cheating via receiving messages through electronic devices has therefore been effectively prevented. The innovation has brought about challenges to item construction, scoring, and equating. The NCETC has worked out an efficient and systematic procedure to ensure the development of a much larger pool of items, which are piloted and calibrated to facilitate the compilation of parallel forms. Quality-control measures are also taken to ensure the consistency of rating scripts on different writing topics and scripts of different source texts for translation. Most importantly, post-test vertical equating for tests given at different times and horizontal equating for the different forms used in the same test are performed using a representative group of anchored students who take an equating test two weeks before the operational test. Effective as they are in combating cheating, "techniques such as multiple versions and multiple forms may provide only a short-term solution to the problem of cheating," because cheating on exams "has its root in the educational and social contexts in which assessment activities take place" (Jin & Wu, 2017, p. 69). In the Ninth Amendment to Criminal Law effected on November 1, 2015, cheating on national exams is seen as a criminal act. Punishment of up to seven years' imprisonment will be imposed on those who cheat and those who assist in cheating. Jin and Wu (2017) pointed out that "in the cat and mouse game of prevention of cheating, legislation is probably the ultimate solution" (p. 69).

Uses of the CET and Its Impact on Teaching and Learning

Since the CET became a large-scale, high-stakes test in the mid-1990s, its implementation has not been without controversy. The debate over the last two decades has centered on its washback or impact on teaching and learning. Having been involved in the development and reform of the test for nearly three decades, I may be considered as an insider of the testing program, hence less capable of providing an unbiased review of its impact. But this is an important element of the history of the CET that cannot be omitted. Therefore, in this part, I will make every effort to conduct an objective evaluation on the uses of the CET and its impact on English language education and support my observations with external evidence where available.

Intended Purposes of the CET

The most important purpose of the CET is to provide feedback for improving teaching and learning. Detailed score reports, therefore, are provided to individuals and groups. At an individual level, the CET reports profile scores of each component skill: listening, reading, translation, and writing, as well as a total score. CET scores across tests given at different times are equated and are therefore comparable. As a norm-referenced test, percentile positions of each component score (listening, reading, translation and writing) as well as the total score are provided on the CET official website (http://cet.neea.edu.cn/). Feedback is also provided at the group level. Each higher education institution receives score reports of its students and performance profiles of students in each academic year. Each provincial or municipal education examinations authority receives reports of each institution in the province or municipality and the reports of the entire province or municipality. The NEEA receives reports of each institution as well as reports of each province or municipality. For reference by institutions and examination authorities, scores of different types of colleges (e.g. key or non-key) are also reported at the group level.

Washback on Teaching and Learning

Although washback was not explicitly articulated as part of the validity argument in the Sino-British cooperative CET validation study in the late 1990s (see *Validation Studies of the CET*), stakeholders' views were elicited through questionnaire surveys to measure the face validity of the test (Yang & Weir, 1998). Educational administrators, teachers, and employers were on the whole positive about the usefulness of the test for promoting teaching and learning and for recruiting new employees. Stakeholders, particularly employers, however, were dissatisfied with the lack of an oral test and assessment tasks of translation, both being important skills for future workplace. Teachers were less satisfied with the large proportion of multiple-choice questions in the test because of its potential negative effect on learning: the heavy reliance on multiple-choice items put a strong psychological pressure on teachers who tended to make excessive use of them for teaching and learning purposes.

It was also found that the CET was used as an important indicator in college league tables, and that college English teachers were evaluated according to their students' performances on the test. In many institutions, however, the simple passing rate (i.e., percentage of students who pass the CET) was used for evaluative purposes. To remedy this deficiency, after the validation study, the NCETC started to use "average graded score" for reporting group performances. Six levels (or grades) were used to describe test takers' performances on the CET, substantially raising the level of granularity of the feedback at the group level. The validation study also revealed that learners' writing performances did not seem to improve over the years. Therefore, a minimum requirement was set for the writing component to encourage progress in learners' writing ability. Test takers who failed to achieve a minimum score of 6 (out of 15) would be penalized by a reduction in their total score, and test takers who did not attempt the writing component (a score of 0) would not be awarded a CET certificate. An analysis of test scores in the following years indicated a steady improvement in students' writing performances (Jin & Yang, 2006).

Alderson and Hamp-Lyons (1996) found in their TOEFL impact study that "(T)ests will have different amounts and types of washback on some teachers and learners than on other teachers and learners" (p. 295). Furthermore, as revealed in recent washback studies (e.g., Garner & Huang, 2014; Watanabe, 2004; Xie & Andrews, 2012), English language teaching and learning has been influenced by language tests via the mediation of a complex set of factors, the top three being those related to students (e.g., educational background), teachers (e.g., quality of teaching), and educational administrators (e.g., perceptions of the relationship between teaching and testing). With the caveat of mediation by factors outlined in these studies, the CET has been shown to have impacted on what is taught in College English classes, how College English is taught, and the priority of and the time spent on College English teaching and learning. The power of the impact however varies from region to region, from institution to institution, and from teacher to teacher.

In a doctoral study conducted in the early 2000s, classroom observation, interviews and questionnaire surveys were used to investigate the CET washback (Gu, 2004, 2007). An interesting finding is that the existence of the CET has established and upheld the status of "College English" as a compulsory course of the foundation stage (the first two years). In Gu's (2004) study, classroom teaching was found to be largely "normal," that is, classroom teaching was not interfered with by test preparation, although in some institutions, the final semester of the foundation stage was devoted to test familiarization and preparation. The CET was also found to have a greater influence on the content and pace of teaching than teaching methodology. The constructs of English language proficiency, however, were sometimes narrowed or underrepresented in teaching and learning because only those frequently assessed were taught and learnt. For example, teachers attached more importance to the reading skill than other skills because reading comprehension took up the largest proportion in the earlier version of the CET. Similar to the findings in Yang and Weir (1998), teachers in Gu's study expressed concern with the large proportion of selected-response items and the lack of a compulsory component of speaking in the CET (see also Jin, 2000). Surveys of teachers' perceptions of the CET in some other studies (e.g., Gu & Liu, 2005; Han, Dai, & Yang, 2004) also raised concern over the problem of test-oriented teaching. As commented in Cheng (2008), "many researchers have advocated that testing should support teaching while in reality the CET drives teaching in China" (p. 32).

Major issues identified in CET washback studies have been addressed in the test's reform projects (see *Revision of Test Content and Format*). The development of the CET–Spoken English Test in the late 1990s and its computerized format in the 2000s was also intended to meet the needs of oral English teaching and learning at the tertiary level (see *Comments on the three speaking tests*).

High-Stakes Uses of the CET

A relevant but high-stakes use of the CET is to require a pass on the CET-4 for graduation or bachelor's degrees and a pass on the CET-6 for admission to master's or doctoral programs. Apart from its uses in the educational context, the CET has been used for making a variety of high-stakes decisions that have little connection with English language education (Jin, 2008, 2014). The validation study reported in Yang and Weir (1998) found that almost all employers (98%) required CET qualifications in recruiting university graduates, even though their employees may not be working in an English-speaking environment. Garner and Huang (2014) looked into the uses made of the CET results by surveying seventy job advertisements for graduating students and interviewing six employers. It was found that "the preferred 'English Certificate' is the CET certificate" (p. 71). Even government departments require CET qualifications for positions in government ministries and bureaus, although there are separate civil service examinations. In the recruitment plan of the National Bureau of Statistics for 2008, for example, all positions had the CET requirement (p. 72). CET qualifications are used by employers as a screening instrument: "We see CET qualification as an indicator of students' learning attitude instead of an indicator of their English ability" (Garner & Huang, 2014, p. 75).

One of the most controversial uses of the CET is as a hurdle requirement for a work or residence permit in first-tier cities such as Beijing, Shanghai, Guangzhou, and Shenzhen. University graduates have to pass the CET-4 in order to be granted a work or residence permit. Without such a permit, it would be very difficult for these graduates to make a living in the cities. Garner and Huang (2014) commented that "The (CET) ball is getting bigger with increasing number of test takers and heavier with the increasing stakes and it becomes more difficult to change the direction (i.e., reform the test)" (p. 85). In the 1997 special issue on test washback and impact published by *Language Testing*, Spolsky (1997) noted that

> [T]ests can provide valuable data for gatekeeping decisions, but must not be left as the sole arbiter . . . we must make sure that gatekeeping

120 Yan Jin

> processes remain under responsible and challengeable human control and not be relegated to the automatic and conscienceless power of mechanical self-propelling tests.
>
> *(p. 246–247)*

Hamp-Lyons (1997) also rightly pointed out that

> [L]anguage learning is not limited to classrooms, and its consequences are not only educational, but also social and political (Pennycook, 1994). The responsibility of language testers is clear: we must accept responsibility for all those consequences which we are aware of.
>
> *(p. 302)*

As the test developer, the NCETC sets the improvement of test validity as its top priority and makes every effort to ensure that the design and implementation of the test promotes College English teaching and learning. As the test provider, or manager, the NEEA considers test fairness and security as its principal responsibility and provides strong support to the NCETC to revise and reform the test based on the changing curriculum requirements. In the next section, research and innovation in the CET will be presented to demonstrate how the test developer and the test provider take up the responsibility for validating the test and improving its efficiency.

Research and Innovation

Validation Studies of the CET

The field of language testing has reached a consensus that test validation is a critical ongoing process for all test providers. Over the past three decades, research has focused on improving the design and efficiency of the CET as well as its educational and social impact. The most significant study to validate the CET was conducted in the 1990s (Yang & Weir, 1998). This Sino-British cooperative project was among the first of its kind in the modern history of language testing in China. Based on the test developer's understanding of validity in the late 1980s and early 1990s, various types of evidence were collected to empirically evaluate the quality of the test and its washback on teaching and learning. For example, content validity was evaluated by inviting language testing experts to make judgment on the coverage of test specifications; criterion-related validity was investigated by correlating CET scores with the rank order of test takers' English proficiency rated by their English language teachers; performances on the constructed-response items were analyzed to demonstrate the so-called response validity; introspective think-aloud studies were also conducted to evaluate the response validity of reading comprehension questions (Jin & Wu, 1997, 1998); surveys were conducted among stakeholders for their evaluation of the usefulness of the test for teaching and learning, providing evidence for the face validity of the test. Although, working within an earlier paradigm, validity was not conceptualized as a unified concept, the varieties of validity evidence and the systematic approach adopted in collecting the evidence have indicated the CET developers' success in their role as a professional testing organization to provide a reliable and valid language testing service. The validation study was presented as a two-hour symposium at the LTRC 2000 in Vancouver and received widespread attention from the field of language testing outside of China (Yang, Jin, Guo, & Xia, 2000).

Innovation in the CET and Related Studies

The use of technology has been a main theme of the innovation in the CET since the early 2000s when the test population reached 10 million a year. In 2003, an online marking system was developed for use in rating the constructed-response items of the CET (see *Rating of Constructed-Response Items*). A number of studies including one doctoral study have been conducted since the implementation of the system in the twelve marking centers (e.g., Huang, 2007; Wang, 2004a, 2004b; Zhang & Yu, 2010). These studies investigated the scoring validity of constructed-response items through analyses of inter- and intra-rater scoring consistencies, raters' decision-making processes, and the effectiveness of real-time online monitoring for improving rater consistency. The online rating system was found to have greatly improved the efficiency of scoring and eliminated the mistakes caused by manual score recording in the traditional paper-based scoring. By incorporating online training and real-time monitoring into the scoring system, rater consistency was also found to have been improved. As the studies were conducted at the time when the online system was newly developed and launched, some teachers were not used to reading and scoring on the computer, eight hours a day for over 10 days. A frequent complaint was eye-fatigue. There were also issues about raters' over-concern with quality-control parameters, which may negatively impact on raters' decision-making process. Based on the results of the studies, improvements were made to the scoring system as well as the quality-control process.

In 2007, to improve the efficiency and the construct validity of the paper-based CET, the internet-based CET (IB–CET) was developed by the NCETC in collaboration with an information and technology company. The most significant improvement in the IB–CET was that it assessed the four major language skills, that is, speaking became an integral part of the test. A comparative study between the IB–CET and PTE–Academic, an internet-based college admission test using largely integrated tasks, was conducted to investigate whether the improvement in task authenticity using integrated tasks would be accompanied by muddied construct validity in language assessment (Jin & Zhang,

2013, 2014). Results showed that the two tests correlated at a quite high level at the total score level ($r=0.84$), but at the level of component skills, the correlations between the tests were relatively low (e.g., $r=0.51$ for speaking, $r=0.59$ for reading), giving rise to concerns with the practice of profiling test takers' communicative skills based on their performances on tasks of an integrated nature in the Pearson Test.

In the writing task of the IB–CET, test takers use the keyboard to type their essays, instead of handwriting their responses, reflecting developments in the real world where students now seldom write out their assignments by hand. A comparative study was conducted to investigate whether the change in the response mode would bring about construct-irrelevant variances. Comparisons were made between test takers' writing performances and processes in the paper-based CET and the IB–CET through text analysis using Coh-Metrix (Version 2.0), survey data analysis, and test score analysis (Jin & Yan, 2017). The study revealed that computer literacy had a facilitative effect on test takers' perceptions of their processes of writing as well as the overall quality of writing in the computer-based writing assessment. More importantly, the authors argued that "the construct of a computer-based language test needs to be reconceptualized by drawing on Chalhoub-Deville's view of local context-bound constructs: computer literacy should be viewed as an important contextual facet interacting with the construct measured in a computer-based language assessment" (p. 1).

In 2013, the computer-based CET Spoken English Test (CET–SET) was implemented nationwide, in which a paired format was designed to assess test takers' interactional competence (Zhang & Jin, 2016). A recent study adopted conversation analysis to investigate test takers' use of communicative strategies in face-to-face and computer-based CET–SET (Jin & Zhang, 2016). The study found that the two modes shared a high degree of similarity in the quantity and variety of communication strategies, although there were minor differences in the frequencies of cooperative strategies. As shown in video clips collected for the CET–SET comparative study, test takers had rich facial expressions and employed a range of body language when engaged in computer-based pair discussion. They listened to their partners carefully and constantly nodded as if they could see each other.

Over the past three decades, a large number of studies have been conducted by Chinese researchers, based in or outside of China, many of which are masters and doctoral students majoring in language testing and assessment. The huge scale of the CET means that it is one of the most controversial testing programs and has aroused considerable interest in discussions of test washback, or more recently, the social dimension of language testing. It is therefore no exaggeration to say that the development and reform of the CET has to some extent promoted research of language testing theory and practice in China.

A Research Agenda for the CET

Innovation has proved decisive in the successful development of the CET. Managing a test with 18 million test takers each year is mission impossible without the application of technology in each and every phase of its development and administration. With recent progresses in the development of machines with human-like intelligence in learning, notably in understanding and producing human language, automated scoring has become an innovation high on the CET research agenda. Through close collaboration with local high-tech companies, the CET has been developing and using automated scoring systems for its performance-based tasks, including for example, read-aloud in the CET–SET, writing and translation tasks in the CET. Validity evidence at this stage comes mainly from correlational statistics of human and machine scores. An argument-based framework for a comprehensive validation of the CET automated scoring systems has been proposed and a research agenda has been set up (Jin, Knoch, & Zhu, 2018).

In addition to technological challenges, a major concern of the test developer is construct-irrelevant variances introduced by test takers' use of test-wise strategies when they know that they are writing or speaking to the machine instead of human raters. To this end, a large-scale survey has been conducted to investigate teachers' and test takers' perceptions of automated scoring and the strategies they are likely to use. Results of the investigation have pointed to the need to inform stakeholders, including teachers and test takers, that they may be misguided by test-wise strategies and that with technological advancement, test-wise strategies may even be counter-productive (Jin, Zhu, & Wang, 2017).

More importantly, the future of the CET, the world's largest English language test, lies in a clearer conceptualization of the constructs to be assessed and a commitment to the continuous improvement of the way we assess the constructs. In a comparative study of local and international language tests, comparisons were made between the TOEFL iBT and the reading and writing tasks of the General English Proficiency Test–Advanced (GEPT-A), a local English language test developed by the Language Training and Testing Center (LTTC) in Taipei (Kunnan & Carr, 2017). The study shows that, although scores on the two tests are highly correlated, "the construct coverage, item scope, and task formats of the two tests are clearly distinct" (p. 1). Similar effects from a local approach can be seen in the CET narrative in this chapter. The comparison between the internet-based CET and the Pearson Test of English—Academic demonstrates an overall strong correlation but clear differences in the constructs being measured (Jin & Zhang, 2014). To conceptualize and operationalize test construct, we need to pay closer attention to both the contextual variables that determine how the test constructs are assessed and test takers' cognitive processing activated when test questions are answered (Weir, 2005). Research has been in progress along the line of factors affecting CET

124 Yan Jin

test performance (e.g., Jin & Cheng, 2013), but further in-depth investigations are needed to disentangle the effect of socio-cognitive factors on the validity of high-stakes tests. As stressed by Weir et al. (2013), "it is important in language testing that we give both the contextual and the cognitive elements an appropriate place and emphasis in test development, resisting any temptation to favor one over the other" (p. 425).

An equally important dimension for the further development of the CET is to adopt Bachman and Palmer's (2010) assessment use argument (AUA) approach to evaluate the uses and consequences of the uses of the CET. Zheng and Cheng (2008) pointed out at the end of their review of the CET that "with the fast increasing number of Chinese students studying in English-medium universities around the world outside China, the impact of the CET on Chinese students' English learning has already gone beyond its intended use and consequences on Chinese society alone. Its impact on test-takers' learning of English needs further research" (p. 416).

Conclusion

This chapter is the first comprehensive documentation of the 30-year history of the development and reform of the CET. The review of this testing program shows that it is a locally developed English language test with distinctive Chinese characteristics that has continuously sought to meet the exacting professional standards set for high-stakes tests in the 21st century.

In this chapter, the development of the CET has been covered by focusing on the most important milestones in the past three decades. It started with a review of the social and educational context in which the test was developed and then charted its growth into an English language test that is probably now the largest in the world. To identify the features unique to the local educational context in China, the interface between the teaching and testing of English in higher education institutions was discussed in detail and a comparative analysis of the local and international English language tests was conducted. Measures taken by the test developer to ensure the quality and fairness of the CET were then introduced. This was followed by a discussion of the high-stakes uses of the test and its impact on teaching and learning. Finally, the research and innovation conducted to improve the validity of the CET were briefly reviewed and a research agenda was set up for further development of the CET.

Weir et al. (2013) regard stability and innovation as "the twin pillars of public examinations" (pp. 422–423). In a similar vein, Fulcher and Davidson (2007) highlight the need for both continuity and innovation in the evolution of language tests, as well as the need to audit that evolution through architectural documentation or a validity narrative (pp. 318–319). The survival and growth of the CET in the past three decades shows that the testing system has met the needs of China's social and economic development. The opportunities and challenges facing the CET remain in the hands of the test developer and the test user. The primary responsibility of the test developer is to enable the local test to meet internationally recognized professional standards. Meanwhile, it behooves test users to team up with test developers to ensure this localized language assessment is being used ethically.

References

Alderson, J. C., Clapham, C., & Wall, D. (1995). *Language test construction and evaluation.* Cambridge, UK: Cambridge University Press.

Alderson, J. C., & Hamp-Lyons, L. (1996). TOEFL preparation courses: A study of washback. *Language Testing, 13*(3), 280–297.

Bachman, L. F., Davidson, F., Ryan, K., & Choi, I.-C. (1995). *An investigation into the comparability of two tests of English as a foreign language: The Cambridge-TOEFL comparability study.* Cambridge, UK: University of Cambridge Local Examinations Syndicate.

Bachman, L. F., & Palmer, A. S. (2010). *Language assessment in practice: Developing language assessments and justifying their use in the real world.* Oxford: Oxford University Press.

Brown, H. D. (2004). *Language assessment: Principles and classroom practices.* London: Longman.

Cheng, L. (2008). The key to success: English language testing in China. *Language Testing, 25*, 15–37.

Council of Europe. (2001). *Common European Framework of Reference for Languages: Learning, teaching and assessment.* Strasbourg: Council of Europe.

Cullen, P., French, A., & Jakeman, V. (2013). *The official Cambridge guide to IELTS for academic & general training.* Cambridge, UK: Cambridge University Press.

Dai, W., & Hu, W. (2009). *Research of the development of foreign language education in China (1949–2009).* Shanghai: Shanghai Foreign Language Education Press.

Educational Testing Service. (2009). *The official guide to the TOEFL test* (3rd ed.). New York, NY: The McGraw-Hill Companies.

Fulcher, G., & Davidson, F. (2007). *Language testing and assessment.* London and New York, NY: Routledge.

Fulcher, G., & Davidson, F. (2009). Test architecture, test retrofit. *Language Testing, 26*(1), 123–144.

Garner, M., & Huang, D. (2014). *Testing a nation: The social and educational impact of the College English Test in China.* Bern, Switzerland: Peter Lang.

Gu, W., & Liu, J. (2005). Test analysis of college students' communicative competence in English. *Asian EFL Journal, 7*, 118–133.

Gu, X. (2004). *Positive or negative? An empirical study of CET washback on college English teaching and learning in China* (Unpublished doctoral dissertation). School of Foreign Languages, Shanghai Jiao Tong University, China.

Gu, X. (2007). *Positive or negative: An empirical study of CET washback.* Chongqing: Chongqing University Press.

Hamp-Lyons, L. (1997). Washback, impact and validity: Ethical concerns. *Language Testing, 14*(3), 295–303.

Han, B., Dai, M., & Yang, L. (2004). Problems with the college English test: Results of a survey. *Foreign Languages and Their Teaching, 2*, 17–23.

Higher Educational Department of the Ministry of Education. (1999). *College English Teaching Syllabus (revised version).* Shanghai: Shanghai Foreign Language Education Press.

Higher Educational Department of the Ministry of Education. (2007). *College English curriculum requirements*. Shanghai: Shanghai Foreign Language Education Press.

Huang, D., & Garner, M. (2009). A case of test impact: Cheating on the College English Test in China. In L. Taylor & C. J. Weir (Eds.), *Language testing matters: Investigating the wider social and educational impact of assessment* (pp. 59–76). Cambridge, UK: Cambridge University Press.

Huang, Y. (2007). A survey of the CET online marking system. *Foreign Language World*, *2*, 82–88, 96.

Jin, Y. (2000). Washback of CET-spoken English test on teaching of oral English. *Foreign Language World*, *4*, 56–60.

Jin, Y. (2008). Powerful tests, powerless test designers?—Challenges facing the college English test. *English Language Teaching in China*, *31*(5), 3–11.

Jin, Y. (2010). The national college English testing committee. In L. Cheng & A. Curtis (Eds.), *English language assessment and the Chinese learner* (pp. 44–59). London: Routledge.

Jin, Y. (2014). The limits of language tests and language testing: Challenges and opportunities facing the College English Test. In D. Coniam (Ed.), *English language education and assessment: Recent developments in Hong Kong and the Chinese Mainland* (pp. 155–169). Singapore: Springer.

Jin, Y. (2017). Construct and content in context: Implications for language learning, teaching and assessment in China. *Language Testing in Asia*, *7*(12). doi:10.1186/s40468-017-0044-1

Jin, Y., & Cheng, L. (2013). The effects of psychological factors on the validity of high-stakes tests. *Modern Foreign Languages*, *1*, 62–69.

Jin, Y., Knoch, U., & Zhu, B. (2018, October). *Developing an argument-based framework for validating the automated scoring systems of the College English Test*. Paper presented at the 21st Academic Forum on English Language Testing in Asia, Shanghai.

Jin, Y., & Wu, E. (2017). An argument-based approach to test fairness: The case of multiple-form equating in the college English test. *International Journal of Computer-Assisted Language Learning and Teaching*, *7*(3), 58–72.

Jin, Y., & Wu, J. (1997). The application of introspection to research of reading comprehension tests. *Foreign Language World*, *4*, 56–59.

Jin, Y., & Wu, J. (1998). Using introspection to validate the validity of CET reading comprehension tests. *Foreign Language World*, *2*, 47–52.

Jin, Y., Wu, Z., Alderson, C., & Song, W. (2017). Developing the China standards of English: Challenges at macropolitical and micropolitical levels. *Language Testing in Asia*, *7*(1). doi: 10.1186/s40468-017-0032-5

Jin, Y., & Yan, M. (2017). Computer literacy and the construct validity of a high-stakes computer-based writing assessment. *Language Assessment Quarterly*, *14*(2), 1–19.

Jin, Y., & Yang, H. (2006). The English proficiency of college and university students in China: As reflected in the CET. *Language, Culture and Curriculum*, *19*(1), 21–36.

Jin, Y., & Zhang, L. (2016). The impact of test mode on the use of communication strategies in paired discussion. In G. Yu & Y. Jin (Eds.), *Assessing Chinese learners of English: Language constructs, consequences and conundrums* (pp. 61–84). Basingstoke: Palgrave Macmillan.

Jin, Y., & Zhang, X. (2013). Skill integration in language assessment: A comparative study of PTE-Academic and IB-CET6. *Computer-Assisted Foreign Language Education*, *6*, 3–10.

Jin, Y., & Zhang, X. (2014). *Effects of skill integration on language assessment: A comparative study of Pearson test of English academic and Internet-based College English Test band-6*. Research Note. Pearson.

Jin, Y., Zhu, B., & Wang, W. (2017, July 19). *Writing to the machine: Challenges facing automated scoring in the College English Test in China*. Paper presented at the 39th Language Testing Research Colloquium, Bogota, Colombia.

Kunnan, A. J., & Carr, N. (2017). A comparability study between the general English proficiency test-Advanced and the internet-Based Test of English as a foreign language. *Language Testing in Asia*, 7(17), 1–16. doi:10.1186/s40468-017-0048-x

Livingston, S. A. (2009). Constructed-response test questions: Why we use them; how we score them. *Educational Testing Service R&D Connections* (Report No. RDC-11).

Nakatsuhara, F., Inoue, C., Berry, V., & Galaczi, E. (2017). Exploring the use of video-conferencing technology in the assessment of spoken language: A mixed-methods study. *Language Assessment Quarterly*, 14(1), 1–18. doi:10.1080/15434303.2016.1263637

National College English Testing Committee. (2016). *College English Test syllabus (revised version)*. Shanghai: Shanghai Jiao Tong University Press.

Pennycook, A. D. (1994). *The cultural politics of English as an international language*. London: Longman.

Sarig, G. (1989). Testing meaning construction: Can we do it fairly? *Language Testing*, 6(1), 77–94.

Spolsky, B. (1995). *Measured words*. Oxford: Oxford University Press.

Spolsky, B. (1997). The ethics of gatekeeping tests: What have we learned in a hundred years? *Language Testing*, 14(3), 242–247.

State Education Commission. (1985). *College English teaching syllabus (for college and university students of science and technology)*. Shanghai: Shanghai Foreign Language Education Press.

State Education Commission. (1986). *College English teaching syllabus (for college and university students of arts and science)*. Shanghai: Shanghai Foreign Language Education Press.

State Education Commission. (1994). *Decision to change the name of the "College English Test Working Group"*. State Education Commission Document [1994] No. 63.

Wang, Y. (2004a). An introduction to the prototype CET online marking system. *Foreign Language World*, 4, 67–73.

Wang, Y. (2004b). An empirical investigation of the CET online marking system. *Foreign Language World*, 5, 74–79.

Watanabe, Y. (2004). Teacher factor mediating washback. In L. Cheng, Y. Watanabe, & A. Curtis (Eds.), *Washback in language testing: Research contexts and methods* (pp. 129–146). London: Lawrence Erlbaum Associates.

Weir, C. J. (2005). *Language testing and validation: An evidence-based approach*. Basingstoke: Palgrave Macmillan.

Weir, C. J., & O'Sullivan, B. (2017). *Assessing English on the global stage: The British Council and English language testing 1941–2016*. Sheffield, UK: Equinox Publishing.

Weir, C. J., Vidaković, I., & Galaczi, E. (2013). *Measured constructs: A history of Cambridge English language examinations 1913–2012*. Cambridge, UK: Cambridge University Press.

Xie, Q., & Andrews, S. (2012). Do test design and uses influence test preparation? Testing a model of washback with structural equation modeling. *Language Testing*, 30(1), 49–70.

Yang, H. (2003). The 15 years of the CET and its impact on teaching. *Journal of Foreign Languages*, 3, 21–29.

Yang, H., Jin, Y., Guo, J., & Xia, G. (2000, March 8). *The National College English Test*. Symposium presented at the 22nd Language Testing Research Colloquium, Vancouver.

Yang, H., & Weir, C. J. (1998). *The validation study of the College English Test*. Shanghai: Shanghai Foreign Language Education Press.

Zhang, L., & Chen, L. (2015). An application of classical test theory and Rasch model in evaluating the quality of the CET-4 test items. *Contemporary Foreign Languages Studies, 10,* 78–85.

Zhang, L., & Jin, Y. (2016). An interactionalist approach to conceptualizing the construct of interactional speaking competence. *Foreign Language Research, 2,* 103–108.

Zhang, S., & Yu, P. (2010). A study of the reliability of the CET online marking system. *Foreign Language World, 5,* 79–86.

Zheng, Y., & Cheng, L. (2008). The College English Test (CET) in China. *Language Testing, 25*(3), 408–417.

APPENDIX 1

TABLE 5.A1 Sub-Skills Assessed in the CET

Listening
A. Understanding information explicitly stated
01 Understanding main ideas
02 Understanding important information or details
03 Understanding views or attitudes explicitly stated
B. Understanding information not explicitly stated
04 Inferring implied meaning
05 Understanding communicative functions
06 Understanding views or attitudes not explicitly stated
C. Understanding by using linguistic contributory skills
07 Identifying prosodic features in connected speech (e.g., pronunciation, stress and intonation)
08 Understanding relationships among sentences (e.g., cause and effect, comparison)
D. Listening strategy use
09 Using appropriate listening strategies to improve comprehension

Reading
A. Understanding information explicitly stated
01 Understanding main ideas
02 Understanding important information or details
03 Understanding views or attitudes explicitly stated
B. Understanding information not explicitly stated
04 Summarizing main ideas
05 Inferring implied meaning
06 Understanding views or attitudes not explicitly stated
C. Understanding by using linguistic contributory skills
07 Guessing meanings of words or phrases by using contextual clues
08 Understanding relationships among sentences (e.g., cause and effect, comparison)

(Continued)

TABLE 5.A1 (Continued)

	09 Understanding relationships among discourses through the use of cohesion and cohesive devices
	D. Reading strategy use
	10 Using appropriate reading strategies to improve comprehension
Speaking	A. Oral production
	01 Stating facts, giving reasons, and expressing opinions
	02 Describing persons, events and phenomena
	B. Oral interaction
	03 Exchanging ideas or views and expressing feelings or emotions
	04 Engaging in debate or argumentation, giving explanations, and making comparisons
	C. Speaking strategy use
	05 Using appropriate oral communication strategies to facilitate oral production or interaction
Writing	A. Idea expression
	01 Presenting main ideas
	02 Providing important details or specific information
	03 Expressing views or attitudes
	B. Discourse organization
	04 Writing narrative, argumentative, or descriptive essays on a given topic with a clear focus
	05 Linking sentences within a paragraph coherently and linking paragraphs into a coherent essay
	C. Use of language
	06 Depth and range of vocabulary
	07 Grammatical accuracy
	08 Appropriate sentence structure
	09 Correct punctuation
	10 Using cohesive devices to express relationships among sentences (e.g., comparison, cause and effect)
	D. Writing strategy use
	11 Using appropriate writing strategies to facilitate written communication
Translation	A. Translation at the sentence level from Chinese into English
	01 Conveying the lexical meaning of Chinese words or phrases
	02 Translating sentences using appropriate syntactic structures of English
	B. Translation at the discourse level from Chinese into English
	03 Being faithful to the original text and ensuring the accuracy of translation
	04 Translating the original text into a smooth and coherent text with a clear structure
	C. Translation strategy use
	05 Using appropriate translation strategies to facilitate the mediation process

Note. Translated from College English Test Syllabus, Revised Version, by National College English Testing Committee (2016).

6

EIKEN AND TEAP

How Two Test Systems in Japan Have Responded to Different Local Needs in the Same Context

Jamie Dunlea, Todd Fouts, Dan Joyce, and Keita Nakamura

Introduction: Framing Our Discussion

Overview of the Chapter

This chapter will introduce two proficiency testing programs produced in and for the context of Japan. The first, EIKEN, is a set of seven level-specific tests developed and administered by the Eiken Foundation of Japan. EIKEN is an acronym derived from the Japanese name for the test system, Jitsuyo Eigo Gino Kentei, which translates as "Test in Practical English Proficiency." The EIKEN website (Eiken Foundation of Japan, n.d.-a) describes the seven tests as providing "well-defined steps that can act as both motivational goals and concrete measures of English ability as learners move through the spectrum of commonly recognized ability levels." EIKEN was first administered in 1963 (Eiken Foundation of Japan, n.d.-b), and has since become firmly embedded within the educational and social fabric of Japan. The development of EIKEN will thus provide a historical framework for the discussion of both tests in this chapter. The second test, the Test of English for Academic Purposes (TEAP), is a much more recent development. TEAP was introduced in 2012 as a collaborative project between the Eiken Foundation and Sophia University with the specific intention of contributing to the reform of university entrance exams in Japan. Each of the following sections will first frame the discussion through the lens of EIKEN—with a longer history of responding to the needs of EFL in Japan and covering a wider range of proficiency levels and test taker groups—before addressing features specific to TEAP.

All tests constitute a set of compromises in which developers set out to balance the sometimes competing demands of the testing context, including the resources available. Dunlea (2016) used the metaphor of music for the test

132 Dunlea, Fouts, Joyce, and Nakamura

development process, likening it to the need to constantly tune instruments and adjust performances according to local characteristics, such as change in temperature and humidity as well as the audience. This requires an evaluation of tensions and synergies in the context and a need to balance these not just as a one-off development exercise but as a continual, ongoing evaluative process throughout the use of an assessment. The two testing programs introduced here provide an interesting case study for the issues associated with developing local, or localized, tests precisely because of the different solutions that the test developers have arrived at in response to different testing purposes and contextual demands within the same overall EFL context of Japan. After elucidating the criterial features of what are posited as "locally appropriate" testing solutions, we shall also consider what locally appropriate means in this context in relation to global standards and trends.

Model of Validation

In embarking on a discussion of how, or indeed whether, a locally developed test is useful for a specific context and purpose, we are essentially engaging in a discussion of validity. Any evidence we purport to show to support our claims of appropriacy for our locally developed tests involves us in the process of validation. We will briefly introduce the socio-cognitive model of language test development and validation as a way of providing us with concrete tools for this purpose. It is beyond the scope or purpose of this chapter to provide an in-depth discussion of the socio-cognitive model or the principles of validity generally. For an in-depth discussion of the socio-cognitive model contextualized against major developments in validity theory over the second half of the twentieth century and first decades of the twenty-first, see Dunlea (2015), which applied the model to a comprehensive validation of the EIKEN testing program.

The socio-cognitive model for language test development and validation was first fully elaborated, with validation frameworks describing criterial features across each of the four skills, in Weir (2005), and has been elaborated and developed further in O'Sullivan (2011, 2012, 2015, 2016) and O'Sullivan and Weir (2011). In its original form, the model identifies five major areas of evidence: *context validity, cognitive validity, scoring validity, consequential validity,* and *criterion-related validity,* with an understanding of the test taker being central to defining both context and cognitive validity. Later iterations of the model in O'Sullivan (2015, 2016) have reorganized the visual presentation of evidence under three core areas of the *test taker,* the *test system*—which includes descriptions of contextual and cognitive features of test tasks—and the *scoring system,* which O'Sullivan and Weir (2011) suggest could usefully subsume criterion-related evidence rather than having this as a stand-alone category (see Figure 0.1 in O'Sullivan's foreword to this book). O'Sullivan and Weir (2011, p. 27) suggest that the model was informed by practical experience in test development and "allows the test developer to define focal language objectives and to collect evidence in a more comprehensive and satisfactory way than earlier models."

Recent iterations of the model by O'Sullivan (e.g., 2015, 2016) are particularly relevant to our discussion of locally developed tests, as they emphasize the complex interaction of features of a test or test system with key stakeholders, and how this interaction leads to impact in both directions (on the test as well as on stakeholders). Both test and stakeholders are embedded within a social context that exerts influence on the nature and direction of that impact. This dynamic interaction is a key part of our discussion of how these locally developed tests are intended to be useful and appropriate responses to the specific demands of the EFL context of Japan.

Historical Context

Overview

We shall present important features of the two testing programs first in outline within a historical narrative. The aim is to understand the local rationale for these test design decisions.

The Social, Educational, and Political Context

Both EIKEN and TEAP have arisen in response to particular demands within a specific context. At the same time, no context is static, and these demands will change over time, particularly in relation to a test such as EIKEN, which has spanned over 65 years of interaction with the educational community in Japan. Sasaki's (2008) 150-year overview of the history of English language assessment in Japan provides a useful backdrop against which to chart the development of EIKEN, before we examine some more recent developments that have impacted on both EIKEN and TEAP. O'Sullivan (2016) suggests we see impact not as a linear process flowing from test, or test innovation, to stakeholders such as teachers and learners, but more as an ongoing cyclical interaction between the stakeholders and test system, with both embedded in a wider social context. The following discussion provides a narrative example of just such a situation, demonstrating the impact on test development that wider changes in society can bring.

Sasaki (2008, p. 65) divides the period from the second half of the nineteenth century through to the early part of the twenty-first century into the following four periods based on differences in the "intended goals and the degree of popularization of school-based English education in Japan":

1. Period 1 (1860–1945): English for the elite.
2. Period 2 (1945–1970): English for everyone.

3. Period 3 (1970–1990): English for practical purposes in the era of rapid globalization.
4. Period 4 (1990–2012): introduction of innovative policies.

Beginning With the Intention of Impact

Three of the current seven levels of EIKEN were implemented in 1963, which falls towards the end of Period 2. (The levels are commonly referred to as *grades*, with the lowest level being Grade 5 and the highest Grade 1, with two bridging levels of Grade Pre-2 and Grade Pre-1. See the next section for a more detailed breakdown of the EIKEN grades.) This period was marked by a rapid increase in the number of students studying English as the first nine years of schooling were made compulsory in post-war Japan. As Sasaki (2008, p. 67) notes, "post-war Japan suffered from a serious shortage of both school buildings and teachers," and this shortage was magnified in the case of English, with teachers from other subject areas drafted in to cover the shortfall. Despite the stated goals of the education ministry, high school and university teachers who produced the influential entrance exams for their institutions tended to maintain a focus on traditional grammar-translation approaches, reflecting their own training and experience (Sasaki, 2008, pp. 67–68).

Two significant features of the EIKEN program can partly be seen as originating in response to these pressures. Firstly, in response to the severe lack of EFL resources and trained teachers, the decision was made to disclose all test materials following administration, with the intention of making high-quality English texts and testing materials available to teachers and learners (Eiken Foundation of Japan, n.d.-c; Fouts, 2013). This practice has become ubiquitous in high-stakes entrance examinations in Japan and has become deeply ingrained as evidence of fairness and transparency by the Japanese public (Yoshida, 1996). As Yoshida (1996) notes, however, this presents serious obstacles to the implementation of modern approaches to quality control in assessment, such as pretesting.

The second significant feature is the inclusion of face-to-face speaking tests from the outset of the EIKEN testing program, which can be considered partly a response to the entrenched influence of the grammar-translation approach noted by Sasaki. While the inclusion of a speaking component may not seem innovative by current standards in EFL teaching and assessment, the education ministry continues to struggle to encourage the introduction of productive skills components into university entrance exams. Indeed, even with receptive skills, listening was only introduced into the influential National Centre Test for University Admissions in 2006, 26 years after that test's implementation (Watanabe, 2013). In this respect, EIKEN can be seen as innovative in the local context in having incorporated a focus on all four skills from its inception, and consistent with the stated intention of the EIKEN program to facilitate positive impact (Eiken Foundation of Japan, n.d.-c).

Rapid Increase in Acceptance and Use in Period 3

At the wider societal level, Sasaki (2008) notes that this period was marked by the rapid economic development of Japan, and an accompanying expansion of the number of Japanese traveling overseas and being exposed to the use of English for real communicative purposes. The EIKEN testing program, too, saw rapid acceptance during this time, with a further three grades (Grades 5, 4, and Pre-1) added to the levels already in place. In 1968, the EIKEN tests received education ministry recognition as authorized proficiency examinations for certification purposes, and by 1987 the number of examinees had grown to 2 million a year.

This period saw growing criticism of the entrance examination system as progressively larger numbers of students continued on from the compulsory schooling system to high school and higher education (Sasaki, 2008). Government responses included encouraging more diverse approaches to high school entrance procedures and introducing a precursor to the current National Centre Test for University Admissions in 1979. An important use of the EIKEN tests that continues today is the use of EIKEN grade certificates in high school entrance applications. This usage contributed to the program's growing popularity.

A further important aspect of the testing program that has contributed to its widespread use is the commitment to accessibility. The EIKEN program from its inception has established public test sites in all areas of Japan, including rural districts, and has maintained a relatively low cost, particularly for the lower grades (Eiken Foundation of Japan, n.d.-d). The network of test sites was made possible by an expanding network of educators that set up test sites at local schools, supervised administration of the tests, and acted as speaking test examiners. This further integrated the test and test developer with the local educational community of English teachers.

Responding to Changing Needs in Period 4

As the demand for access to the tests rose, a system of group test sites was started to complement the public test sites at which the exams had been administered from their outset. Group test sites are institution-specific test sites catering solely to the students at a particular institution (Eiken Foundation of Japan, n.d.-d). Period 4 also saw the addition of Grade Pre-2, completing the seven-level testing program. The latter part of this period also saw a series of revisions to test structure and content, leading to the current standardized formats for the First Stage tests (test specifications are available online at www.eiken.

or.jp/eiken/en/grades/). Tests are currently administered three times during the Japanese academic year, which runs from April to March. Tests at public test sites are offered on Sundays only. Tests at group test sites are offered over a three-day period from Friday through to Sunday, which has also increased the number of test forms required for each grade.

Sasaki (2008) notes that Period 4 has been dominated by a series of policy initiatives by the Ministry of Education, Culture, Sports, Science, and Technology (MEXT) aimed at the way English is taught and assessed in schools, and importantly at the way English is assessed for high-stakes, high school, and university entrance purposes. Several of these initiatives have had direct effects on the development of the EIKEN testing program during this period.

In 2003, MEXT published the "Action Plan to Cultivate Japanese with English Abilities." A significant development in the Action Plan (MEXT, 2003) was the use of EIKEN grades as recommended benchmark levels of proficiency for graduates of junior and senior high school, as well as for professional contexts including proof of English proficiency for teacher certification. These recommendations have been reiterated in later policy documents such as MEXT (2011) and are shown in Table 6.1. Prior to the publication of the action plan, preparation materials for EIKEN grades included very general level descriptions pointing to the formal education level for which the test was considered most relevant. For example, Grade 3 was described as being targeted at a level appropriate for graduates of junior high school. The move towards using the EIKEN grades as external benchmarks of proficiency by MEXT in turn highlighted the need to develop more explicit test specifications, as reliance on the implicit understanding of content specified by the Courses of Study curriculum documents was no longer sufficient for the growing expectations of stakeholders.

The Action Plan (MEXT, 2003) also included recommendations for universities to consider using external proficiency exams such as EIKEN and other international exam systems as standardized measures of English proficiency in place of the English sections of entrance exams, which were generally produced in-house by each institution. As Sasaki (2008) notes, the entrance exams have been subject to a great deal of controversy. While some authors (e.g., Mulvey, 2001; Watanabe, 1996) have pointed out that the relationship between the exams and the impact on teaching and learning is not necessarily as clear-cut as is sometimes assumed, the variable quality, lack of clear specifications, lack of standardization in terms of content, and inappropriate level of difficulty in relation to the targeted population have been consistently highlighted as problematic (e.g., Brown & Yamashita, 1995; Kikuchi, 2006). The recommended use of the EIKEN exams by MEXT as an alternative to in-house entrance exams increased the expectations of stakeholders in terms of specification and validation evidence.

The Action Plan (MEXT, 2003) also included a number of initiatives to specifically increase the number of Japanese high school and university students studying abroad. In response to this, the EIKEN testing program began investigating the possibility of receiving recognition for EIKEN certificates as proof of English proficiency for admissions purposes by foreign universities (Fouts, 2013). Fouts (2013) suggests that a significant hurdle faced by many students hoping to study abroad, particularly in rural areas of Japan, was the high cost and general lack of accessibility to the international proficiency exams most widely used for entrance purposes in English-medium universities at the time. The cost of taking the upper grades of the EIKEN exam was less than half of the cost of these exams, which were also only available in major population centers. The EIKEN testing program was now presented with possible uses and interpretations that were not part of the original design. In addition, this new use introduced new stakeholders who would not be familiar with common reference points such as the MEXT Courses of Study curriculum guidelines or expected levels of attainment in the Japanese educational system. These new stakeholders, international educators, and assessment experts also expected to see validation evidence collected according to best practice in the international context. These new demands on the testing program led to a number of initiatives, for example predictive and criterion-referenced validity studies to investigate the appropriacy of using the tests for these purposes (Brown, Davis, Takahashi, & Nakamura, 2012; Hill, 2010).

By the end of Sasaki's (2008) Period 4, then, the EIKEN grades had thus become firmly embedded in the educational and societal context of Japan, as well as developing new uses beyond that local context and involving stakeholders outside the groups of local educators and learners with whom the testing program had previously developed a close interaction. These various uses are described in more detail on the Eiken website (Eiken Foundation of Japan, n.d.-e).

Recent Developments and the Introduction of TEAP

Much public discussion remains critical of language teaching in schools and of the proficiency levels of Japanese school leavers (Aoki, 2017; Negishi, 2012). A key target of these concerns has continued to be university entrance examinations. A constant theme of exam reform has been the demand to incorporate four-skills testing to encourage a focus on productive skills in the classroom. This priority was a key feature in the development of TEAP and continues to be a major impetus for change at the level of language policy in Japan. TEAP, as with EIKEN, has from the outset posited positive impact as an important and explicit goal (Green, 2014). TEAP was intended to provide a high-quality entrance exam system that would alleviate many of the perceived problems with the current exams. It was also intended to provide a model of language proficiency that would have positive impact on the teaching and learning of English in high school, as well as on the expectations of stakeholders in relation to assessment best practice.

During this same recent period, certain elements of the EIKEN tests have also undergone changes and adjustments, very often in response to the same features of the social context that gave rise to the development of TEAP. A set of revisions was introduced across the skill papers and grades of the system in 2016 (Eiken Foundation of Japan, n-d.-f). While the overarching framework of the seven-level set of tests remains largely intact, some of these adjustments could be interpreted as attempts to incorporate features more readily identified with international assessment practices, such as the development of a scale score to connect the separate EIKEN Grades onto a common, Item Response Theory based scale. Other changes, such as moves to revise the writing assessments at the key high-stakes Grades 1, Pre-1, and 2 levels, could be seen as a rebalancing of the demands of meeting the practical realities of large-scale testing with the desire for enhanced validity.

Features of Localization

Overview

This section will look in more depth at some of key features for EIKEN and address features of TEAP developed specifically to enhance the usefulness of that test for the local context. We can usefully employ the categories of the socio-cognitive model to help us illustrate these features. We will examine the features of the tests mainly from the perspective of contextual and cognitive aspects of test design, both falling within what O'Sullivan (2015, 2016) refers to as the test system, as well as aspects of scoring validity, or the scoring system. In relation to contextual features, we will separate these into two distinct areas: contextual features of the actual test tasks and content, an area of evidence that overlaps with the traditional definition of content validity. Stepping back from the internal specification of the test tasks, we will also identify locally appropriate contextual features of design related to administration and other peripheral aspects of the test system.

EIKEN: Locally Relevant Contextual, Cognitive and Scoring Features

Peripheral Features of the Test System

It is beyond the scope of this chapter to provide a detailed breakdown of test content, and interested readers should consult the EIKEN website for test specifications at each grade level. Here, we will begin by looking at features of the EIKEN program that we can loosely define as contextual parameters within the secondary area noted earlier in this chapter, those related to aspects of test administration outside the internal contextual parameters of the test content.

Some of the key features of the test that have arisen as responses to the local context reside in this category and act as defining characteristics impacting on test-internal contextual features as well as cognitive and scoring parameters.

A defining feature of the EIKEN test program is its structure comprising seven stand-alone tests targeting separate levels of proficiency, the seven grades, from Grade 5 through to Grade 1 (with the two bridging grades of Pre-2 between Grades 3 and 2, and Pre-1 between Grades 2 and 1). Appendix A provides an outline of the test structure. (Note that Grades 4 and 5 both offer test takers the choice of an optional speaking assessment via computer, but this is not required for certification at this level and is taken in a low-stakes, un-invigilated environment of the test taker's choice.)

The separation into grades has been a prominent feature of the system from the beginning. The grade system is not unique to Japan. Indeed, the Cambridge English Qualifications are also built around a five-level system that, in a developmental pattern similar to EIKEN, added grades over a period of time. Another test locally developed in East Asia, the GEPT, which is also described in this volume, is also based around a similar level-specific framework. Breaking the test into manageable grades allowed for the test content to be specified in a way that would be relevant to the perceived key learning benchmarks the tests were meant to reflect and support.

As noted earlier, the public release of test materials has been a key feature of the testing program from the beginning. This is an entrenched feature of the testing culture in Japan that comes with a cost: it imposes serious limitations on certain technical aspects of test development, such as item banking and pretesting. Nonetheless, it is easy to see the benefits from the perspective of learners and teachers, who can access high-quality materials for reading and listening practice either in the classroom or for individual study. EIKEN test takers can take their question papers home (from public test sites), and answer keys are made available online for self-checking one's own responses.

Another peripheral aspect of the test system is the intensive involvement of the local educational community in the ongoing production and administration of the EIKEN tests. The integration of the wider educational community has obviously had benefits in terms of accessibility and affordability. The very large number of test sites, particularly for group sites, has only been achievable with the collaboration of teachers and schools.

However, we would posit a further benefit to the inclusion on a large scale of the local educational community in the test production and administration. Green (2007) has suggested that achieving positive washback on teaching and learning for a well-designed test will be facilitated if teachers are teaching not to the test but to the construct underpinning its test design. We would suggest that the closer integration of teachers in the validation of the test through their involvement in review and editorial committees, but perhaps even more importantly through their extensive involvement as examiners for

140 Dunlea, Fouts, Joyce, and Nakamura

the second-stage speaking test, presents a valuable opportunity for teachers to understand the principles behind the test and to transfer important principles of the construct, not just superficial features of task format, to the classroom. The use of the mostly local teaching population from junior and senior high schools, for whom English is also a foreign language, presents further possible benefits in line with those suggested by Hill (1996). Examiners embedded within the local context with a clear understanding of the demands on local EFL learners may provide a more accurate assessment of their performance, as well as more useful interpretation of any shortcomings or difficulties encountered.

Looking Inside the Test

The seven grades that comprise the system are shown in Table 6.1. In addition to the name of each grade, the table gives an indication of level in terms of what the test developer, the Eiken Foundation, considers to be a relevant level of the Common European Framework of Reference for Languages (CEFR), along with local uses, including recommended uses as benchmark levels by MEXT. The putative relationship to the CEFR will be discussed in more detail under the topic of validation evidence later. It is relevant here, however, to help orient readers to the targeted proficiency levels of each grade. We will suggest that the process of evaluating what might constitute locally appropriate content will need to be closely integrated with the targeted proficiency levels and the intended uses and interpretations of a test—both of which change in distinctive ways as one moves up through grades in the EIKEN system, as shown in Table 6.1.

Dunlea (2015) provides an in-depth analysis of both contextual and cognitive features of the EIKEN tests. Amongst these features, contextual parameters in particular lend themselves to adaptation to take account of local learning priorities and circumstances. Features covered in Dunlea (2015) include vocabulary levels and topics as well as other key criterial features, quantitative measures such as readability indices, and cognitive processing demands targeted by

TABLE 6.1 Overview of Proficiency Levels of EIKEN Grades

EIKEN Grade	CEFR comparison	Example of recognition/use
1	C1	International admissions to graduate and
Pre-1	B2	undergraduate programs; MEXT benchmark for English instructors (Pre-1)
2	B1	MEXT benchmarks for high school graduates
Pre-2	A2	
3		MEXT benchmark for junior high school graduates
4	A1	
5		

items at different levels as judged through expert judgment protocols. Interested readers are pointed to that study for details, and we shall limit ourselves to describing some of the key findings.

Clearly vocabulary and topics are two key areas amenable to localization. Vocabulary learning targets for EIKEN grades in the past, as with those provided by MEXT in the Courses of Study curriculum guidelines, were given as very broad quantitative targets. Details were left to teachers, learners, and preparation materials providers to flesh out, and in practice the relationship was often very closely linked to the vocabulary used in the limited number of widely used text books. However, from the early 2000s, internal test-item writing and quality-assurance processes began to incorporate more systematic and explicit vocabulary resources in item development and review. Dunlea's 2015 study includes the results of detailed vocabulary analysis of reading and listening texts across the EIKEN grades, and clearly shows that the vocabulary levels are constrained to be consistent across test forms within grades administered over time, and with the distinctions showing clear incremental increases across levels. The broad levels in terms of the BNC 14 lists produced by Paul Nation (2006) also show consistency with a number of studies in the literature examining tests targeting similar levels of ability and analyses of real-world reading demands (such as Nation, 2006). There is a very clear distinction between the approach to moderating vocabulary between the upper grades and lower grades, with Grade 2 clearly being a pivotal grade in terms of transitioning from the more controlled and supported classroom environment to the independent language use contexts associated with CEFR B2 and above.

The analysis of EIKEN items included topics and other quantitative measures of text complexity, along with criterial features relying on expert judgment such as level of abstractness. In addition, measures of cognitive demand were operationalized through the evaluation of the "key information" function, the degree of integration of information required across a text to successfully answer a test item. The EIKEN grades clearly show increasing cognitive demand as the target level of the grade increases.

Dunlea's (2015) study also demonstrated clear distinctions across levels in terms of the relationship between grades and levels of the CEFR. As Dunlea notes (2015, 2016, 2017), the CEFR itself was intended to be localized, with important criterial features appropriate for particular educational contexts added and expanded as it is adapted for local use. That applies equally to diverse contexts within Europe as it does without to places such as Japan. Perhaps the most visible area of localization occurs in the areas of vocabulary and topics and situations used for input texts in the tests. Two categories in Dunlea's, 2015 study are the degree to which background knowledge would be required to access particular topics or vocabulary items, or whether the same topics or vocabulary items may have a particularly local interpretation which could differ from other contexts. Adapting texts to avoid culturally specific references which might not be accessible to EFL students is not unique to EIKEN or other local tests, and similar classification categories are utilized in a number of publicly available test specifications and analysis grids (e.g., Council of Europe, 2009; Geranpayeh & Taylor, 2013; Khalifa & Weir, 2009; O'Sullivan & Dunlea, 2015; Shaw & Weir, 2007; Taylor, 2012, 2014; Wu, 2014). Green and Hawkey (2011) note in their description of item writing in relation to the IELTS test that this is a key feature of adapting texts for that high-stakes international test.

For EIKEN, it is particularly at the lower grades that such evaluation becomes an important part of ensuring not only accessibility of test content, but valid use and interpretation of test results in terms of relevance to the primary TLU of typical test takers. Dunlea (2009) outlined a case for clearly defining the classroom as an important part of the TLU for EFL learners in Japan. Indeed, we would suggest that, even within an international proficiency framework such as the CEFR, the criterial features of descriptors defining proficiency levels A1 and A2 clearly delineate a TLU that is very much local and restricted. Descriptions of typical communicative activities in the CEFR at these levels reference concepts such as "everyday," "routine," and "familiar." A very similar set of defining features is seen also in the extensive list of empirically scaled descriptors developed for the EIKEN grades in the Eiken Can-do List (Dunlea, 2010; Eiken Foundation of Japan, n.d.-c). In order to interpret these in practice and operationalize them in terms of actual teaching and learning goals and test specifications, we need to understand clearly who our learners are, where they are likely to encounter and interact with the target language, and what *everyday* will mean for them in practice. For Grades Pre-2 through to 5, this is a particularly strong aspect of item writing and quality review.

Topics and situations also provide a useful place to adapt local tests, and once again it is at Grades Pre-2 through to 5 that this is most prevalent. While many test specifications state that no background knowledge is required, in actual fact some background or content knowledge is *always* required to interpret language, whether or not it is connected to a test item. The distinction is really one of whether the background and content knowledge required can reasonably be expected to be present in a typical test taker without any special instruction or experience. Based on our key words associated with the lower levels of the EIKEN grades, and the understanding of who typical test takers are for these grades, situations and topics familiar to the test takers can easily be defined, and in some very clear ways, these will be locally specific. An example might be a listening dialogue between two junior high school students in which the question asks the listener to identify what the two speakers agree to do before school. In the context of Japan, this might reasonably be meeting at a very early time to attend a club activity before school starts, or equally participate in such organized school activities on a regular basis on weekends. Such situations will be readily recognizable to typical Japanese learners, allowing them to employ their real-world schema and focus on aspects of the text required for comprehension, but may not be so easily recognizable to a typical lower-secondary school student in a different context where such regular, organized school activities may not be familiar.

From Grade 2 onwards, the uses and interpretations of the tests are increasingly outward-looking and intended to provide an indication of a test taker's ability to participate in independent learning and language-use contexts outside the classroom. Indeed, as Yanase (2009) has posited, engaging in language use outside the classroom will be a key variable in facilitating movement from B1 to B2. Yanase (2009) provides a useful diagrammatic representation of the interaction between contextual features such as text complexity, topic range, and level of abstractness, as well as cognitive demand in terms of the complexity of processing required to access and demonstrate understanding of more complex ideas and themes. He then links these to levels of the CEFR through overlap with key words and concepts that indicate both qualitative and quantitative changes as CEFR levels increase. Yanase (2009) further goes on to draw parallels between the EIKEN grades and these criterial features of the CEFR. Dunlea (2015) notes that Grade 2 is

> a pivotal level in terms of transitioning from the more restricted lower grades to the more advanced grades relevant to B2 and C1 on the CEFR. This interpretation lends support to claims by Yanase (2009) of the pivotal nature of this level for EFL learners and of the importance for learners at this level to expand the nature of their exposure to and use of the target language in order to move through this transition zone.
>
> *(p. 298)*

What we see, then, as we move through the EIKEN grades, is a gradual change in the balance of features appropriate for each grade. Some of those adjustments can be defined in generic terms as being pertinent to different levels of proficiency, making reference to features, for example, described in widely applied frameworks such as the CEFR. Others, such as taking account of vocabulary likely to be taught and learned in a local, formal-education context, or cultural concepts, situations, and topics likely to be familiar and accessible for lower-level learners in those formal-education learning contexts, will be more specifically local. As we move from Grade 2 (CEFR B1) through Pre-1 (CEFR B2) to Grade 1 (CEFR C1), the prominence of locally specific features becomes less of a priority.

TEAP

Peripheral Features of the Test System

TEAP provides an interesting example of how locally appropriate features may be related more to peripheral features of the test and less to the actual content

144 Dunlea, Fouts, Joyce, and Nakamura

in terms of visible features such as vocabulary and topics. Appendix A provides an overview of the test structure, which will be discussed further in this section. As illustrated earlier, TEAP was developed as a direct response to local priorities in terms of the perceived need by key stakeholders for entrance exam reform in higher education. Key goals for the test are described in Weir in the following way:

> A long term aim of the TEAP is to have a positive impact on English education in Japan by *revising and improving* (emphasis added) the widely varying approaches to English tests used in university admissions, and by serving as a model of the English skills needed by Japanese university students to study at the university level in the English as a foreign language (EFL) context of Japan.
>
> *(2014, p. 4)*

At the same time, TEAP was developed more recently than EIKEN, allowing the developers to take account of not only the extensive history and experience of the EIKEN tests, but also of current thinking and best practice in language test design and validation. This has given rise to a number of features that distinguish the test from other local assessment solutions in Japan, including EIKEN.

Green (2014) presents a detailed overview of the areas that the test developers intended TEAP to have a positive impact on. Importantly, this goes beyond just a list of intended impact and extends to detailing what aspects of the test design are intended to facilitate each kind of intended positive impact. As can be seen by evaluating this list, many of the features of TEAP that can be considered local responses to local priorities relate to what we have in this chapter labeled secondary contextual parameters associated with aspects of test administration and the overall test system. In the case of TEAP, many of these are aimed at explicitly changing locally accepted assessment practices to enhance technical quality in ways that would align the test with international best-practice guidelines. University entrance exams are extremely high-stakes test uses and receive intense scrutiny, including from the media. In addition, there was an explicit intention to provide TEAP as a model to facilitate positive washback by encouraging teachers to teach to the construct underpinning it and, as noted, to introduce international best practices in assessment. For these reasons, international testing experts from the Centre for Research in English Language Learning and Assessment (CRELLA) were approached to participate in the design and validation of the test. The interaction between global and local perspectives is thus seen also in this fruitful collaboration between local development partners (the Eiken Foundation and Sophia University) with international assessment experts. Five features of the test design will be discussed here, outlining similarities and differences to EIKEN and the local rationale for each design decision.

Firstly, the test is designed as a multi-level assessment which aims to measure accurately proficiency levels from A2 through to B2, differing from the level-specific approach of EIKEN. The rationale for this resides in its intended use for university entrance, and once again, the intention to change the way these tests had been delivered and used. Obviously, the test would need to distinguish between students from a range of levels. A key intention of TEAP was to provide meaningful feedback to test takers beyond simply passing or failing.

Secondly, the test content is not released publicly after use in the examinations, something which still distinguished TEAP from almost all locally developed high-stakes tests used for entrance purposes, including EIKEN and the National Centre Test. TEAP intended from the outset to employ best practice in terms of technical quality, and ensuring that test version comparability could be maintained across multiple test forms was a key concern. To ensure this, all items are pretested, analyzed with Rasch to place the items onto a common scale of difficulty, and placed in an item bank for test construction.

Thirdly, TEAP is offered at public test sites multiple times a year, and the scores from a single administration can be used by a test taker to apply to multiple institutions. The rationale here is first to overcome the anxiety and perceived unfairness of the entrance exam system in which a student has only one chance at a very high-stakes exam. At the same time, under the system prevalent at the time of the development of TEAP, test takers were required to take different tests for every institution to which they applied. Although all students would take the National Centre Test as a first stage, they would then be required to take a different English test, written to completely different designs, in second-stage tests instituted by individual universities. In many cases, different departments within the same university would also employ different exams.

Fourthly, TEAP provides two kinds of feedback in the form of a scale score and external criterion proficiency framework, the CEFR. This feature cuts across contextual and scoring parameters in terms of our model. In terms of EIKEN, it is interesting to note that EIKEN has also begun to adopt these features. EIKEN traditionally provided a pass/fail decision at each grade level, along with the number of items answered correctly. As Dunlea (2015) notes, the raw scores provided meaningful feedback because they were provided in conjunction with publicly released test content to facilitate revision. Dunlea (2015) also provides a description of how the pass/fail line for each grade was adjusted through post hoc analysis to ensure comparable results across test administrations in terms of pass/fail decisions. As a part of the 2016 revisions however, EIKEN has introduced a common scale as a part of feedback. The rationale for TEAP's design decisions also calls on international best practice. Kolen and Brennan (2004) note that raw scores can lead to misunderstanding,

146 Dunlea, Fouts, Joyce, and Nakamura

as test forms may differ in difficulty. Scaling and equating provide a way of ensuring the meaning of test results is consistent across multiple test forms designed to the same specifications. At the same time, TEAP included the CEFR into test design from the outset to provide meaningful reference points for interpretation of scale scores in terms of what test takers could be expected to achieve with the language at different levels of proficiency.

Fifthly, TEAP included clear and explicit test specifications incorporating design features derived from the socio-cognitive model. The rationale was once again to employ best practice in the field to provide a model for reform. One important criticism of university entrance exams has been the lack of clear or consistent test specification, with test formats changing over years, and criterial features of content also differing. By developing and providing clear and explicit approaches to specification, the developers intended to facilitate better preparation by test takers through a more detailed understanding of what to expect.

Looking Inside the Test

The test purpose and use for TEAP is summarized in Weir as:

> to evaluate the preparedness of high school students to understand and use English when taking part in typical learning activities at Japanese universities. The target language use (TLU) tasks relevant to the TEAP are those arising in academic activities conducted in English on (Japanese) university campuses.
>
> *(2014, p. 4)*

One of the key features impacting on test content from the perspective of criterial contextual and cognitive parameters is the decision to employ the CEFR in test design from the outset and focus specifically on levels A2 through to B2. As already noted, MEXT had presented EIKEN Grade 2 (CEFR B1) and EIKEN Grade Pre-2 (CEFR A2) as attainment goals for high school students. The B1 level of TEAP thus, in effect, looks back to the content and proficiency levels that we can expect high school students to be reasonably well acquainted with. The B2 level looks forward, extending and challenging higher-performing students, while also acting as a model to demonstrate aspects of academic English proficiency that might also be amenable to future teaching and learning. Clearly, the important transitional B1 level described in Yanase's model is in the center of the proficiency levels measured by TEAP. As such, we would expect there to be less locally specific adaptation in relation to vocabulary and topics as the test moves from B1 to B2, taking an increasingly outward-looking approach, similar to the features of EIKEN grades from Grade 2 and above noted earlier. Detailed data similar to that provided for EIKEN in Dunlea

(2015) on contextual parameters such as vocabulary levels and readability measures are presented for TEAP Reading and Listening tasks in Taylor (2014). Studies documenting the development of the Writing and speaking components are described in the following paragraphs, and interested readers are referred to these studies for in-depth analysis of the tasks and test-taker output. The productive skills components are central to the design of TEAP given the central part these skills play in MEXT reform measures.

First, the writing component was designed to take into account features of the local educational context, while also targeting features identified by Weir (2014) as crucial for academic writing. In terms of writing instruction in Japanese high schools, Kobayashi and Rinnert (2002) and Rinnert and Kobayashi (2001) have demonstrated that students not only lack experience in extended writing in English, but that their experience of writing in their L1 (first language) is also often limited to personal reflections. Weir (2014) identified reading-into-writing tasks, in particular summary tasks and the ability to inform writing through knowledge transformation rather than simply knowledge telling, as key skills necessary for effective academic writing. The TEAP writing component attempts to address these through two reading-into-writing tasks, one targeting B1-level performance, and one B2-level performance. The B1-level summary task, which is constrained across a range of contextual features to be accessible to high school students, requires students to summarize key features of a single text. Importantly, reference was made to B1-level descriptors in the CEFR, particularly in the *Processing Text* scale. In designing the task, the rating criteria were also explicitly designed to take into account the wording in descriptors relevant to the level of the task, for example the following B1 descriptor: "Can paraphrase short written passages in a simple fashion, using the original text wording and ordering" (Council of Europe, 2001).

The second writing task was designed to fulfill the aim of looking forward to the more demanding context of university and to provide a model for key features of academic writing at the B2 level. The task requires the processing of four texts, two graphs, and two longer written verbal texts. Test takers have to be able to identify overlapping and unique information relevant in all four texts and incorporate this appropriately into their summary to demonstrate a B2 level. For a detailed description of the development and validation of these tasks, see Weir (2014).

Speaking also provided the opportunity to incorporate features addressing local priorities, while incorporating key features of speaking relevant to the B1 and B2 levels of proficiency. A key aspect of the speaking test development was the use of function checklists to aid in both task design and validation. Drawing on surveys of speaking functions considered important by both high school and university teachers (Nakatsuhara, 2014a), a series of four speaking tasks were developed. One of the innovative aspects of the speaking is Task 2, in which test takers have to take the role of questioner. The rationale for this task drew on the results of the surveys in Nakatsuhara (2014a), which identified questioning as important. At the same time, the task was designed to promote the development of speaking skills through allocating a more proactive role for the learner. At the same time, in the same way as the B1 writing task described earlier, contextual and cognitive features were constrained to make this task achievable at B1 level, once again making reference to CEFR descriptors for carrying out an interview when designing the task and rating scales. In terms of what we have referred to previously as scoring aspects of validity, the TEAP speaking test also incorporates explicitly description of interactional effectiveness (Eiken Foundation of Japan, n.d.-g). While this draws on the CEFR and the literature on speaking assessment as described in Nakatsuhara (2014a), it is specifically designed to promote aspects of speaking considered to be weakly addressed in the local educational context, and to do so in ways which can be constrained to make the tasks accessible to learners at an appropriate level.

Impact

In relation to impact, it is useful to once again refer to the reconfigured visual representations of the socio-cognitive model provided by O'Sullivan (2016; see also Figure 0.1 from O'Sullivan's foreword to this book), in which he visually represents the dynamic relationship and interaction between stakeholders, test system, and the social context in which all of those are embedded. For both of the testing programs discussed in this chapter, impact has been an important, and significantly, explicit aim from the outset. We have already discussed in some detail how these aims have in fact impacted directly on the tests, reflecting O'Sullivan's suggestion that the direction of impact extends in both directions, not just from test to stakeholders.

The EIKEN program has obviously had a visible and large impact on the educational landscape of Japan, as measured simply by the footprint it leaves with test taker numbers. We can add to this the large number of teachers involved, whether in direct content production roles such as review committees; as one of the more than 10,000 speaking test examiners; in administering the tests, particularly at any of the 18,000 group test sites; or as a consumer in terms of using the test materials as teaching and learning materials generally or in direct preparation of students for the tests. Another indicator of impact is the widespread recognition of the tests for entrance purposes at school and university level. The tests have also had direct interaction with, if not impact on, MEXT guidelines. The move by MEXT to refer to EIKEN grades to help to define proficiency attainment targets for junior and senior high schools has had a direct impact on the testing program, playing a significant role in many of the validation activities undertaken since 2000 and which will be discussed later. In effect, the change to looking to EIKEN as a benchmark placed a greater onus on the test developers to demonstrate clearly what the levels mean in practice and facilitate learning and teaching of skills and knowledge relevant to those levels.

While there are thus very visible signs of the impact of the EIKEN program, in terms of what is often referred to as washback, that is, the impact specifically on teaching and learning practices, much remains anecdotal without clear empirical evidence to provide insight into the effectiveness of the program. This may be partly related to the sheer familiarity of the program, perhaps leading to an acceptance of some claims without questioning. Given the effort that has been placed by EIKEN from its inception in 1963 to both remain affordable and accessible while offering a direct, live, face-to-face interview test, a more targeted research agenda into the impact of the speaking assessments on teaching and learning would be beneficial. EIKEN has faced a difficult balancing act with the speaking tests, which has impacted on the test design, for example in the two-stage format to allow for speaking tests to be delivered as a part of certification down to Grade 3. However, a counterclaim to the validity argument, and particularly to the claim for positive impact through the inclusion of speaking, may come from the compromises that need to be made to carry out this balancing act on such a large scale. The tests are tightly constrained, particularly at the lower levels. Thus this careful balancing of priorities to maintain wide accessibility could lead to unintended consequences if teachers teach directly to these tightly controlled test tasks, without understanding the imperatives that have led to their design.

TEAP is a newer test administered on a smaller scale than EIKEN at present, and as such there is less scope for evaluating measurable impact. At the same time, this has presented valuable opportunities, which the test developers have exploited. Most importantly, Green (2014) was a valuable attempt at gathering baseline data on teachers' and learners' perceptions of important parts of the TEAP test design, including those secondary contextual features described earlier. We have already noted that part of the intended impact of TEAP is to explicitly promote change in the assessment practices for high-stakes university entrance exams. There are indeed tantalizing indications that the rather bold decision to deliberately do away with some of those expected practices in favor of promoting internationally accepted guidelines for ensuring technical quality in the tests is in fact being noticed, and indeed accepted. One key example of such decisions is the decision not to publicly release test content after administration to enable pretesting and item banking. Figures for the number of test takers are not made publicly available, however the test is recognized for entry purposes by over 100 universities (Eiken Foundation of Japan, n.d.-h), indicating that a key set of stakeholders, universities themselves, have accepted the design decisions made.

Given the prominence of positive impact in the design and development of both EIKEN and TEAP, further empirical validity evidence to support impact claims needs to be collected. TEAP has made a promising start through Green

150 Dunlea, Fouts, Joyce, and Nakamura

(2014), and it would be extremely instructive not just for the local context but more widely to carry through with further studies to evaluate the impact of both TEAP and EIKEN over time.

Innovation

Innovation needs to be considered through the prism of the local context in which these testing programs were designed and operate. Innovation should not only be interpreted as novel, unique, or groundbreaking from a global perspective. Certain aspects of the test design and implementation may indeed not be earth-shattering from a global perspective, but make an important contribution at the local level to introducing a focus on skills not developed elsewhere or by promoting good assessment practices that might otherwise not be accepted. In the case of EIKEN, we would offer the example of the effort to include speaking assessments as evidence of the former kind of innovation and point to TEAP's deliberate introduction of international best-practice approaches to pretesting while shedding the local expectation of publicly releasing test materials as an example of the latter.

In terms of TEAP, we have already highlighted a number of key test design decisions that could be considered bold and innovative in the context of Japan. Faced with the expectation to maintain the practice of releasing test materials to the public, the decision for TEAP to move in the opposite direction, albeit a direction bringing it closer to accepted best practice at an international level, is indeed an important step. In terms of internal test design, we have already discussed in some detail particular aspects of speaking and writing which are innovative in the context of Japan. We would point to the writing test, particularly Task B, as being innovative at a global level. Weir (2014) highlighted the lack of international tests incorporating reading-into-writing tasks that can adequately target key aspects of academic writing ability. The test design for TEAP, and the in-depth validation studies accompanying it, can indeed be considered important contributions not just to Japan but to the field generally. Similarly, the approach to test design for speaking is also instructive. Needs analysis surveys employing function analysis were combined with criterial features defined in the CEFR to design tasks that elicit key aspects of speaking relevant for the academic TLU of TEAP. These tasks at the same time constrain key contextual and cognitive parameters to make them accessible to high school students.

Validation and Quality Assurance

EIKEN

Within Sasaki's Period 4, as described earlier, we might define a sub-period from the early 2000s as an intensive period of validation research for the

EIKEN tests. As already noted, the impetus for the intensive focus on validation research during this period came from two directions. One was the move to explicitly reference EIKEN grades as external criterion benchmarks of proficiency. The second was the move to support MEXT calls to increase the number of students studying abroad by seeking recognition from foreign universities for EIKEN certificates as proof of English proficiency. With both of these developments, the demand grew, both from within Japan and externally, for clearer descriptions of the EIKEN grades and for validity evidence to support the claim that the grades indeed were "well-defined steps that can act as both motivational goals and concrete measures of English ability as learners move through the spectrum of commonly recognized ability levels." (Eiken Foundation of Japan, n.d.-a)

The Eiken website (Eiken Foundation of Japan, n.d.-c) provides an overview of the key studies undertaken in this period, many of which had implications on further test development, including on TEAP. One of the first of these was the EIKEN Can-do project, a large-scale project to develop empirically scaled descriptors in the form of can-do statements for the different EIKEN grades. The project is described in some depth in Dunlea (2010). This project, which made explicit reference to other major international projects to develop similar descriptive proficiency frameworks, including the ALTE Can-do project and the CEFR (Dunlea, 2010), also initiated a period of outward-looking validation research in which the Eiken Foundation began to look to collaboration with international expertise to inform research. This process was accelerated by the need to provide evidence to foreign universities to support the recognition of EIKEN grades. This led to an important study in 2008 by J. D. Brown. Brown (2008) describes the process by which he embedded himself within the EIKEN test production teams and was given wide access to internal test materials, test data, and staff for interviews. While employing a different approach and model to validation than the socio-cognitive model, the approach taken by Brown, in which the test system is seen to be embedded within a social context and intimately connected to the key stakeholders, has clear and striking connections to the socio-cognitive approach. Brown undertook further research to support the use of EIKEN tests for entrance purposes, including carrying out an innovative vertical scaling study with Rasch to place the different, stand-alone, EIKEN grades onto a common scale in order to facilitate a criterion-related validity study examining the relationship of EIKEN grades to the TOEFL®iBT (Brown et al., 2012). The experience of working with vertical scaling can be seen to have provided important groundwork for the more extensive study reported in Dunlea (2015) and for the recent introduction of the Common Scale of English (Eiken Foundation of Japan, n.d.-h). Another important validation study in terms of supporting the use of EIKEN for study abroad was Hill (2010). Hill carried out an in-depth, longitudinal study of students using EIKEN grades to enter a community college in Hawaii. The study was innovative in that it combined not only quantitative measures but also a range of qualitative research methods to build a detailed picture of the students and the variables that can impact on study success for foreign students in an English medium environment.

However, by far the biggest and most comprehensive validation study for EIKEN is Dunlea (2015), which employed the socio-cognitive model to drive a research agenda addressing the contextual and cognitive profiles of EIKEN grades, with a large-scale vertical scaling study utilizing over 22,000 items administered over 8 years to empirically validate the claim that the EIKEN grades do indeed represent empirically distinct proficiency levels that align with definable criterial contextual and cognitive features. The study further addressed the issue of external criterion relevance by carrying out multiple standard setting studies to investigate the relationship of EIKEN grades to the CEFR, finding strong evidence to support the relationship reported in Table 6.1. Further evidence to support this relationship was obtained in an international collaborative study reported in Dunlea and Figueras (2012).

TEAP

TEAP has from the outset incorporated a collaborative approach to test development and validation that has included leading international researchers. The project to develop TEAP also benefited from the ability to incorporate an explicit model of test development and validation to drive both design and data collection for validation purposes. A number of important studies, already referenced earlier in this chapter, have documented not only the theory underpinning design, but the comprehensive piloting, analysis, and revision that accompanied that development. Key studies are Weir (2014) on writing, Nakatsuhara (2014a) on speaking, Taylor (2014) on reading and listening, and Green (2014) on washback. The speaking test also provides another interesting example of the iterative nature of test development and how ongoing features of the context need to be evaluated against the stated goals and priorities of the test. Nakatsuhara (2014a) describes how the test was originally intended to be a live, face-to-face interview that would be videotaped and double rated separately by trained raters. The videotaping was intended to provide more useful input to support the evaluation of interactional effectiveness. Nakatsuhara (2014b) describes the process whereby the original design decisions were reviewed to rebalance practicality in the face of increasing numbers of test takers with the ability to adequately measure the targeted construct. This led to a decision to abandon video rating in favor of sound recordings. At the same time, double rating was maintained, but a holistic rating was elicited from the interlocutor conducting the test, and this was followed by a single, detailed analytic rating from a separate rater using the sound recordings. Nakatsuhara (2014b) provides an interesting discussion of the process of how these decisions were made and how the assumptions underpinning them were checked and validated through a follow-up rating study. TEAP continues to be the subject of collaborative research between the test development research team and external researchers inside and outside Japan, for example In'nami, Koizumi, and Nakamura (2016).

Quality Assurance in Item Writing and Content Production

Quality assurance in relation to content production has evolved over the years. An important feature that has become more prominent since the early 2000s is the approach to test specification. Approaches to test specification used for the development of TEAP, which drew heavily on the socio-cognitive model, have in turn been adapted and applied to the item-writing process for EIKEN. Earlier, we described the comprehensive validation study carried out by Dunlea (2015). This study noted how the internal item-writing and review teams that form part of the Editorial Department had developed a high degree of standardization and consistency across a range of criterial features for the EIKEN tests without the kind of specification approach later employed by TEAP. Dunlea (2015) recommended that, going forward, these criterial features should be specified more explicitly, a recommendation that has been taken up. Another key outcome of this validation program was the creation of an extensive digital item-banking system. All of the items tagged for the criterial features noted in Dunlea (2015), and additionally for the other skills not described in that study, were included in a comprehensive, searchable item bank, along with statistical information on empirical difficulty and item discrimination. This has greatly facilitated quality assurance and allows the test development teams to review items and item features systematically.

Lessons Learned and Improvements Needed

The examination of EIKEN and TEAP within the same chapter has provided a useful example of how lessons can be learned and applied over time, not only within but also across testing programs. As described earlier, changes introduced to EIKEN in 2016 include aspects such as a common scale score to connect grades that not only built on earlier studies such as Brown et al. (2012), but undoubtedly drew on the experience of using Rasch scaling in the development of TEAP. The examples described in detail earlier in this chapter, particularly the narrative description of the interaction of context and test design and revision, provide graphic examples of the tensions and synergies inherent in test use and design suggested by Dunlea (2016) and the interaction of stakeholders, test design decisions, and the social context as described by O'Sullivan (2016). These examples demonstrate the iterative, ongoing need to balance the tensions and synergies of the testing context, and how that balance may need to change over time. Nothing is written in stone, and nothing should be considered a one-off development exercise. The constant need to evaluate and adjust also highlights Kaftandjieva's caution regarding standard-setting, which we would suggest is indeed a fitting caveat to test development generally:

> There is no gold standard, there is no true cut-off score, there is no best standard setting method, there is no perfect training, there is no flawless implementation of any standard setting method on any occasion and there is never sufficiently strong validity evidence. In three words, nothing is perfect.
>
> *(2004, p. 41)*

For EIKEN and TEAP, an important issue that needs to be considered is the balance of resources for validation, research, and dissemination. We have already noted that the early 2000s were something of a "golden age" for validity research for EIKEN and TEAP. This golden age was preceded by a period in which the majority of resources, understandably, were devoted to validation through an iterative consensus approach to ensuring content relevance for key stakeholders. The relationships with those key stakeholders remain imperative, while resources for validation will always remain finite. As the wider social context in which the tests function changes, evolving priorities may impact on how resources are allocated to validity research and dissemination. One area that is particularly susceptible to such changing priorities is that part of the research agenda aimed at reaching the international research community. Output from these activities may be less accessible, or indeed relevant, to the immediate priorities of important local stakeholders. Balancing priorities, of course, is not necessarily restricted to locally developed tests; test developers across contexts and regardless of scale will face such choices at some point. In embarking on validation studies, we very often need to ask ourselves not "what is next?"—as there will potentially always be more evidence that can be collected—but rather, "when should we stop?" In that respect, it is worth remembering Cronbach's criteria for evaluating potential validation studies:

1. Prior uncertainty: Is the issue genuinely in doubt?
2. Information yield: How much uncertainty will remain at the end of a feasible study?
3. Cost: How expensive is the investigation in time and dollars?
4. Leverage: How critical is the information for achieving consensus in the relevant audience?

(as cited in Kane, 2013, p. 165)

For EIKEN and TEAP, then, questions of balancing the local with the international extend not just to the test design but also to the validation and research agenda employed to support that test design. We would emphasize that engaging with the international research community is not just for the purpose of establishing the credibility of the testing programs. It is an important way of contributing lessons learned and experience gained in one local context to an international discussion of what constitutes best practice in assessment, knowledge of which may indeed be of use for others struggling with similar issues in different contexts. We thus hope that resources will continue to be found to maintain a commitment to transparency and research dissemination both locally and globally for EIKEN and TEAP.

Localization: Balance Between Local and Global

A theme that has run through this chapter is the concept of balancing the tensions and synergies of a dynamic testing environment. This concept overlaps with the visual representation in O'Sullivan (2016, and this volume) of the cyclical interaction between stakeholders, test systems, and the wider social context of use in which they are embedded. Our discussion has shown that the socio-cognitive model provides a powerful way of considering a taxonomy of explicit variables, or parameters, across a range of validation evidence categories, which are amenable to manipulation in a systematic way to help us reach the balance we deem appropriate and acceptable to stakeholders.

Our discussion has further demonstrated that the balance between local and global, the degree to which a test moves towards one or other end of the continuum, is not fixed by the national or cultural context, but once again is rather connected to the uses and intended test takers within that context. As we have seen, even within the same testing system, such as EIKEN, the acceptable balance of features will need to change as we move up and across proficiency levels and also extend and expand the expected range of uses of the test into more generic, international contexts. Our intention has been to illustrate with two real-world, dynamic examples how the concepts of local and global can inform how we balance the particular tensions and synergies of our own testing context and need not be considered as black-and-white choices between opposing extremes.

References

Aoki, M. (2017, April 6). Japan's latest English-proficiency scores disappoint. *The Japan Times*. Retrieved from www.japantimes.co.jp/news/2017/04/06/national/japans-latest-english-proficiency-scores-disappoint/

Brown, J. D. (2008). Testing-context analysis: Assessment is just another part of language curriculum development. *Language Assessment Quarterly, 5*(4), 275–312.

Brown, J. D., Davis, J. McE., Takahashi, C., & Nakamura, K. (2012). *Upper-level EIKEN examinations: Linking, validating, and predicting TOEFL®iBT scores at advanced proficiency EIKEN levels*. Retrieved from www.eiken.or.jp/eiken/group/result/pdf/eiken-toeflibt-report.pdf

Brown, J. D., & Yamashita, S. O. (1995). English language entrance examinations at Japanese universities: 1993 and 1994. In J. D. Brown & S. O. Yamashita (Eds.), *Language testing in Japan* (pp. 86–100). Tokyo: Japan Association for Language Teaching.

Council of Europe. (2001). *Common European Framework of Reference for Languages: Learning, teaching, assessment.* Cambridge, UK: Cambridge University Press.

Council of Europe. (2009). *Relating language examinations to the Common European Framework of References for Languages: Learning, teaching, assessment.* Strasbourg: Language Policy Division.

Dunlea, J. (2009, May). *Maximizing test usefulness: A framework for addressing the needs of EIKEN test takers.* Paper presented at the 8th JALT PanSIG Conference, Tokyo.

Dunlea, J. (2010). The EIKEN Can-do list: Improving feedback for an English proficiency test in Japan. In L. Taylor & C. Weir (Eds.), *Language testing matters: Investigating the wider social and educational impact of assessment* (pp. 246–260). Studies in Language Testing, 31. Cambridge, UK: Cambridge University Press.

Dunlea, J. (2015). *Validating a set of Japanese EFL proficiency tests: Demonstrating locally designed tests meet international standards* (Unpublished doctoral dissertation). University of Bedfordshire, UK.

Dunlea, J. (2016, October). *Tensions and synergies in standardized testing: Making the numbers meaningful.* Keynote presentation at the 4th New Directions in English Language Assessment conference, Hanoi, Vietnam.

Dunlea, J. (2017, November). *Setting standards: The role of assessment in implementing the CEFR in education reform.* Keynote presentation at the 20th National Association of Foreign Language Educators Annual Conference [中国教育学会外语专业委员会第20次学术年会], Beijing, China.

Dunlea, J., & Figueras, N. (2012). Replicating results from a CEFR test comparison project across continents. In D. Tsagari & I. Csepes (Eds.), *Language testing and evaluation: Volume 26. Collaboration in language testing and assessment* (pp. 31–45). Frankfurt am Main: Peter Lang.

The Eiken Foundation of Japan. (n.d.-a). *EIKEN grades.* Retrieved from www.eiken.or.jp/eiken/en/grades/

The Eiken Foundation of Japan. (n.d.-b). *History.* Retrieved from www.eiken.or.jp/eiken/en/association/history/

The Eiken Foundation of Japan. (n.d.-c). *Research.* Retrieved from www.eiken.or.jp/eiken/en/research/

The Eiken Foundation of Japan. (n.d.-d). *Eiken test administration.* Retrieved from www.eiken.or.jp/eiken/en/eiken-tests/administration/

The Eiken Foundation of Japan. (n.d.-e). *Recognition.* Retrieved from www.eiken.or.jp/eiken/en/recognition/

The Eiken Foundation of Japan. (n.d.-f). *Examinee statistics.* Retrieved from www.eiken.or.jp/eiken/en/eiken-tests/stats/

The Eiken Foundation of Japan. (n.d.-g). 問題構成・見本問題 [Test format/sample questions]. Retrieved from www.eiken.or.jp/teap/construct/

The Eiken Foundation of Japan. (n.d.-h). The *EIKEN CSE score.* Retrieved from www.eiken.or.jp/eiken/en/eiken-tests/overview/cse/

Fouts, M. T. (2013, July). Building bridges to the international community: The EIKEN example. In L. Bachman (Chair), *The challenges and issues in developing English language tests in the Asian EFL context.* Symposium conducted at the 35th Language Testing Research Colloquium, Seoul, South Korea.

Geranpayeh, A., & Taylor, L. (Eds.). (2013). *Examining listening: Research and practice in assessing second language listening.* Studies in Language Testing, 35. Cambridge, UK: Cambridge University Press.

Green, A. (2007). *IELTS washback in context: Preparation for academic writing in higher education.* Cambridge, UK: Cambridge University Press.

Green, A. (2014). *The Test of English for Academic Purposes (TEAP) impact study.* Retrieved from www.eiken.or.jp/teap/group/report.html

Green, A., & Hawkey, R. (2011). An empirical investigation of the process of writing academic reading test items for the International English Language Testing System. *IELTS Research Reports, 11,* 273–374.

Hill, K. (1996). Who should be the judge? The use of non-native speakers as raters on a test of English as an international language. *Melbourne Papers in Language Testing, 5*(2), 29–50.

Hill, Y. Z. (2010). *Validation of the STEP EIKEN test for college admission* (Unpublished doctoral dissertation). University of Hawai'i at Manoa, Manoa, HI.

In'nami, Y., Koizumi, R., & Nakamura, K. (2016). Factor structure of the Test of English for Academic Purposes (TEAP) test in relation to the TOEFL®iBT test. *Language Testing in Asia, 6*(3), 1–23.

Kaftandjieva, F. (2004). Standard setting. In Council of Europe (Ed.), *Reference supplement to the pilot version of the manual for relating language examinations to the Common European Framework of Reference for Languages: Learning, teaching, assessment (CEF).* Strasbourg: Language Policy Division.

Kane, M. T. (2013). Validating the interpretations and uses of test scores. *Journal of Educational Measurement, 50*(1), 1–73.

Khalifa, H., & Weir, C. J. (2009). *Examining reading: Research and practice in assessing second language reading.* Studies in Language Testing, 29. Cambridge, UK: Cambridge University Press.

Kikuchi, K. (2006). Revisiting English entrance examinations at Japanese universities after a decade. *JALT Journal, 28*(1), 77–96.

Kobayashi, H., & Rinnert, C. (2002). High school student perceptions of first language literacy instruction: Implications for second language writing. *Journal of Second Language Writing, 11*(2), 91–116.

Kolen, M. J., & Brennan, R. L. (2004). *Test equating, scaling, and linking: Methods and practices* (2nd ed.). New York, NY: Springer-Verlag.

Ministry of Education, Culture, Sports, Science, and Technology. (2003). *Regarding the establishment of an action plan to cultivate Japanese with English abilities.* Retrieved from www.mext.go.jp/english/topics/03072801.htm

Ministry of Education, Culture, Sports, Science, and Technology. (2011). *Five proposals and specific measures for developing proficiency in English for international communication.* Retrieved from www.mext.go.jp/english/elsec/1319701.htm

Mulvey, B. (2001). The role and influence of Japan's university entrance exams: A reassessment. *The Language Teacher, 25*(7), 11–17.

Nakatsuhara, F. (2014a). *A research report on the development of the Test of English for Academic Purposes (TEAP) Speaking Test for Japanese university entrants—Study 1 & study 2.* Retrieved from www.eiken.or.jp/teap/group/report.html

Nakatsuhara, F. (2014b). *A research report on the development of the Test of English for Academic Purposes (TEAP) Speaking Test for Japanese university entrants—Study 3 & study 4.* Retrieved from www.eiken.or.jp/teap/group/report.html

Nation, P. (2006). How large a vocabulary is needed for reading and listening? *The Canadian Modern Language Review, 63*(1), 59–82.

Negishi, M. (2012). *The development of the CEFR–J: Where we are, where we are going.* Retrieved from www.tufs.ac.jp/common/fs/ilr/EU_kaken/_userdata/negishi2.pdf

O'Sullivan, B. (2011). Language testing. In J. Simpson (Ed.), *Routledge handbook of applied linguistics.* Oxford: Routledge.

O'Sullivan, B. (2012). Assessment issues in languages for specific purposes. *Modern Language Journal, 96,* 71–88.

O'Sullivan, B. (2015). *Aptis test development approach* (Aptis Technical Report TR/2015/001). London: British Council.

O'Sullivan, B. (2016). Adapting tests to the local context. In C. Saida, Y. Hoshino, & J. Dunlea (Eds.), *British Council new directions in language assessment: JASELE journal special edition.* Tokyo, Japan: British Council.

O'Sullivan, B., & Dunlea, J. (2015). *Aptis General technical manual version 1.0* (Aptis Technical Report TR/2015/005). London: British Council.

O'Sullivan, B., & Weir, C. (2011). Test development and validation. In B. O'Sullivan (Ed.), *Language testing: Theories and practices* (pp. 13–32). Oxford: Palgrave Macmillan.

Rinnert, C., & Kobayashi, H. (2001). Differing perceptions of EFL writing among readers in Japan. *The Modern Language Journal, 85*(2), 189–209.

Sasaki, M. (2008). The 150-year history of English language assessment in English education in Japan. *Language Testing, 25*(1), 63–83.

Shaw, S., & Weir, C. J. (2007). *Examining writing: Research and practice in assessing second language writing.* Studies in Language Testing, 26. Cambridge, UK: Cambridge University Press.

Taylor, L. (Ed.). (2012). *Examining speaking: Research and practice in assessing second language speaking.* Studies in Language Testing, 30. Cambridge, UK: Cambridge University Press.

Taylor, L. (2014). *A report on the review of test specifications for the reading and listening papers of the Test of English for Academic Purposes (TEAP) for Japanese university entrants.* Retrieved from www.eiken.or.jp/teap/group/report.html

Watanabe, Y. (1996). Does grammar translation come from the entrance examination? Preliminary findings from classroom-based research. *Language Testing, 13*(3), 318–333.

Watanabe, Y. (2013). The National Centre Test for University Admissions: Test review. *Language Testing, 30*(4), 565–573.

Weir, C. J. (2005). *Language test validation: An evidence-based approach.* Oxford: Palgrave.

Weir, C. J. (2014). *A research report on the development of the Test of English for Academic Purposes (TEAP) Writing Test for Japanese university entrants.* Retrieved from www.eiken.or.jp/teap/group/report.html

Wu, R. Y. F. (2014). *Validating second language reading examinations: Establishing the validity of the GEPT through alignment with the Common European Framework of Reference.* Studies in Language Testing, 41.Cambridge, UK: Cambridge University Press.

Yanase, K. (2009, May/June). 話題・題材の「広がり」と「深み」 [Topics: Breadth and depth]. *STEP Eigo Joho.*

Yoshida, K. (1996, January 15). Language testing in Japan: A cultural problem? *The Daily Yomiuri* (Educational Supplement).

APPENDIX A

TABLE 6.A1 EIKEN Test Format

Level	Module	Test format	Items	Time allotted	Max score	Passing score
Grade 1	Reading	Sentence completion	25			
		Gap fill in passages	6			
		Q&A based on passages	10	100 min.		
	Writing	English composition (200–240 words)	1			
	Listening	Q&A based on dialogues	10		3400	2630
		Q&A based on monologues	15	30 min.		
		Q&A based on extended interview	2			
	Speaking	Conversation				
		Short speech		10 min.		
		Q&A based on speech				
Grade Pre-1	Reading	Sentence completion	25			
		Gap fill in passages	6			
		Q&A based on passages	10	90 min.		
	Writing	English composition (120–150 words)	1		3000	2304
	Listening	Q&A based on dialogues	10	25 min.		
		Q&A based on monologues	15			
	Speaking	Short narration				
		Q&A		8 min.		

(Continued)

TABLE 6.A1 (Continued)

Level	Module	Test format	Items	Time allotted	Max score	Passing score
Grade 2	Reading	Sentence completion	20			
		Gap fill in passages	6			
		Q&A based on passages	12	85 min.		
	Writing	English composition (80–100 words)	1		2600	1980
	Listening	Q&A based on dialogues	15	25 min.		
		Q&A based on monologues	15			
	Speaking	Short narration Q&A		7 min.		
Grade Pre-2	Reading	Sentence completion	20			
		Gap fill in dialogues	5			
		Gap fill in passages	5	75 min.		
		Q&A based on passages	7			
	Writing	English composition (50–60 words)	1		2400	1728
	Listening	Conversation completion	10			
		Q&A based on dialogues	10	25 min.		
		Q&A based on monologues	10			
	Speaking	Oral reading Q&A		6 min.		
Grade 3	Reading	Sentence completion	15			
		Gap fill in dialogues	5			
		Q&A based on passages	10	50 min.		
	Writing	English composition (25–35 words)	1		2200	1456
	Listening	Conversation completion	10			
		Q&A based on dialogues	10	27 min.		
		Q&A based on monologues	10			
	Speaking	Oral reading Q&A		5 min.		
Grade 4	Reading	Sentence completion	15			
		Gap fill in dialogues	5			
		Q&A based on passages	10	35 min.		
		Word reordering	5			
	Listening	Conversation completion	10			
		Q&A based on dialogues	10	25 min.	1000	622
		Q&A based on monologues	10			
	Speaking (internet-based recorded interview)		Oral reading Q&A	4 min.		

Level	Module	Test format	Items	Time allotted	Max score	Passing score
Grade 5	Reading	Sentence completion	15			
		Gap fill in dialogues	5	25 min.		
		Word reordering	5			
	Listening	Conversation completion	10			
		Q&A based on dialogues	10	20 min.	850	419
		Matching	10			
	Speaking (internet-based recorded interview)		Oral reading Q&A	3 min.		

Table 6.A2 TEAP Test Format

Module	Test format	Items	Time allotted	Max score*
Reading	Sentence completion	20		
	Q&A based on graph or chart	5		
	Q&A based on notice, announcement, or e-mail	5		
	Q&A based on short passages	10	70 min.	100
	Gap fill in passages	2		
	Q&A based on extended passage	1		
	Q&A based on extended passage (including graph or chart)	1		
Listening	Q&A based on short dialogues	10		
	Q&A based on short monologues	10		
	Q&A based on short monologues (including graph or chart)	5	50 min.	100
	Q&A based on extended dialogues	3		
	Q&A based on extended monologues	3		
	Q&A based on extended monologue (including graph or chart)	1		
Writing	Summary (70 words)	1	70 min.	100
	Essay (200 words)	1		
Speaking	Interview			
	Role play			
	Monologue		10 min.	100
	Extended interview			

Note. Japanese universities set their own minimum **TEAP** score requirements for admission based on the total score for all four skills (maximum of 400).

7

THE ENGLISH LANGUAGE PROFICIENCY ASSESSMENT FOR THE MALAYSIAN PUBLIC SERVICE

Kadeessa Abdul-Kadir

Developing the ELPA

Introduction

The development of the English Language Proficiency Assessment (ELPA) under the "English for the Malaysian Civil Service (EMCS)" project was a collaborative effort between the National Institute of Public Administration (INTAN) and the British Council. Initially limited to assessing workplace use of English among junior- and middle-level management officers in the Administrative and Diplomatic Service (PTD), it was developed with the Testing and Evaluation Unit (TEU), Centre for Applied Language Studies, University of Reading. It is administered by INTAN's English Language Unit (ELU) and is part of the requirements for development and promotion exercises in the public service.

Evolution of the ELPA

The ELPA was developed by a small group of English language trainers with the Public Service Department of Malaysia (PSD). From initially assessing the English language competency of PTD officers numbering about 5,000, the test was later extended to include other government agency officers. The test is unique in being the first to be developed specifically for the Malaysian public service.

Purpose of the Test

ELPA focuses on "job-specific" language proficiency and enables INTAN and the PSD to evaluate the English language proficiency of public service employees in their placement, training, and promotion planning exercises.

Early Test Development Phase

Its development phase covering a two-year period included conducting a language-needs survey, preparing the test specifications, and developing and field-testing test items. These stages provided the validity evidence required for test use on the target population. The project officially commenced in 1997, when testing experts from Reading University identified and funded partly by the British Council established the specifications and timelines for rolling out the first version of the ELPA. This project was in line with the Council's global commitment to developing indigenous English language test overseas (see Weir & O'Sullivan, 2017, Chapter 2.) The involvement of the experts helped with capacity building of INTAN's ELU staff many of whom were involved in multiple roles as test developers, administrators, and raters for the different components. Though members of the ELU were qualified TESL or TESOL trainers, none had experience in large scale testing. All members of the newly formed testing team were, however, teaching staff of the ELU and completely familiar with the language needs of the public service.

Testing Needs Analysis

The early stage in the test development phase involved determining the needs of the test-taking population through a questionnaire survey of 213 officers representing 18 government agencies. This *a priori* validation process (Weir, 2005) determined the nature and frequency of English language use in selected agencies including the PSD, Ministry of Foreign Affairs, the Ministry of International Trade and Industry, the Education Ministry, and the Prime Minister's Department. The needs analysis enabled the testing unit to decide on the purpose, content, method, and level of the assessment. Activities identified as being more frequently carried out in English included reading job-related reports, journals, periodicals, reference books; reading and writing reports and letters; making telephone conversations; and participation in discussions and meetings.

The testing team also conducted interviews with heads of departments of various ministries and senior officers in the PSD to determine the testing needs of the target population. Based on the survey and interview data, a set of assessment specifications was drawn up comprising reading, writing, and speaking modules. Each module was designed in terms of its task types and task conditions to bring the test in line with target situation analysis. As the purpose of the assessment was to measure "job-specific" proficiency, task-based, directives, and actual materials simulating public service occupational settings were used as far as possible. The test specifications underwent numerous reviews and revisions and much care was taken to ensure that all important and relevant information derived from the survey data was translated into clear and explicit language specifications for the test-writing phase. In this way, test validation was seen as a continuous process that went directly into the item-writing phase.

164 Kadeessa Abdul-Kadir

Item Writing Based on Test Specifications

The writing of assessment tasks and items for each of the three modules for the first version of the ELPA followed the needs-analysis phase. Item writing included examining and reviewing the test items, test layouts, and test rubrics. Once the team was satisfied with the items and rating scales for the different modules, feedback questionnaires were prepared for each module during the pre-trialing of the test. The questionnaires sought as much feedback as possible and were designed to provide further evidence for validating the test construct of the items for the modules. Among areas of concern at this stage were:

1. suitability and relevance of assessment tasks, materials, and topics;
2. appropriateness and effectiveness of the different methods of assessment;
3. appropriateness of the coverage of language skills;
4. adequacy of time allocation for each task/item and for each module;
5. clarity of test instructions and item rubrics;
6. the suitability of performance scales used for assessing candidates' performance; and
7. logistical constraints in administering the different test modules.

Several test forms were developed and trialed from 1997 to 1998. The use of a validated grammar test on loan from Reading's TEU together with ELPA's test provided evidence for *concurrent* validity. The grammar test developed was shown to correlate highly with each of the skills components of Weir's Test in English for Academic Purposes (Weir, 1983).

The reading module explored facility values, discrimination indices and internal reliability of items, and section and reading tests as a whole. Analyses between performances and data from feedback questionnaires were carried out as they provided important and useful information on test takers' attitudes and perceptions of the test and their abilities and whether this affected performance on the reading test. For the writing and spoken interaction, besides correlations between test performances and perceptions of test takers about the test, the testing team was also interested in inter-rater reliability of rating consistency. Between June and November 1998, the team finalized the different test versions including producing relevant documentation to provide information on the assessment for potential user-departments and candidates. Once this was completed, ELPA was launched in November 1998.

ELPA Reporting

Once rolled out in 1998, the reporting of test scores was done as in other established assessments. The practice has been to report ELPA as separate bands for the three skills with a band for each skill and a composite score. This is in line

The ELPA for the Malaysian Public Service **165**

with findings that language ability is better explained in a three-factor (divisible) rather than a general (unitary) model (Abdul-Kadir, 2008). Stakeholders, on the other hand, prefer a composite score for ease in decision-making. The composite score allows ranking to be broken down to the different levels of proficiency: Band 5 (Expert), Band 4 (Competent), Band 3 (Adequate), Band 2 (Limited), and Band 1 (Extremely Limited).

Localization of ELPA to Reflect the Language Needs of the Intended Test Population

The ELPA has evolved over the years. For ease of comparison the original ELPA is termed ELPA 1.0 and the new model as ELPA 2.0 (see Table 7.1). The changes were necessary to enhance the overall effectiveness of the test type and tasks and to accommodate the competencies and needs of the current test-taking population although both ELPAs retain their three skill components.

ELPA 1.0

ELPA 1.0 consists of 3 modules: reading, writing, and speaking. The reading module assesses the ability to read quickly using skimming and scanning strategies to retrieve information while the careful reading seeks to extract main ideas and lexical meaning, and to make inferences from the text. The texts used in this module are 700–800-word extracts from journal and magazine articles, newspapers, and non-fiction books. Topics are broadly professional and drawn mainly from the fields of management and administration, and are specific to public service work settings while applicable to all ministries and departments. This component is dichotomously scored and test takers are provided with a reading profile based on their performance on both sections.

The writing module comprises two sections involving writing a formal letter and a formal report. For the former, test takers provide a 150–200-word response as a letter in reply to a given situation. Topics are mainly drawn from administration and management fields and in general include expressing opinions or an apology, providing information, directions, explanation, instructions, and advice, seeking clarification or assistance, and making or replying to complaints.

In the formal report task a 400–600-word description of a situation is provided for which a report has to be produced. The situations draw upon public service work settings and simulate them as far as possible. They include presenting proposals for solving a problem, presenting justifications or arguments for or against a course of action, evaluating a situation or problem, making deductions and comments, and providing solutions.

These tasks are rated on a six-criteria analytical rating scale comprising task fulfillment, organization, grammar, vocabulary, style, and mechanics. The scale

166 Kadeessa Abdul-Kadir

is quite similar to that used in large scale testing such as IELTS and TOEFL. The rating scale for writing was developed based on the different needs of assessing written output for the public service context. However, an important criterion that sets it apart from others is style. In the context of the public service, the use of appropriate register is incorporated into the style of writing when addressing the different stakeholders in the hierarchy.

A successful candidate, for instance, will demonstrate the use of style and register that is appropriate for the intended reader. As the public service consists of a distinct hierarchy, the tone and style would need to be appropriate to the different levels of stakeholders. This provides insight into the experience and competency level of the candidates. Candidates who have more experience and exposure in working with different ministries and agencies perform better than those who do not have this exposure. As entry and mid-level officers their jobs include preparing all types of correspondence that are then checked by their superiors for suitability of content and style. This "on the job training" helps officers sharpen their letter writing skills and adopt a suitable style that is appropriate to their ministry or agency.

Like most rating scales the descriptors used for assessing style are quite general. However, for each task, the examiner is given the scoring guide for each of the criteria. This is also the case for the assessment of style. As in the example earlier, the style for writing to a counterpart might be different from writing to someone higher up in the public service. One example is that in every invitation letter, there is always information provided in the letter on whom to contact if the recipient requires further information. If the recipient is a counterpart or someone of equal standing, then the sender would provide that information. If the recipient is someone higher up such as the Chief Secretary or a Secretary-General, then the appropriate style would be to offer the office as the contact for confirmation. Both the writing tasks are weighted equally. An average score of the two writing tasks is converted to a band of 1 to 5 and test takers receive a profile of their writing ability using the rating scale descriptors.

Finally, the speaking module consists of a telephone conversation, discussion, and interview. All three involve two-way communication with another officer and, in the case of the third task, officers engage in an interview with the interlocutor to converse about their work experience and academic qualifications. The interlocutor will ask questions based on a completed pre-interview questionnaire given earlier to the test takers.

Like the other components, topics for the situations are drawn mainly from the fields of administration and management and typically include providing information, explanation, clarification via the telephone and addressing a problem and seeking solutions via discussion.

A 6-point holistic rating scale assesses performance on all three tasks and the results are combined and reported as bands on a scale of 1 to 6. Like the writing tasks, the speaking tasks are weighted equally. It is interesting to note that both

The ELPA for the Malaysian Public Service **167**

speaking and writing use holistic and analytical rating scales respectively. The choice between holistic and analytical was based on consultations with the testing experts and what the team thought might work best at that time.

The ELPA 1.0 provides the basis for a widely accepted model of a localized English language assessment and continues to be the preferred choice for such assessment for agencies in identifying and recommending customized training programs for their officers. INTAN's ELU tradition for institutionalizing a strong testing program built on a continuous effort to maintain test validity and reliability has been well recognized within the public service.

ELPA 2.0: A Move to a More Specific Local Test

ELPA 2.0 involves an innovation in terms of accommodating emerging competencies for the public service specifically for assessing the language ability of officers fast-tracked for promotion. It is another PSD initiative to recruit talented officers to fit key posts without going through the normal time taken to reach higher grades. While the rigor and comprehensiveness of the assessment for the three components are maintained, modifications include increasing the word length for the response attribute for both the letter and report writing tasks. This allows for greater output for both tasks and provides a better sample of the writing ability of test takers. This modification is based on an observation of raters' perceptions that longer writing tasks provide a more stable and better indicator of writing ability (Abdul-Kadir, 2008).

Another modification was to change the one-word or short responses of the reading module to multiple-choice responses. This was initiated in 2008 in response to having an answer key allowing several answers to be accepted due to the wide differences in vocabulary and choice of words for expressing ideas when answering the skimming, stated main idea, or inferential type of question. By changing the short responses to multiple-choice responses, checking for test reliability became easier and enabled the team to improve the overall reliability of the reading component. Although the reading and writing modules were modified, the main difference between ELPA 1.0 and 2.0 lies in the speaking module. In ELPA 2.0, all three tasks were replaced with a Read and Respond Task and an Individual Short Talk. The rationale for including two very different tasks was based on discussions with stakeholders where officers identified for fast-track need different skill sets such as giving talks or briefings. Similarly, the ability to react and respond critically and to offer opinions on management and leadership topics relevant to the public service are also considered important skills for success in the workplace.

ELPA 2.0 also introduced the use of a task-specific rating scale in addition to the holistic rating one used in the speaking module. For the Individual Short Talk, test takers expound for three minutes on a given topic. Time is provided for them to prepare their talk such as using their smartphones or devices to

TABLE 7.1 Comparison of ELPA 1.0 and 2.0

Reading Module

Section	Focus	Item Type	Time	Dimensions of Sample	Weighting	Response Attributes	
						ELPA 1.0	*ELPA 2.0*
A	Reading quickly	Scanning for details: 5 multiple-choice questions	4 mins	1 to 2 texts	50 %	One word/ short answer	MCQ
		Skimming for gist: 2 multiple-choice questions	6 mins	2 texts			
B	Reading carefully	Extracting main ideas, making contextual inferences: 5 short answer questions	20 mins	1 to 2 texts	50 %		
		Inferring lexical meaning: 5 short answer questions		1 to 2 texts			

Writing Module

Section	Task Type	Time Allowed	Weighting	Dimensions of Sample ELPA 1.0	Response Attributes ELPA 2.0
A	Formal Letter	30 mins	50 %	One task; length 1 page (150–200 words)	One task; length 1 page (200–250 words)
B	Formal Report	45 mins	50 %	One task; length 2–3 pages (400–600 words)	One task; length 4–6 pages (600–800 words)

Speaking Module

ELPA 1.0	Task Type	Mode	Time	Weighting	Dimensions of Sample
	Interview	Candidate-to-interviewer; face-to-face	5 mins	50%	One task
	Telephone conversation OR Discussion	Candidate-to-candidate; no visual contact OR Candidate-to-candidate; face-to-face	5–7 mins	50 %	One task

ELPA 2.0	Task Type	Mode	Time	Weighting	Dimensions of Sample
	Read and Respond to Text	Candidate-to-examiner; no visual contact	5 mins	50%	One task
	Individual Short Talk	Candidate-to-examiner; face-to-face	7–10 mins	50%	One task

google for information. The task-specific rating scale incorporates all aspects of task fulfilment and delivery and is used together with the holistic rating scale. The use of both holistic and analytical rating scales for speaking strengthens the validity of speaking ability interpretations. Table 7.1 summarizes the main features of ELPA 1.0 and 2.0.

Shifting to a More Localized Test

Several reasons explain the gradual shift to a more localized test like ELPA for the Malaysian public service in place of internationally recognized tests like TOEIC. The first is that ELPA is fairly unique in that it addresses the specific English language needs of officers in a public service setting as opposed to other established assessments such as TOEFL or IELTS, which had been used quite regularly in the past for a variety of purposes.

Another reason for the use of a more localized test like ELPA is also due to a recognition given by Cambridge Assessment English to another local test developed to assess the level of English proficiency for entrance to public universities in Malaysia. This Malaysian University Entrance Test (MUET), administered by the Malaysian Examinations Council (MEC), was officially recognized for its initiative to align with the Common European Framework of Reference for Languages (CEFR), an international standard for describing language ability. With the alignment to CEFR, MUET is set to enter the international market and become one of Malaysia's products in language assessment. A recognition from an established body like Cambridge is important as it gives credence to the Malaysian Examinations Council's capability to develop and deliver language tests. Also Cambridge has had a long-standing relationship with the Ministry of Education and the Government of Malaysia for providing O- and A-level qualifications through the local equivalents in the Malaysian Certificate of Education (MCE) and the Higher School Certificate in Education (HSC). With the success of MUET, the government encourages ELPA, developed as a home-grown product like the MUET, to venture into aligning with CEFR since it has become a high-stakes assessment. Though starting out small ELPA has proven to be another important local assessment.

As ELPA is considered an assessment of language for a specific or occupational purpose, the localization argument can be further supported by how the team decided on the generality or specificity of the assessment with respect to the public service context. Questions as to how the specific needs of the discourse community, in this case each ministry or agency, were reconciled makes a strong case for the use of a local assessment like ELPA. Bachman and Palmer (1996), Douglas (2000), and Stansfield and Wu (2001) agree that the testing of language for specific or occupational purposes (LSP) derives its test method and content from the analysis of the target language use (TLU) domain.

For INTAN's ELU to adopt a working definition of testing of English as a specific or occupational purpose, the definition or framework put forward by Douglas (2000) is relevant where LSP should be assessed over general language proficiency when the situation merits. As interpretations of test takers' abilities vary from performance to performance, language performance varies with both context and text type including the competencies needed to perform the tasks. For this reason, Douglas (2000) asserted that test takers should be given authentic tasks in which language ability and knowledge of the field interact with the test content. Once this is achieved, interpreting a person's performance as evidence of language ability on tasks that represent the target situation can then be supported with the proper arguments.

To add to the localization argument, Douglas (2000) further argued that a high degree of precision in the control of language is demanded of people who work in any highly specialized field. This precision is translated into the way members of discourse communities access the specific language in order to function effectively. To further extend this notion of precision, organizations and workplaces forming a certain discourse community sharing common purposes and objectives in the ways they enact social meaning also require their members to perform communicative acts in specific ways (Bazerman, 2004; Blyler, 1999).

For the Malaysian public service where the larger discourse community can be disaggregated into discrete communities (specific ministries and agencies, and schemes of services) which may or may not have their own TLU domain, the decision was to keep the test tasks as general as possible but is still within the public service context. This meant that regardless of which ministries or schemes the officers serve, the test tasks would reflect the likelihood they would engage in such tasks in the workplace.

Based on the different components, some theories of testing the discrete skills such as writing, reading, and speaking offer support for the use of ELPA as a localized test over other more established international assessments. The following explains how the application of theories for assessing the different skills fit the contextual needs of the test population.

Content Localization: Application of Theories in Assessing Different Skills to Fit the Contextual Needs of the Target Group

Testing Writing

For the writing module, the argument for localization is centered on the premise that organizations, like individuals, have writing processes that are unique to their particular discourse community. As these communities share common purposes and objectives in how they enact social meaning in which writing is

The ELPA for the Malaysian Public Service **171**

performed in certain ways or processes as described earlier (Blyler, 1999), the *Genre Approach* sees ways of writing as purposeful, socially situated responses to particular contexts and communities. Since writing letters and reports are generally the types of activities that public officers engage in across the ministries and agencies, it was the preferred choice for the component. In addition, the time needed to complete both writing tasks under assessment conditions had to be factored in so that candidates feel that producing letters and reports within the given time reflects actual writing experience in their workplace setting.

For ELPA the *Genre Approach* resonates well with workplace assessment in a public service context keeping in mind the need to avoid very technical forms and subject- or genre-specific tasks such as engineering, scientific, or economic writing that would require skills and the technical knowledge to produce them. For example, some officers spend most of their careers doing work requiring writing such technical reports and remain in these departments until suitable replacements with the skills and competency required to perform such tasks are available.

An important consideration for this module is to ensure that test takers are assessed on their facility with the use of English in writing. If the general idea was to get them to demonstrate their language facility using workplace-appropriate tasks, then it would make sense to provide as much information in the prompt as possible. This would ensure that they only needed to demonstrate their ability to elaborate on the content and to organize ideas as well as show facility with language use in terms of grammatical and vocabulary structures to fulfil tasks that best reflect workplace writing. As mentioned earlier, style is also included as an important criterion for judgment.

Research on assessing writing ability has also established that it can be separated into "discrete" elements (Hamp-Lyons, 1991) such as grammar, vocabulary, spelling, punctuation, and orthography. These were included in our criteria for judgment. But more importantly two other facets, namely task fulfilment and style, were also included to reflect the illocutionary and propositional features of workplace writing. This could not have been described without performing the textual analysis of both types of writing. The judgment of the tasks then would include task fulfilment, content as in elaboration of ideas, organization, range of grammatical structures, vocabulary range, use of appropriate style or register, and mechanics.

A notable difference between assessment and actual workplace writing is the extent to which the composing process plays out in these different settings. Under assessment conditions, in this specific case, some aspects of the process were deliberately incorporated into the tasks to provide the officers some practice before the required text was turned in. This was done by making them aware of the stipulated time for planning and drafting and that space is provided in the test booklet for drafting their outlines. The interaction between the test takers and the text is one area that needs to be considered. For example, how

172 Kadeessa Abdul-Kadir

do they respond and negotiate the meaning of the tasks (in this case the prompt and the instructions from the examiners) to actually produce the required text as there are no opportunities for feedback from anyone? How do test takers revise and edit their writing? How do they shift forward and backwards during the act of composing? Perhaps the time limit makes it difficult to display the complexity of the composing process, and under assessment conditions this would be a major limitation for observing the process.

Finally, the other tension, or one that might be perceived as such, is the extent to which genre theory can explain these two different scenes, which are assessment and non-assessment conditions. As in the assessment, the steps taken by the testing team to arrive with the right kinds of tasks for the assessment have been detailed. There was much textual analysis of the types of genre conducted to ensure that these tasks reflect as much as possible some of the types of workplace writing the officers would engage in. The textual analysis did represent "felicity" conditions (Bazerman, 2004) that would be appropriate and suitable to meet the needs of the public service and included studying the propositional and illocutionary features of the text. As such, much of the process of typification (Bazerman, 2004) where test tasks are standardized to fit the practices within the public service was largely the result of the textual analysis.

Using genre to guide workplace assessment did make sense despite the constraints of the assessment conditions. It would have been extremely difficult given logistical and resource constraints as well as ensuring a reliable measure to have officers perform on more productive tasks requiring multi-level processes and incorporate the interplay of other texts and people for assessing workplace writing. Perhaps what is most important is that the testing unit was aware that writing is exploratory, generative, and recursive and is a complex process rather than a linear route leading to a pre-determined product.

Testing Speaking

As with the writing module, ELPA's speaking module is also grounded in the LSP tradition of addressing speaking activities that are characteristic of the public service context. All the test tasks conform to the various specifications spelled out such as test takers' language knowledge and the strategic competence needed to successfully perform the tasks. For the different test tasks, fluency is measured as part of linguistic knowledge. The size and accuracy of the use of grammatical structures and vocabulary is also a feature of the linguistic knowledge assessed, and the extent of test takers' background knowledge in general public service topics can impact task performance. They must be familiar with public service topics to enable them to participate actively in the interview, telephone, or discussion test tasks. Apart from test takers' attributes, task characteristics also contain features of the construct in question. This includes the rubric, input text or situation, expected response, and the relationship

The ELPA for the Malaysian Public Service **173**

between input and the expected response. From the use of the different features in the specifications for the speaking and writing modules, it is possible to have an idea of the potentially rich output in terms of the specific-purpose language ability that test takers could contribute.

The speaking module was initially meant as a test of speaking ability and, as such, performance would be linguistically oriented. However, over the years the shift to include some aspects of public service knowledge was necessary to reflect the quality of test takers competent not only in the language but also knowledgeable in public service matters. As such the introduction of an analytical rating scale to address the features specific to a particular task including knowledge was introduced in ELPA 2.0 to provide a more comprehensive assessment. Some of the criteria in the rating scale include the ability of test takers to coherently present arguments on a public-service-related topic. The arguments must reflect depth in knowledge about the particular subject matter area. On a different note, the test takers are also allowed to google for information on the given topic as this is also reflective of current or emerging skills needed for digital capability readiness. It has been observed that the lack of such researching skills can affect test takers' performance in the individual short talk task.

Testing Reading

For testing reading, much of the task of defining the reading construct as well as the types of reading were informed by the findings of the testing needs analysis as well as by the testing consultant. Theories on the nature of reading and the essential variables that affect the development of the reading component were brought to bear during this phase. The nature of reading in the public service context where quick reading strategies such as skimming and scanning as well as reading for explicitly stated main ideas, inferencing, and understanding vocabulary from contextual clues were also deemed necessary skills for this purpose.

Another important consideration in the development of the reading module was the large number of domain areas in the public service. For example, it would have been almost impossible to provide suitable texts covering all domains and address the exact discourse for each of the 21 schemes of public service and their sub-discourse contexts. The testing team had to ensure that the texts were general enough for a wide swath of officers and were drawn mainly from leadership, management, and social domains. The use of a pro-forma document to check relevant and suitable content as well as determine the appropriate length of texts proved to be useful for addressing the nature of reading in the public service. In addition, consideration for the nature of texts and how they lend themselves to testing the different sub-skills are continuously being examined. For each text, the team would always employ a set of

174 Kadeessa Abdul-Kadir

criteria. For example, longer texts with facts and figures and explicit details would lend themselves well to quick reading as opposed to texts with more main ideas and supporting details for careful reading.

Just as reading is difficult to master it is also equally difficult to perform well on it. This is evidenced by the performance of test takers on the three different skills of the ELPA. Data on the performance of officers selected for fast-track purposes from 2015 to 2017 shows that only 20% of the 1,000 test takers scored at Band 4 and above on the reading component as opposed to 40% and 50% respectively on the writing and speaking components. This low performance on reading can be attributed to several factors and, as noted by Hawkey (2006), reading is perhaps among the more difficult skills to master as in IELTS.

The time constraint placed on the reading-quickly section makes it difficult for the test takers. For this section, test takers are constantly instructed to start and stop reading after answering item(s) on each text. This type of testing experience is new to many and raises anxiety levels. In addition, text familiarity is also a factor. As mentioned earlier, although texts are sourced from very general public-service-related domains, some test takers would not have prior knowledge of the topic to answer correctly. Another factor that could contribute to the low reading performance is that the texts employed have to lend themselves to the different sub-skills tested; for example, texts used for scanning items need to have many facts and figures and be fairly lengthy. In addition, the difficulty level of the texts might also contribute to the low performance on the reading module. Since this is a workplace assessment of language competency, the choice of texts must to a certain extent reflect the types of reading done there. From one-page letters to lengthy reports, these documents need to be read and processed quickly or carefully to enable the officers to perform other tasks.

Context-Specific Problems and Overcoming Challenges

The ELPA continues to find a niche in the world of public service assessment and INTAN's ELU is faced with several challenges to ensure that it remains effective and valid. One concern is the rise in the number of entry level officers taking the assessment. This is the direct result of the PSD's policy to fast-track eligible officers through either individual initiatives or departmental nominations. ELPA was initially developed for mid-level managers having at least a few years' work-related experience, and entry level officers identified for fast-track purposes will find the assessment challenging since they are unable to relate to the workplace context as required by the different test tasks. As such, the low number of such officers who performed either at adequate or limited level as context appropriate on the ELPA is reflected in the test tasks.

The test itself is reflective of workplace use of English. As such, officers who are required to use English in a public service context would only be able to do so once they are in the system. This comes with years of experience and working in an environment where English is used in a variety of communicative settings. Graduates from local universities who are not proficient in English will enter and remain at that level unless they are posted to agencies and ministries which require more regular English language usage in their daily operations. Numerous opportunities are available for officers to improve and enhance their English competency but many shy away since there is no intrinsic motivation for them to use the language. As such the present educational system does not prepare them for the context specific discourse in the public service.

Another challenge faced by the ELU is the overuse of ELPA for different purposes since it is the only means available for assessing workplace use of English for the public service. From 2003 onwards the ELPA was repurposed for a wider test population to assess officers for fast-track lateral entry to the PTD scheme and also for those vying for Federal scholarships. This is certainly positive as the stakeholders now recognize the usefulness of this home-grown product. However, for the ELU, the pressure is mounting to produce and administer several versions of the tests. The surge in the number of test takers in 2003 and subsequently from 2015 onwards has far-reaching implications on the operations of the ELU. An immediate impact of these changes is the overwhelming number of requests from PSD's Service Division for the test to be administered to their officers in an effort to comply with the new directive. The role of ELU as test developers and administrators expanded significantly which in turn exerts tremendous pressures on the ELU to effectively manage this assessment. This is important and warrants serious attention if the scores on the test are to be used to interpret and generalize the English language abilities of public sector officers.

Can One Test Fit All Public Service Employees?: Using an Innovative Interpretive Argument Approach to Establish Test Validity

The Different Uses of ELPA

Since it was developed with the public service in mind, the ELPA has been used for a variety of purposes. Initially it was to put in place a training or development mechanism for PTD officers based on their performance on it. For this target group, the number of test takers did not exceed 500 after it was introduced in 1998. A shift in policy in 2003 saw ELPA being extended to other services. This shift was to address firstly the growing concerns over the perceived weakness in English language of lower and middle management officers that was seen as compromising their competitiveness in matters of governance and public management. The second reason was to fulfil the requirement for a comprehensive remuneration package comprising, among others, an assessment of competency levels including in the English language. Up till 2008, the impact of repurposing of ELPA to include these uses was examined in a comprehensive validity inquiry using Kane's (2006) Interpretive Argument approach which will be described in detail in the subsequent paragraphs. As part of a continued quality control process, the testing team provides internal reports of test performance to management and stakeholders on a regular basis. Each of these reports contains the different claims according to the argument structure put forward. Many of the evidence provided for the support of the claims are based on quantitative methods using reliability analysis, Generalizability theory and others. A complete illustration of the use of the different measurement instruments is showcased in validity inquiry study in Abdul-Kadir (2008).

Another surge in numbers of test takers was in 2015 with the introduction of a policy to fast-track highly talented and competent civil servants to key positions in government with INTAN being tasked to conduct English language assessments on them. This policy outlining the processes and procedures as well as the prerequisites for agencies affect the career prospects of more than sixty thousand federal public officers from across 21 schemes of service and four grade levels. With this policy, ELPA is officially used as the first screening instrument for the fast-tracking.

Another initiative in the wider use of the ELPA was for assessing officers applying for in-service training from 2018 onwards. One of the responsibilities of the PSD is to manage human capital development by providing opportunities for public officers to pursue postgraduate studies locally or abroad. Annually around 500 officers are selected for the Federal Training Award for masters or doctoral studies. While those awarded scholarships to study in the UK, the U.S., or Australia will still need to take either TOEFL or IELTS, those applying to local universities have to show proof of English language proficiency. Stringent measures taken ensure that only the best and brightest are offered such scholarships. In March 2018, of the 497 potential in-service scholars from 12 schemes of service who sat for the ELPA, 14.1% attained Band 4 (Competent User), 73.6% were placed at the Adequate User (Band 3), and the remaining at Band 2 (Limited User).

Maintaining Quality and Fairness vis-a-vis Different Groups

The previous section shows that ELPA is well on its way to becoming the test of choice for assessing public service officers. With the numerous groups of officers assessed under different purposes, ascertaining ELPA's test validity in assessing, interpreting, and generalizing their English language ability and its impact on the public service is important. When it was first developed, efforts were made to ensure that evidence of test validity was sought by instituting routine procedures during the test development phase. During this phase, the nature of the validation was mostly to confirm the appropriateness and relevancy of the test constructs from measures such as a needs-analysis survey prior to the development of test tasks to using feedback questionnaires during field testing. Other measures included involving test takers in ensuring that different reading texts and samples of writing tasks were provided to garner their feedback.

As the demand for ELPA increases, mechanisms will be required to be placed to ensure validity of test score interpretations. One means of testing validity is the use of Kane's (2006) Interpretive Argument Approach. This large-scale validity inquiry opted for such an approach that claims to offer a systematic and pragmatic means to test validation and explicate evidence from a network of inferences and assumptions leading from observed performance to test impact. This was first used in 2008 in conducting a comprehensive study on ELPA's test validity and is now incorporated in the test development and test use phase to provide continuous checks and balances.

The 2008 study addressed some concerns on the issue of validity of test-score interpretations and accountability where an assessment intended for a particular target population (PTD) is extended to groups having possibly dissimilar discourse needs as a result of the 2003 policy shift. In utilizing this validation approach, the study examined the claims for the use of the test based on a network of inferences forming the basis for the validity argument. This included examination of the evidence from scoring procedures, generalization of observed scores to universe of scores, extrapolation of observed scores to non-test behavior, and investigating the impact of the test on the public service. The argument-based approach is a pragmatic means to assess validation and serves the development and appraisal stages where the goal is to develop a validity model that supports test use interpretations. Given that during the test development phase the efforts are mainly confirmatory, the appraisal stage is where the proposed interpretations are critically evaluated. The three functions that the interpretive arguments serve include providing a framework where test developers can indicate the assumptions that are to be met, a framework for validity arguments, and a basis for evaluating the validity argument.

For the interpretive argument to work an argument is set up for each level of inference containing elements such as *warrant*, *backing*, and *data* based on Toulmin's model of inference (2003). These are needed to support any claims made about the test for each level (see Table 7.2). The interpretive argument structure for each level of inference with its claims, assumptions, and backings was spelled out as clearly as possible and the evidence supporting the inferences collected. The evidence included analyses of test data, interviews with stakeholders, test developers, and raters and an online feedback from test takers. In ensuring test usefulness and test validity, quality control, and fairness is of paramount importance. An example of how each level of inference was set up can be seen in Figure 7.1. Similar argument structures were set up for each level of inference (see Figure 7.2). For this study, a total of nine argument structures were framed where evidence was sought for the different levels of inference (Abdul-Kadir, 2008). For this chapter, Level 1 argument structure

178 Kadeessa Abdul-Kadir

TABLE 7.2 Interpretive Argument for a Trait Interpretation

Scoring: from observed performance to an observed score
- A 1.1: The scoring rule is appropriate.
- A 1.2: The scoring rule is applied accurately and consistently.

Generalization: from observed score to universe score
- A 2.1 The observations made in testing are representative of the universe of observations defining the testing procedure.
- A 2.2 The sample observation is large enough to control sampling error.

Extrapolation: from the universe score to target score
- A 3.1 The universe score is related to the target score.
- A 3.2 There are no systematic errors that are likely to undermine the extrapolation.

Implication: from target score to verbal description
- A 4.1 The implications associated with the trait are appropriate.
- A 4.2 The properties of the observed scores support the implications associated with the trait label.

Note. Adapted from "Validation" by M. Kane (2006), *Educational Measurement*, New York: Macmillan.

and its corresponding evidence to support the claims are reproduced to illustrate the depth and systematic nature of the Interpretive Argument Approach. For subsequent level of inferences, only some are reproduced for reference.

Table 7.3 presents the overall interpretive argument evidence to either support or negate the continued use of ELPA for different groups of test takers. Through the mixed method approach of using quantitative and interview data, the plurality of findings suggests that ELPA provides an effective and fair indicator of English language competency regardless of the service being assessed. Using the argument structure to guide the different types of evidence needed for each level of inference, the following paragraphs summarize the findings as an illustration of the depth and comprehensiveness of Kane's (2006) Interpretive Argument Approach to test validity.

Fidelity of Scoring Procedures

The fidelity of the scoring procedures as the first level was supported by evidence from the test takers and ELPA administrators. Generally, positive feedback was received from the test takers. While having some reservations on the management of the ELPA and certain procedural aspects especially on the scoring of the different components and its impact on overall reliability and fairness, the administrators were overwhelmingly in agreement on the usefulness of the assessment.

Generalizability

The use of classical test theory, generalizability theory, and multi-facet analysis findings for the generalization inference suggests moderate to high

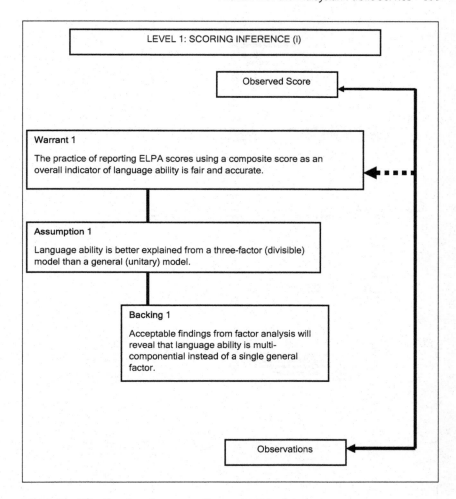

FIGURE 7.1 The Scoring Argument Structure: Level 1

Source: Adapted from Chapelle, Enright, and Jamieson 2007, p. 24

inter-rater reliabilities as well as high G and Phi coefficients. This indicates that for most of the analyses, test takers' ability contributed to the largest magnitude of variance although other facets associated with the assessment were also examined. An interesting finding on the use of analytical and holistic scoring suggests that, across different raters and groups, the analytical scores proved to be less stable than holistic scores if each of the rating scale criteria was incorporated in the analyses. The largest source of variance was contributed by rater-by-item (criteria) interaction that implicates the way the raters used the rating scale for each test taker. Further analyses from FACETS reveal that rater severity, although present, was not an issue. In

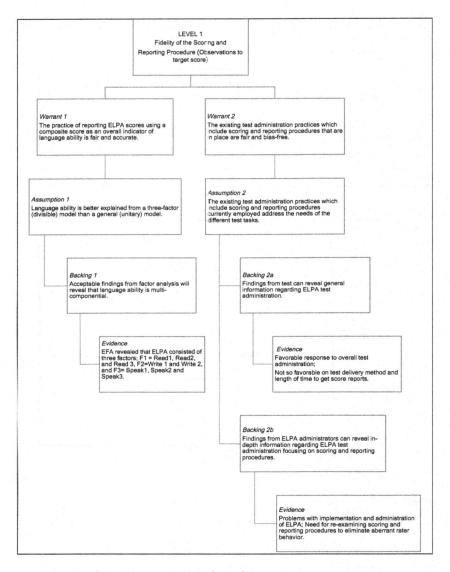

FIGURE 7.2 Evidence Supporting Level 1 Inference

addition, although no raters were found to be misfitting, some were inconsistent in their own ratings.

Extrapolation

Findings for the extrapolation inference, among others, confirmed the underlying structure of ELPA to be a three-factor correlated model where the sub-tests

The ELPA for the Malaysian Public Service **181**

TABLE 7.3 Overall Interpretive Argument Evidence (Levels 1 to 4)

	Support	*Counter-support*
Level 1	• Test takers' perception of overall administration of test as positive	• Test dimensionality challenged current practice of reporting composite of language ability • Internal problems in managing as well as inconsistencies in rater behavior may affect reliability of scoring.
Level 2	• Estimates of raters' consistency and reliability from multiple methods remained high for generalizability data.	• Questions about size of sample for generalizability inference • Manipulation of the ELPA test cycle which did not reflect operational scenario
Level 3	• Confirmed structure of ELPA to be three-factor correlated model and hence implications on reporting of results • Some link established between test scores and actual use of English at the work place (Model A better than Model B)	• Structural models did not take into account test takers background such as service, or grade level which might reveal measurement invariance as an important condition to achieve validity of inferences. • Context of language use was not ascertained and therefore linking test scores to domain of interest might be problematic for tested models.
Level 4	• Positive feedback from test takers, ELPA administrators, policy makers from all four services about test use and impact	• ELPA administrators and policy makers agreed that alternate forms of assessment to address insufficiency of the ELPA test should be considered.

and test tasks performance indicators were found to measure the three latent traits quite well. The writing component was the most reliable while speaking was found to be the least reliable. In an attempt to validate the construct of ELPA by extrapolating test scores to actual use of language at the workplace, the data of two competing structural models suggest a weak-to-modest fit. Non-performance indicators such as frequency and type of activities that require the use of English in the workplace suggest a weak-to-moderate relationship to the performance indicators.

Test Use and Impact

The fourth level of inference included findings for test use and impact, an area often neglected in validity inquiry. Feedback from three stakeholders suggests that on the whole, the ELPA has had a positive impact on the public service.

182 Kadeessa Abdul-Kadir

Test takers and policy makers alike provided insights as to the reasons for the application of the ELPA to a wider group such as meeting the higher objectives of enhancing language competency in the public service. More on test use and impact will be explained in the next section.

Evaluation of the Interpretive Argument Approach

Overall, the interpretive argument framework for test validation as proposed by Kane (2006) worked well for the intended purpose of the study. These included the demands for comprehensiveness and the multitudes of evidence needed to evaluate the strength of the validity argument for examining test use and impact and whether these demands can be met effectively by a single researcher in a single study. Although ELPA is a localized test, the processes and procedures to ensure test validity are comparable to any other established international proficiency tests.

Continuous efforts to ensure quality and fairness have been instituted and followed. First the ELPA is very much specification-driven as a means to ensure standardization of the different versions in terms of content, test taker attributes, and response attributes. Either version, whether ELPA 1.0 or 2.0, goes through rigorous review sessions in which the testing members discuss issues from text suitability to item effectiveness for each skill tested. A checklist drawn up for every aspect of test development helps guide current and new members on the processes and procedures during the test development and administration phases.

Like the other international testing companies, INTAN's ELU endeavors to be transparent in disseminating information to various stakeholders on test performance and findings from internal research with regular reports being presented to the highest level of government. Test takers are provided with test information before any test administration and test-familiarization sessions are held upon request. In addition, rater-training is an integral part of the process since inter-rater reliability affects the dependability and generalizability of test scores. Finally, where possible, internal research into the validity of test score interpretations is regularly carried out using modern validity theory (Kane, 2006; Messick, 1989) to support arguments that score inferences from the tests are valid for the intended use.

Test Use and Impact

As mentioned, the one area that is often neglected in validity inquiry is test use and impact. For the ELPA this was one of the areas investigated in 2008 and continues to be looked into. From time to time, evidence for test use and impact is sought from the various stakeholders including the test takers. This final level of inference in Kane's (2006) Interpretive Argument Approach centers on the use of tests for decision-making and how these decisions impact different stakeholders especially test takers. According to Weiss (1998), impact is defined as "the net effects of a program" (i.e., the gain in outcomes for program participants minus the gain for an equivalent group of non-participants). Impact may also refer to program effects for the larger community but "more generally, it is a synonym for *outcome*" (Weiss, 1998). From an evaluation perspective, Weiss differentiated between *processes* and *outcomes or products* with the former focusing on "what goes on while a program is in progress" while the latter studies measures and describes "the end result of the program." Varghese (1998) differentiated *impact* and *evaluation* studies that focus on the effects or changes and on program achievements, respectively.

Although the definitions of impact as articulated here are derived from an evaluation perspective, in language testing research much of the awareness raised in impact studies is linked to the concept of "washback" which generally refers to the influence of a test on teaching and learning. This way of defining impact has been criticized as being too narrow and some researchers have proposed that general education and educational measurements should employ a broader term which includes effects beyond the classroom as well as impacts on the educational system and society as a whole (Hamp-Lyons, 1997; Turner, 2001). Hamp-Lyons further reiterates that "the responsibility of language testers is clear: we must accept responsibility for all the consequences which we are aware of" (p. 302). Turner (2001) points out that empirical studies conducted on washback have demonstrated that this phenomenon "cannot be articulated in a simple theory" (p. 139) and that its definition has evolved into a multi-faceted concept. Many studies have noted that in performance testing, washback effects on certain participants can be observed even during the test development phase and is not necessarily the end result of testing. Although this has not been documented systematically, the consideration for potential washback effects during the testing cycle warrants attention.

As studies on washback in educational settings continue to be the focus of language testing research, there have not been any that examine impact from other perspectives such as tests developed for specific or occupational purposes. This is especially so for high-stakes assessments where the results are used to make important decisions having immediate and direct effects on test takers and other stakeholders (Qi, 2005). Nonetheless, studies on washback can certainly inform the methodology for investigating impact in test situations not directly related to the classroom and teaching such as in the case of the high-stakes matriculation English test in China where Qi (2005) employed interview and questionnaire methods for collecting data.

Using Kane's Interpretive Argument Approach to further study test use and impact, a triangulation approach of data analysis from three stakeholders was used to gather evidence for this level. For Level 4 inference, the complete argument structure with the evidence is illustrated in Figure 7.3 (Abdul-Kadir, 2008).

The three groups of stakeholders addressed the issue of test use and consequence by providing their own perspectives. The type of data available controlled the amount and type of information for this level of inference. Through the questionnaire test takers were asked about the suitability and relevancy of ELPA for assessing workplace use of English in the public service. In addition, responses to items about test use and impact were also sought.

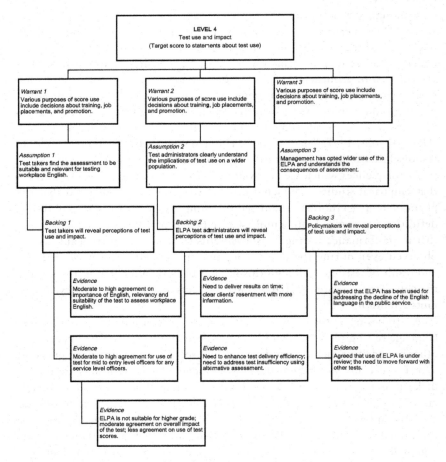

FIGURE 7.3 Evidence Supporting Level 4 Inference

The ELPA for the Malaysian Public Service **185**

Findings for this level as illustrated in Figure 7.3 suggest that test takers were positive about the use and the impact of the assessment on the public service. They also suggest slight differences in perceiving the criticality of English use at the workplace. While the Research and Development and PTD services thought use of English to be critical, the Education and Legal services did not share that view. Similar positive perceptions of test relevancy and suitability were evident across the four groups with all agreeing that ELPA should be used for entry to mid-level officers and not for senior level officers. As for items that enquired about test impact in general, test takers across all the four services were again generally positive about its impact. Moderate agreement about test use, test relevancy, test effectiveness, as well as test as a good indicator of language ability was noted for the whole group. However, test takers were less in agreement on the amount of information given on how the test scores would be interpreted and used. This was also echoed by ELPA administrators thus suggesting that information on test scores does not get to the end users who are the test takers. The current practice is for test scores to be provided as reports to the client agency for it to disseminate to their officers. Currently, the PSD provides test scores online for test takers to check.

Most criticism of test use and impact was from the ELPA administrators themselves although they provided a rich perspective of the internal goings-on in the world of test administration. Several issues with respect to test use and impact were raised including the need to enhance test delivery efficiency, allay client fear or resentment with more information, and address test insufficiency with alternate forms of assessment. Enhancing test delivery efficiency was a theme that came up repeatedly during the interviews.

From assignment of raters to the use of the different procedures and from preparation of test scores to the time to produce the reports, these processes need to be re-examined and improved. As for the overall perception of test administration as revealed in Level 1 inference, test takers were less favorable about the use of a paper-based test as currently practiced. This may suggest a need to use alternative forms of test delivery such as an online test. The ELPA administrators viewed insufficiency in terms of not having enough assessments to address the needs of different groups or services. This arose out of concerns for having to use ELPA on pockets or groups of officers who might find the test inadequate to address their needs especially for those who performed poorly. However, this view was not shared by the test takers. From the questionnaire data as reported earlier, test takers were generally in agreement that the ELPA test content was relevant to their workplace English language needs.

The findings from policy makers on test use and impact focused on several themes. The first was the overall purpose of using ELPA to address the decline of English language in the public service. This was perhaps the overarching goal

186 Kadeessa Abdul-Kadir

of using ELPA as well as encouraging and, in some cases, making it compulsory for English language competency testing of officers in an effort to promote the importance of being proficient in the language for global competitiveness. The policy makers needed an instrument regardless of its initial intended use and through ELPA they perceived that this has been achieved. They were in agreement that whatever policy instituted in relation to the assessment be reviewed based on feedback. The policy makers were also in agreement with ELPA administrators on the need to look for alternative forms of assessment although they differed on what these should take.

Research and Innovation

ELPA has been in existence for 20 years and much has evolved during that time. First there is the move from the original ELPA or ELPA 1.0 to ELPA 2.0. This change showed that the team was confident to move away from what was prescribed earlier to a model better suited to current needs. Bold measures such as introducing new tasks and moving away from what worked and what did not have become the way the team experimented with ELPA for it to remain relevant. With the need to assess different groups for different purposes such as those going for in-service training, INTAN's ELU will have to consider other test tasks for the different components to meet the needs of the various test takers. There has been much research and innovation since then, most of it for internal use and therefore not publicized outside the public service.

Using Multiple Rating Instruments

Research is being carried out on the need to revisit the scoring procedures to include both analytical and holistic scoring for the speaking module and to assess officers for different competencies and not just for linguistic purposes. For officers in the public service, the need to use strategic competence in their speaking and writing is being looked into and where possible, analytical rating scales for certain tasks introduced for the speaking module. Similarly for writing, we recognized the need to re-examine the analytical scale to remove some of the less appropriate discrete criteria such as mechanics and replace them with categories more appropriate to testing communicative writing. Findings from the interpretive argument approach (Abdul-Kadir, 2008) seem to suggest that raters viewed mechanics differently when scoring the writing tasks. Some were lenient and others were strict on errors such as spelling and punctuation. In addition, there is a general belief that given the time limit, first draft errors are expected in a paper-and-pen-based test such as ELPA.

Differentiating Further Language Abilities

There is currently a need for the testing team to re-examine the levels of proficiency since a larger number of officers fall in the "Adequate" rather than in the "Very Limited" bands. This could suggest some form of under-specification or under-valuing of the level of proficiency which could be a source of testing error (Fox, 2004). This could be addressed by broadening the levels in the Adequate band (High and Low) and eliminating the Very Limited band. Performance data collected since ELPA 2.0 was introduced seem to support this initial finding. Research into this area is being carried out using all the test scores from the different administrations including looking at the performance of officers on the Pre-ELPA online and correlating it with the ELPA scores for those who were selected. This research will change the way the ELPA results are reported and provide a more indicative way of describing proficiency levels as more officers fall in the broader Band 3 category. This will also implicate the way development or training is provided for all the band levels.

Digitizing ELPA

Efforts have also been undertaken to introduce an online version of the ELPA using available software. The problem was with the reading module where we faced certain constraints. One was the difficulty to place long texts for the reading-quickly section with candidates practically having to scroll to skim or scan for information within the time given. The other was the limited function of the interface available to actually ensure that the test items were presented in a way that is acceptable to the candidates.

Utilizing a Pre-ELPA Screening Test

The development and use of the Pre-ELPA Online Test provides another measure to validate ELPA's test score interpretation. This is seen as an innovative move to lessen the burden on INTAN's ELU and allow only test takers with a certain level of proficiency to take the ELPA. The results have been encouraging. Of the total number who sat for the online test and subsequently qualified for the ELPA, almost 30% made it to Band 4 and above with none being placed in the "Limited" or "Very limited" bands.

This online test consists of reading and structure items. It is a one-hour test with 50 multiple-choice questions. The ELU provides the online test development team with a steady bank of items for delivery of several versions of tests administered twice or three times a year depending on the number of candidates identified for fast-tracking. Currently efforts to make this online test more adaptable is being explored with results reporting on test reliability and internal consistency of the different versions.

188 Kadeessa Abdul-Kadir

Examining Emerging Competencies

An immediate task is to revisit the 1997 needs-analysis survey to determine whether there are emerging communication competencies required for the 21st century. This will be done through a public-service-wide online survey. The competencies required must also be in line with the needs of the public service. Currently, the move to Industry 4.0 and the requirement for digital capabilities is being studied and addressed in INTAN. There is very much the need to address new communicative competencies that are in line with individual digital capability readiness.

Exploring Qualitative Approaches to Test Validity

While much of the evidence to support the development and use of newer test versions rest heavily on the use of quantitative approaches such as item reliability, inter-rater estimates using correlations, rater severity using RASCH Model as well as looking at sources of variance using Generalizability Theory (G-Theory), very little qualitative approaches are used in ensuring content validity apart from using a standard pro-forma or a set of criteria as mentioned earlier for text selections. The use of discourse analysis through the applications of computational linguistic analysis will be explored. We are looking into the use of Coh-Metrix as way to analyze texts at multiple levels especially texts sourced for the reading assessment. Information from this type of analysis can certainly inform the testing team on the suitability of the texts used for reading quickly or reading carefully.

Another area of research that is greatly needed is to benchmark ELPA to the Common European Framework of Reference for Languages (CEFR) and other international language tests. Currently, there is a working reference on ELPA to tests relevant for comparison such as IELTS, TOEFL, and TOEIC based on the advice from and consultations with local experts.

An area that needs to be linked to the assessment is personal development. With so many assessments being administered, the future development of officers following the assessment is equally important. Since INTAN is a training organization, its ELU runs a range of courses addressing different skills as well as proficiency levels. One effort is to place these courses on the CEFR levels and also ELPA bands. At the moment, there is a recommendation for training for officers depending on their test scores such as remedial and enhancement training mainly for those who scored Band 3 and below. For those who scored in top Band 3 and also Band 4, enhancements which cater not only to their workplace needs but also their level of proficiency are recommended. More courses in line with the emerging competencies are in the pipeline especially those that require the embracing and mastering of digital capabilities in communication.

The ELPA for the Malaysian Public Service **189**

Perhaps the most important innovation and ongoing research is the use of the Interpretive Argument Approach in guiding and informing the different decisions taken during the test development, test appraisal, or evaluation phases. In each test version, the argument structure for the different levels of inferences is set up. As an example, the ELPA that was administered for potential In-service Training Scholarship holders has moved from the development to the evaluation phase. In the development phase, Levels 1 and 2 were investigated in terms of the scoring procedures and the generalizability of the test scores. The team is currently looking into the extrapolation phase where factors such as test takers' characteristics (grade level, scheme of service, and years of experience) affect performance on ELPA. As for test use and impact, perceptions of these are being sought from test takers and the different stakeholders.

More focused and continuous research into test development and management will be instituted to enable ELPA to be the sole measure of English competency for the public service. Efforts at strengthening the delivery of English language training and assessment for the public service have been stepped up with the establishment of the Centre for Language Excellence in August 2017 in INTAN. This will see the expansion of the English Language Unit with additional staffing and a more dynamic organizational structure focusing on research and language assessment as a core activity.

Critical Analysis

Some issues remain to be addressed in the efforts to make ELPA the sole localized measure of English competency for the public service. One is the totally home-grown and internal use of ELPA. Because ELPA is used within the Malaysian public service as an internal assessment, many outside the public service do not have access to the internal goings-on in its development and management. As there are few language testing experts in the public service outside of INTAN, members of the testing unit play a tripartite role as test developers, managers, and evaluators. In many validity inquiry situations, the responsibility for providing evidence for test use often rests with the test developers and it is during the test development phase that validity evidence is rigorously sought. For the ELPA, the testing members have the opportunity to be involved in every stage of test development including at its operational stage thus enabling them to view the issues related to test validity from a unique and multi-dimensional perspective. However, for the test to be credible and receive international recognition, it needs to be benchmarked against more established assessments through collaboration with other public services that offer similar assessments.

The other issue is the separation of the role of INTAN's ELU and the other stakeholders. The ELU is seen as the implementing body of ELPA whereas the other stakeholders are the decision-makers. As such in any policy or initiative made with respect to the assessment of English competency either through ELPA or other tests incorporated in the leadership development and assessment programs, the "wisdom of the stakeholders" overrides the professional advice given. For example, ELPA as a first screening instrument for fast-track purposes has to be used with caution since there are other factors that could affect or explain leadership success although language competency is one of them.

INTAN needs to expand the knowledge of the concept of validity to multiple stakeholders involved in the use of ELPA test results. Different stakeholders have a vague idea of validity of test score interpretations as evident when multiple requests for ELPA are made for administration in a short amount of time. Stakeholders and policy makers are often unaware of the different stages of the test development and also in the appraisal or test evaluation stage (Kane, 2006). Ensuring that they understand that validity is multi-faceted, ranging from concerns of construct representativeness, consistency between test construct and the target domain to issues of test use and impact, is important so that they are better informed for decision making. In addition, a better understanding of the concept of validity when they are directly or indirectly affected by the scores of an assessment would allow them to scrutinize the assessment using the same yardstick (or language) as do the validity theorists.

A final issue that needs to be addressed is the inclusion of the reading module in the ELPA assessment. The latest administration of ELPA to potential in-service scholarship holders reported that reading is the least relevant skill to be tested. Time pressure was noted as the factor that would affect performance on reading. This is because the test takers are expected to answer one or two questions within a short time period before being instructed to move on to the next question. The ELU needs to investigate the value of assessing the different skills as discrete skills or strategies. Perhaps it is time that reading should be considered a skill that is needed to perform a productive act such as writing or speaking. For ELPA integrating reading and writing might be an option or way forward to make reading reflect a more authentic workplace activity.

Developed as an instrument to assess the language proficiency of a small number of public service officers, ELPA is now the main driver in the English Language Testing System for the Malaysian Public Service. The experience in all aspects of test development and delivery over the last 20 years and the ability to continue to use ELPA as a useful and effective tool for assessing workplace language proficiency has helped INTAN's ELU to be recognized as a credible language testing provider for the public service. It is hoped that this recognition will enable INTAN's ELU to continue to strengthen and improve its operational excellence in the area of language testing locally and internationally.

References

Abdul-Kadir, K. (2008). *Framing a validity argument for test use and impact: The Malaysian public service experience* (Unpublished doctoral dissertation). University of Illinois at Urbana-Champaign.

Bachman, L. F., & Palmer, A. S. (1996). *Language testing in practice: Designing and developing useful language tests.* Oxford: Oxford University Press.

Bazerman, C. (2004). Speech acts, genres, and activity systems: How texts organize activity and people. In C. Bazerman & P. Prior (Eds.), *What writing does and how it does it: An introduction to analyzing texts and textual practices* (pp. 309–340). Mahwah, NJ: Lawrence Erlbaum.

Blyler, N. (1999). Research in professional communication: A post-process perspective. In T. Kent (Ed.), *Post-process theory: Beyond the writing-process paradigms* (pp. 65–79). Carbondale, IL: Southern Illinois University Press.

Chapelle, C. A., Enright, M. K., & Jamieson, J. (2007). *From validation research to a validity argument.* Paper presented at the 4th European Association for Language Testing and Assessment Conference, Sitges, Spain.

Douglas, D. (2000). *Assessing languages for specific purposes.* Cambridge, UK: Cambridge University Press.

Fox, J. (2004). Test decisions over time: Tracking validity. *Language Testing, 21*(4), 437–465.

Hamp-Lyons, L. (Ed.). (1991). *Assessing second language writing in academic contexts.* Norwood, NJ: Ablex Publishing Corporation.

Hamp-Lyons, L. (1997). Washback, impact and validity: Ethical concerns. *Language Testing, 14*, 295–303.

Hawkey, R. (2006). *Impact theory and practice.* Cambridge, UK: Cambridge University Press.

Kane, M. (2006). Validation. In R. L. Brennan (Ed.), *Educational measurement* (4th ed., pp. 17–64). New York, NY: American Council on Education and Macmillan.

Messick, S. (1989). Validity. In R. L. Linn (Ed.), *Educational measurement* (3rd ed., pp. 13–104). New York, NY: American Council on education and Macmillan.

Qi, L. (2005). Stakeholders' conflicting aims undermine the washback function of a high-stakes test. *Language Testing, 22*(2), 142–173.

Stansfield, C. W., & Wu, W. (2001). Towards authenticity of task in test development. *Language Testing, 18*(2), 187–206.

Toulmin, S. E. (2003). *The uses of argument* (updated ed.). Cambridge, UK: Cambridge University Press.

Turner, C. (2001). The need for impact studies of L2 performance testing and rating: Identifying areas of potential consequences at all levels of the testing cycle. In C. Elder, A. Brown, E. Grove, K. Hill, N. Iwashita, T. Lumley, T. McNamara, & K. O'Loughlin (Eds.), *Experimenting with uncertainty: Essays in honour of Alan Davies.* Cambridge, UK: Cambridge University Press.

Varghese, N. (1998). Evaluation vs. impact studies. In V. McKay & C. Treffgarne (Eds.), *Evaluating Impact* (pp. 47–54). London: Department of International Development.

Weir, C. J. (1983). The associated examinng board's test of English for academic purposes: An exercise in content validation events. In A. Hughes & D. Porter (Eds.), *Current developments in language testing* (pp. 147–153). London: Academic Press.

Weir, C. J. (2005). *Language testing and validation: An evidence-based approach*. Houndmills: Palgrave Macmillan.

Weir, C. J., & O'Sullivan, B. (2017). *Assessing English on the global stage*. Sheffield, UK: Equinox Publishing.

Weiss, C. H. (1998). *Evaluation: Methods for studying programs and policies*. Upper Saddle River, NJ: Prentice-Hall.

8

GLOBAL, LOCAL, OR "GLOCAL"

Alternative Pathways in English Language Test Provision

Cyril J. Weir

In the volume so far we have examined closely a number of individual tests developed locally in Asian countries. We have discussed the merits of each as regards their local appropriateness; underpinning validity research and evidence of innovation; quality management; and beneficial impact. It seems fitting in a conclusion chapter to consider where such tests sit in the wider scheme of things and whether we might favor the approach they have adopted as compared to other options. Accordingly, in this final chapter we reflect critically on the various pathways individual countries might take with regard to the provision of English language tests in their own systems. Three approaches are considered: the global, the local, and the "glocal," a more recent amalgam of the two. This concluding chapter also attempts to tease out some of the additional threads that emerge from Chapters 2–7; these threads link themes that are repeated across the chapters and they trace a picture which points to the positive impact and legacy of localized or glocalized tests.

The Globalized Test

Globalization describes:

> a situation in which available goods and services, or social and cultural influences, gradually become similar in all parts of the world.
>
> *dictionary.cambridge.org (n.d.)*

So far in this volume, we have looked at tests, which were developed specifically with their local context in mind *ab initio*. We start this final chapter by reminding ourselves that as well as these localized test products, there are global

194 Cyril J. Weir

test providers operating across the language proficiency range whose stated mission is to increase recognition of their own global tests all around the world. We would emphasize straightaway that neither type, local or global, can automatically be considered superior to the other. Their value and attractiveness are dependent on the extent to which they individually exhibit *fitness for purpose* in terms of the desiderata used throughout this volume for a good test: that they exhibit quality management; are underpinned by validation research; provide positive impact; have an alertness to innovation possibilities; and demonstrate appropriateness for the local context.

There are a number of tests on the market that have globalization as their intention, and we will briefly describe the best known and most reputable of these: TOEFL iBT, Cambridge English Examinations, and IELTS. The purpose of this exercise is to clarify what a global test is and does and for whom, so that a comparison can be made with the local tests detailed in this volume. However, as we have noted, no inferences should be drawn *a priori* about their being in any way innately superior to local tests.

Internet-based Test of English as a Foreign Language (TOEFL iBT)

The TOEFL iBT is a test of Standard American English (SAE) primarily intended to measure the English language ability of non-native speakers wishing to enroll in English-speaking universities, but is also used for immigration purposes in a number of countries, for example, Australia. Since its introduction in late 2005, the iBT format has progressively replaced the computer-based tests (CBT) and paper-based tests (PBT), although paper-based testing is still used in selected areas (see www.ets.org/toefl/ibt/about).

TOEFL iBT measures the ability to use and understand Standard American English (SAE) at the university level, evaluating how well listening, reading, writing, and speaking skills can be combined to perform academic tasks. TOEFL iBT targets a range of English language proficiency levels (rather than just a single level), covering the B1, B2, and C1 levels of the CEFR. Candidates are tested on all four skills and have to perform tasks that integrate more than one skill, such as reading and listening in order to speak or write in response to a question prompt. The Reading test (60–80 minutes) involves reading passages from academic texts and answering questions. The Listening test (60–90 minutes) involves listening to lectures, classroom discussions and conversations, then answering questions. The Writing test (50 minutes) involves writing two essay responses based on reading and listening input to support an opinion. The Speaking test (20 minutes) comprises six short tasks requiring a candidate to express an opinion on a familiar topic and to speak or answer questions drawing on reading and listening input. The Speaking test is taken on a computer in response to recorded input, and it is therefore not reciprocally interactive in the way that a face-to-face interview with a human interlocutor can be.

TOEFL iBT is produced and administered by Educational Testing Service (ETS) in the U.S. and test scores are accepted by more than 10,000 universities, colleges, agencies, and other institutions in over 130 countries around the world. More than 30 million people have taken TOEFL since its inception.

Cambridge Assessment English Examinations

Cambridge Assessment English Examinations offer another example of the global approach to English language testing (www.cambridgeenglish.org). For over a hundred years, Cambridge has been a respected purveyor of international English tests (see Weir, Vidaković, & Galaczi, 2013, for a full history covering 1913–2012). The University of Cambridge Local Examinations Syndicate (UCLES) first entered the market in 1913 with the advanced level *Certificate of Proficiency* in English (CPE) administered to three candidates. Weir (2013) provides detail of the efforts of Cambridge English, ably abetted by the British Council, to spread British influence around the world over the course of the 20th century through the promotion of its international English language examinations:

- 1913: Certificate of Proficiency in English (CPE) (C2 Level CEFR)
- 1939: Lower Certificate in English (LCE), rebranded as First Certificate in English (FCE) in 1975 (B2 Level CEFR)
- 1980: Preliminary English Test (PET) (B1 Level CEFR)
- 1991: Certificate in Advanced English (CAE) (C1 Level CEFR)
- 1994: Key English Test (KET) (A2 Level CEFR)
- 1989: IELTS (in cooperation with the British Council and IDP Australia)

The late 20th century multi-level developments in Cambridge Examinations were a result of the changing political and economic context in Europe. Progress towards integration with the European Economic Community from the 1970s onwards, with its focus on *standardization* across national boundaries, was accompanied by a perceived need on the part of governmental agencies to define language teaching and learning goals more precisely at different levels of proficiency. This required the specification of linguistic performance at differing levels of ability from beginner to advanced (A1 to C2 in CEFR terms). European developments had a marked effect on the work of examination boards in the United Kingdom, not least in the way they had to conceptualize language constructs in a more granular fashion, in order to accommodate multi-level tests.

Together with the Can-do Project of the Association of Language Testers in Europe (ALTE), the development of the Common European Framework of Reference for Languages (CEFR) (Council of Europe, 2001) provided a clearer definition of what these global "general" proficiency levels meant, both in

196 Cyril J. Weir

English and in other widely spoken European languages. As a result of attempts to link Cambridge examinations to the five ALTE levels and subsequently to the six Council of Europe levels, the UCLES General English test proficiency levels were to become clearer and more explicit (see Jones, 2000, 2001, 2002; Jones & Hirtzel, 2001, for details of the ALTE framework; Alderson, 2002; Council of Europe, 2001; North, 2000, 2002, for details of the CEFR).

By relating examinations to a single common framework (i.e., the CEFR), the interpretation of levels by the end users of test certificates, such as employers, was facilitated. This made these qualifications more global and usable and increased people's potential mobility within the European Community and beyond.

The growth of Cambridge English Examinations in the international market place went hand in glove with the seemingly inevitable rise of English as a global language. Weir and O'Sullivan (2017, p. 10) describe how a combination of economic, political, social, and technological factors contributed to the global spread of English in the 19th and 20th centuries (British Council, 2013; Brutt-Griffler, 2002; Howatt & Widdowson, 2004). This globalization of English was increasingly accompanied by a growing interest in securing recognized qualifications in the language in upwardly mobile sections of society in many countries; the attraction of passing a reputable international English language test linked to a prestigious university was clear. The Cambridge Assessment English website (www.cambridgeenglish.org), January 2018, evidences the global reach of Cambridge English language tests:

> Over 5 million Cambridge English exams are taken each year in 130 countries. Around the world, more than 20,000 universities, employers, government ministries and other organisations rely on Cambridge English qualifications as proof of English language ability.

The development of Cambridge Assessment English examinations in the 20th century provides a good example of a globalized, English-language, knowledge product which Cambridge with the help of the British Council sought to spread around the world. A number of governments have adopted the Cambridge General English examinations as a global alternative and incorporated them into their own educational systems especially in Europe (see Hawkey, 2006; Hawkey & Milanovic, 2013).

IELTS

Another highly researched and generally admired global product managed by Cambridge Assessment English (in partnership with the British Council and IDP Australia) is the IELTS test, primarily used for establishing the language proficiency of students wishing to enter tertiary level English medium study.

As the test became better known and increasingly accepted by receiving institutions around the world, the numbers taking IELTS grew rapidly from 14,000 candidates when it was first administered in 1989. By 2015, more than 2.7 million IELTS tests were completed annually by candidates in around 140 countries (www.ielts.org/media_centre.aspx) and in 2018 the numbers exceeded three million. Almost three-quarters of IELTS candidates are seeking to prove their English language ability for academic purposes, but the test is also used to meet English language qualification requirements for professional and immigration purposes. The growth in test numbers reflects the strong growth in the number of organizations turning to IELTS to meet their needs for language proficiency assessment. As of August 30, 2016, more than 9,000 education institutions, faculties, government agencies, and professional organizations around the world recognized the IELTS test (see Weir & O'Sullivan, 2017, for details).

But Are These Global Tests Fit for Purpose?

The attractions of adopting well respected global examinations for use in one's own country are not hard to understand: they are general, broad-spectrum proficiency tests based on reasonably clear specifications of the level(s) of proficiency that is (are) being targeted; they are usually professionally produced and validated by world-leading, well-resourced examination boards with considerable history, expertise and experience; they are internationally transportable qualifications with high currency; they are, with few exceptions, administered securely and efficiently across the world by respected and prestigious international organizations and in many cases an online version of the examination is available; they are systematically linked to international standards like the CEFR and ALTE; and, they are developed with the support of effective quality management systems. For example, each of the Cambridge examinations is supported by the extensive research detailed in the four volumes on constructs in the Studies in Language Testing (SiLT) series (Shaw & Weir, 2007, on writing; Khalifa & Weir, 2009, on reading; Taylor (Ed.), 2011, on speaking; Geranpayeh & Taylor (Eds.), 2013, on listening). TOEFL is similarly underpinned by an extensive research program (for example Biber et al., 2004; Cumming, Grant, Mulcahy-Ernt, & Powers, 2004; Cumming et al., 2005; Enright et al., 2000; Hamp-Lyons & Kroll, 1997; Hudson, 1996). These global tests meet the professional expectations of the language testing field (ALTE standards, 2007; American Educational Research Association et al. Standards, 2014; EALTA Guidelines, 2006; ILTA Code of Ethics, 2000/2018).

As regards most of the key desiderata for a language test discussed in this volume in terms of quality management, validation research, innovation, and impact, TOEFL iBT, the Cambridge General English tests, and IELTS would seem to meet the expectations of fitness for purpose, *but with one telling exception*: they are general, broad-spectrum proficiency tests intended for multiple

198 Cyril J. Weir

users in many different contexts. In other words, they are not *localized* for a particular context (either country or specific domain). In Hamlet's immortal words, *there's the rub.*

Globalization has inevitably led to English native speaker linguistic standards and cultural norms, especially those of the "inner circle" countries, such as the UK or the U.S., being included in these global tests as the goals for the "norm-dependent" or "third and expanding circle" countries where English is being learned as a foreign language for the purposes of international communication, for example, China, Japan, Korea (Kachru, 2005; Kumaravadivelu, 2008). In inner-circle-produced tests, European or American styles of living, learning, and thinking are often introduced as standardized and desirable. As Dendrinos (2013, p. 5) explains:

> The content of international testing is not questioned either, with regard to whether or to how well it responds to the experiences, literacies and needs of local stakeholders. Nor is it read critically for its ideological underpinnings, even though it is without doubt that tests are not value-free or ideology-free products. . . . Texts and images used in tests carry ideological meanings, while the choice of subject matter and text type, as well as the linguistic choices in texts, construe worlds and realities for the test-taker.

Dendrinos (2013, p. 13) cites Balourdi (2012) as having "provided ample linguistic evidence to support the claim that there are ideological inscriptions in test texts that linguistically construe different realities." The issue for Dendrinos is the question of whom within a society "should have control over the linguistic construction of reality."

She crucially identifies the potentially fatal flaw in the global test (2013, p. 6):

> The final point to be made with regard to international proficiency testing is that it is by default a monolingual project. It does not involve adjustments to the cultural, linguistic or other needs of particular domestic markets because this would mean that the same product could not be sold in different cultures.

Dendrinos (2011, pp. 50–53) argues that "the exam papers of the international exam batteries are always constructed as monolingual instruments, intended to measure test-takers' language competence or performance in a single language," and there is "a need for the development and assessment of literacies required in an increasingly globalized world, with its diversity of communication technologies and its multilingual contexts." She advocates more examination batteries for language competence certification include tests or activities aiming to measure test-takers' performance in written and spoken mediation.

Global, Local, or "Glocal" 199

To be strictly accurate, Cambridge CPE had mediational translation tests into and out of English in numerous languages, in the countries where the exam was administered, for over 60 years from 1913 in two exams each lasting two hours. However, in the end the practical considerations of catering for large numbers of languages saw their demise in 1975. So "always constructed" was not strictly true for the past, but holds true for the present. It is thus one area where the localized test has a clear advantage in that it can cater to a small number of other languages to be used for written and spoken mediation alongside English.

There is a growing body of opinion (including the proponents of the test developments described in this volume) which questions globalized tests and instead advocates the importance of including local content, norms, and values into teaching materials and tests (see Brown & Lumley, 1998; Canagarajah, 2006; Clyne & Sharifian, 2008; Dendrinos, 2011, 2013; Gray, 2002; Hino, 2016; Lowenberg, 2002; Tsou, 2015; Zafar Khan, 2009). The reaction is against the earlier "one-size-fits-all" global approach to language testing in favor of a bespoke test, where the aim is for best fit with the particular needs/demands of a local context (either specific domain or culture).

Though fitness for purpose is a testing mantra that is sometimes "more honor'd in the breach than the observance," the current research and thought leaders at Cambridge Assessment English are clearly aware that "one test does not fit all." Cambridge English's *Principles of Good Practice* (2016) details how Cambridge has developed tests both for general and specific purposes (see Davies, 2008, on IELTS; O'Sullivan, 2006, on Business English tests for examples of the latter). Now with a portfolio of over twenty different exams, Cambridge aims at "providing the right assessment for the right person." Cambridge English's *Principles of Good Practice* (2016, p. 3) unequivocally states that "Tests need to be fit for purpose, offering users a range of solutions that meet diverse needs." However, even with these best intentions, Cambridge has not been immune from criticism of the uses made of some of the many tests for which it is responsible. For example, the fitness for purpose of IELTS, for certain of its user groups, has been questioned.

Moore, Morton, Hall, and Wallis (2015) looked at the suitability of IELTS for use with those involved in professional work across a range of occupational areas as well as those in the academic domain (see also Read & Wette, 2009, for similar findings). While noting a number of similarities in literacy demands between the two groups, they found (2015, p. 1):

> The main differences noted related to the highly transactional nature of professional communications.

And they suggest a radical solution might be to

> work towards developing a separate IELTS test for general professional employment purposes.

The use of IELTS in the teaching profession has also been the subject of research. Sawyer and Singh (2011) investigated stakeholders' perceptions of the role of IELTS in the selection process of international students for teacher education courses in Australia. This study found that the student teachers required a wide range of English language/communication skills for practicum classes beyond those needed for academic success, including familiarity with colloquial idiom in a school context and the discipline-specific discourse of particular subjects, as well as the ability to respond spontaneously in classroom interactions with students.

As well as concerns about its suitability for assessing medical staff and other professions, further questions have been raised, for example, about its suitability for assessing lower level EAP students in the Middle East. Morrow (2017, p. 1) notes:

> [IELTS] does not appear to fully address the specific needs and issues of students and universities in the United Arab Emirates . . . its influence on instructional and assessment practices has grown . . . in ways that do not seem to be completely congruent with the needs of low-level English learners who are about to begin studies in English-medium universities . . . the advanced linguistic demands of the IELTS exam, its equal weighting of scores from the four skill-based sections, and the exam's general communicative orientation are not well-suited for making valid and reliable decisions about the readiness of Arab students to begin college-level studies in English.

In fact this desire for contextually appropriate and financially affordable local EAP tests has led to the development of home grown alternatives to TOEFL iBT and IELTS, in many countries worldwide for example: the Malaysian University English Test (MUET) (Malaysian Examinations Council, 2015); the Test of English for Academic Purposes (TEAP) in Japan (see Green, 2014; Nakatsuhara, 2014a, 2014b; Taylor, 2014; Weir, 2014); the Diagnostic English Language Assessment (DELA), University of Melbourne, the University of Auckland's Diagnostic English Language Needs Assessment (DELNA) (See Read, 2015, for discussion of these and further examples of other locally produced diagnostic EAP tests); the Exaver test in Mexico (Abad Florescano, Dunne, & Grounds, 2004); internal tests in Turkish universities, for example, at Boğaziçi (Hughes, 1988) and Bilkent (Kantarcıoğlu, Thomas, O'Dwyer, & O'Sullivan, 2010; O'Dwyer, 2008), and at Zayed University in the UAE (O'Sullivan, 2005).

Read (2015) argues convincingly that in many cases the motivation for these institutional localized tests was the need for a post selection diagnostic instrument (as in fact performed previously by ELTS the precursor of IELTS when it was used by the British Council 1980–1989 to select students for awards and then to determine how much language help was needed by recipients of awards before programs started. See Read, 2015, p. 126). This function had been lost in the transformation of IELTS into to a pre-admission gate-keeping instrument testing general proficiency rather than academic English, the so called "IELTS compromise" post 1995 (Read, 2015, pp. 4, 29–30).

It is not to say that global tests, such as IELTS, can never be locally appropriate, but this is not a given especially with their general rather than academic orientation. Any such claims for local appropriateness would need to be based on rigorous empirical evidence rather than assertion.

From our examples, it is clear that the use of broad-spectrum global tests (e.g., iBT TOEFL, IELTS, or Cambridge English Qualifications) may not always provide the best fit for specific/local (domain or culture) testing needs. Where this is the case, a different local pathway is required. We next turn to the scenario of localized tests that has been the focus of the earlier chapters in this volume. We reflect on how far these localized tests have furnished evidence that they are fit for purpose in their own particular local contexts.

The Localized Test

Contributors to this volume were asked to critically evaluate the ways their tests were localized, that is, made congruent with the socio-cultural contexts in their own countries. They were asked to explore in what ways and why these localized tests were more appropriate than global tests aimed at similar categories of students, which were international in orientation and not country specific.

As well as financial considerations, with the locally developed tests being more affordable for local candidates, a number of clear lines of argument emerged. Firstly, many of the tests were seen to fulfill an important role in the delivery and evaluation of the national English language curriculum, meshing closely at various levels with a country's educational system. With the GEPT in Taiwan and the EIKEN Tests in Japan, the tests at the various CEFR levels are intended to match the English language curriculum in the school system. In China, the CET is intended to address the same specification as the College English program for tertiary level students. As such they might be readily conceived of as achievement tests rather than broad-spectrum general language proficiency tests, and crucially more fit for purpose than externally available general proficiency tests, such as the Cambridge General English tests.

Another clear example of localization is the job-related English for Specific Purposes test developed for use in a very specific context in-country. Such a localized test was developed for public service employees in Malaysia where the specification for the ELPA test was based on a target situation analysis of what these employees had to do in their jobs in the Malaysian Public Service.

202 Cyril J. Weir

Specific Linguistic Features That Appeared in One or More of the Local Tests

Arising out of a close relationship between test and local context, not surprisingly the linguistic and cultural features of the localized tests in Chapters 2–7 are often in line with specific local language norms and features of language use in the classroom or work situations. Localization impacts on cognitive and contextual parameters in different ways in each test.

Linguistic features:

- Phases and levels of cognitive processing across the four skills have been adapted.

    For example, the TEAP test in Japan for university entrance was deliberately aimed at the B1 level to match the level of students exiting the secondary system, with B2 tasks to differentiate the better performing students. Compare this with IELTS where items tend to focus on the B2 and C1 levels and iBT TOEFL with a focus on B1 to C1, which is beyond the level at which most Japanese school leavers are capable of operating.
- Focus has been targeted on problematic lexico-grammatical areas particular to a country, as in the Korean TEPS test.
- Certain key words including proper nouns, words describing institutions and words that reflected unfamiliar cultural practices have been changed into words that are more familiar to the participants (Al-Fallay, 1994; Chihara, Sakurai, & Oller, 1989; Sasaki, 2000; Steffensen, Joag-Dev, & Anderson, 1979). Changing words that might be associated with a specific culture, according to these authors included references to

    a. names for specific people, places and products (Rice Krispies; the city of Chicago);
    b. specific historical events or periods (the Norman Conquest; football-related violence in the 1970s);
    c. local institutions (the probation service; the House of Lords);
    d. locally familiar objects (breakfast cereals; sharp suits);
    e. locally situated social practices (window shopping; children in the classroom undertaking problem-solving activities in pairs); and
    f. idiomatic language including culturally specific references (milestone research; professional soap boxes).

- Localized rating scales are used. For example, pronunciation in speaking might relate to local norms. This is the case for the GEPT and the CET. They accept local accent as long as the production is comprehensible. They do not expect native-like pronunciation.
- Local raters are attuned to local variants.

Global, Local, or "Glocal" **203**

- Rubrics can be used in the host language as is the case with the lower levels of the GEPT.
- Familiar local names can be used, especially in listening.
- Local accents can be used in some listening tests to cut down the time and effort candidates need to attune. This is not the case with the CET or GEPT.
- Topics are accessible and selected with regard to local needs.
- Visuals that are culturally, socially, and geographically appropriate to the country may also be included.
- There is cultural affinity of test content; cultural experiences of specific groups of learners and teachers can be taken into account (Dendrinos, 2013).
- Content knowledge is appropriate to the test taking population. For example, consideration is given to students in rural areas who have not followed a standard curriculum. Content can relate to learners' "previous experiences, competencies and skills, areas of life world knowledge, types of literacies and social needs." (Dendrinos, 2013)
- "Localized tests can avoid the preoccupation with typical or even stereotypical aspects of British or American culture, most people using English in their own countries to communicate with others for whom English is also a foreign language." (Dendrinos, 2013)
- Testing of different foreign languages, not just English, can be done in a uniform manner as is described in the chapter on VSTEP in Vietnam, using the same specifications, under the same quality management system.
- Cross-linguistic mediation can be tested. Dendrinos (2006, 2011, p. 3) describes mediation as the "act of extracting meaning from visual or verbal texts in one language, and relaying it in another, so as to facilitate communication." This is the case for the task of picture description in the elementary level of GEPT Writing and the intermediate level of GEPT Speaking. A visual prompt accompanied with rubrics in Chinese are provided. CET written tests in both Band 4 and Band 6 have tasks of "paragraph translation": a 30-minute task of translation from Chinese into English.

Non-linguistic features:

- Local tests ensure accessibility to all test-takers by providing numerous test centers nationwide.
- The fees of local tests are kept lower than those of international tests to ensure affordability for local test-takers. See Chapter 4 for VSTEP's pricing structure in Vietnam.
- Tests are administered at multiple times throughout the year or within the same day.
- Information regarding the tests is provided to stakeholders in the local language.

204 Cyril J. Weir

More Than Just a Local Test?

In our earlier discussion of globalized tests, we identified a number of activities as being necessary for a language test to meet international standards. The contributors to this volume were each asked to address the most important of these dimensions in relation to influential local language tests they had conceived of and developed for use in their own countries. We next provide an overview of the tests in terms of four core desiderata: quality management, validation research, innovation, and impact and washback.

Quality Management

Whoever develops a test, whomever a test is developed for, and whatever type of test is on offer, the quality of the product is paramount. The localized test developers who contributed to this volume are all well aware that they have the same responsibility as global test developers to ensure that generic quality standards are met. They all recognize the need to create and implement a Quality Management System (QMS) whose purpose is to improve the products and/or services of their organization in order to meet the requirements of their customers in the most effective and appropriate ways, and to do so in a well-planned and focused manner.

The Association of Language Testers in Europe (ALTE) provides clear and specific guidelines for achieving test quality. It has made strenuous efforts to define a quality threshold for the examinations produced by its members. One of ALTE's aims since 1990 has been to establish common standards for all stages of the language-testing process (see ALTE, 2007). To achieve this, members are audited by other ALTE members against a set of minimum standards for establishing quality profiles in ALTE examinations. ALTE members are now required to explain how their examinations meet these standards. Evidence to back up the argument is also required (see also ALTE, 1993/2001, 1994, 1998; ALTE/Council of Europe, 1997; Van Avermaet, Kuijper, & Saville, 2004). Evidence of quality has to be generated in the areas of

- test construction;
- administration and logistics;
- marking and grading;
- test analysis; and
- communication with stakeholders.

The developers of the tests reviewed in this volume have similarly addressed quality control and management issues in these areas in relation to their own tests. Some, like EIKEN, GEPT, TEPS, and the CET already have highly developed quality management systems in place, others like the ELPA and

VSTEP are consciously developing their systems in the right direction. For each of the examinations in this volume, developers identified any areas of quality management that are in need of improvement in the final section at the end of each chapter and made suggestions as to how this will be achieved.

In the Academic Forum on English Language Testing in Asia (AFELTA), discussion is taking place about developing a set of standards that will be more suitable than ALTE's for the Asian context. This is one of the future directions which all of these six local tests need to consider soon.

Validation Research

The extensive research carried out on the CET and the GEPT is impressive. EIKEN and TEPS too, in the 21st Century, have embarked on a similar research based path towards validating their suites of tests, and the new TEAP in Japan is beginning to build a body of research evidence for validity claims regarding the scores produced. Smaller tests such as the ELPA and VSTEP do not have the same resources or personnel to match these large-scale testing institutions, but there is evidence of a commitment to carrying out solid research (e.g., in the argument based approach to validity in the ELPA and VSTEP) to enhance the validation of each test.

It is perhaps worth noting at this point how in-country initiatives to create local "home-grown" tests, such as those described and discussed in this volume, have proven an important catalyst for the development of local research capabilities across Asia over the past two decades. In some parts of the region at the start of this century there existed relatively little home-based knowledge and expertise relating to test development and validation activity. Research skills and opportunities could sometimes only be accessed and acquired if Asian test developers and students travelled abroad to countries such as the UK, the U.S., and Australia in order to complete a PhD or to work for an extended period overseas as a visiting scholar or "research apprentice." The situation is very different today, however. A number of key figures in the language testing communities in Asia may have originally acquired their research training and experience overseas but since then they have successfully developed or expanded the research capacity and capabilities in their own contexts and a strong professional cadre of researchers can be found within local assessment agencies and universities. During the Language Testing Research Colloquium (LTRC) in Amsterdam in June 2014, a working group of language assessment specialists in Asia decided to form an association to promote language assessment activities in their region. After an initial meeting, the Asian Association for Language Assessment (AALA) was established and an Executive Board was formed. Since then, AALA has grown steadily and now boasts over 300 individual members from various countries and regions not only in Asia but also in

206 Cyril J. Weir

other parts of the world. The general purpose of the association is to promote language assessment in Asia by:

- offering students and faculty in colleges and universities opportunities to understand and present current research and practice;
- offering professional staff in assessment agencies opportunities to understand and present current research and practice;
- conducting an annual conference and other events in the region to promote interaction and communication among students, faculty, and professionals;
- promoting professional publications that advance theory and practice; and
- advocating for the ethical use of assessments and assessment use.

Since its establishment in 2014, annual AALA conferences have been held in Hangzhou, Bangkok, Bali, Taipei, Shanghai, and Hanoi. In 2016 the association established two student awards, the AALA Best Student Paper Award and the AALA Best Student Poster Award, as well as the AALA Outstanding Dissertation Award. The AALA Student Committee publishes a biannual newsletter, *In Conversation*, in order to promote engagement of Student Members in the association's activities. The establishment and rapid growth of AALA testifies to the energy and commitment of language testing professionals in Asia, many of whom now promote and support international research projects (the list of current Executive Board members makes impressive reading!). Their breadth of experience and expertise is also likely to stimulate more locally initiated and locally conducted research into assessment, suggesting a bright future for language testing validation research across Asia.

Innovation

Just as it is difficult to turn around an oil tanker, global testing organizations which have been in existence a long time often find it more difficult to make changes. A case in point is the IELTS, where the listening and reading components have not changed very much since it was launched in 1989 despite the fields of listening and reading having moved on considerably in that period.

The tests featured in this volume have been able to respond in a more innovative fashion to developments in the field of language teaching and applied linguistics. We have seen how early in the 21st century, the GEPT introduced state-of-the-art features into its tests, namely, a dedicated *expeditious* reading paper and integrated reading-into-writing tasks assessing the ability to build an intertextual interpretation from multiple non-verbal and verbal sources. The CET has resorted to technology to combat malfeasance, to improve its marking systems, and to deliver speaking tests on an industrial scale. Eiken has developed TEAP, a state-of-the-art English for Academic Purposes test, where, in its writing test, the candidate's ability to cope with intertextuality is the central focus. *Knowledge transformation* is required rather than *knowledge telling*, as seen in other tests such as IELTS. The construct measured is thereby considerably closer to the construct of writing in academia. Tests which are locally produced are often more easily able to incorporate innovative approaches, whether in terms of creating new and relevant task formats involving the skills of mediation or multimedia input, or in terms of developing sophisticated procedures for test delivery and processing. Other sources for innovation in test design could include the application of locally developed corpora of learner language or teaching materials (see, for example, Chapter 2 and the role of corpora development with regard to GEPT).

Impact and Washback

Alderson and Wall (1993, p. 121) suggest that the term "washback" should be limited to the influences the test might have on teaching, teachers, and learning (including curriculum and materials), and this seems now to be generally accepted. Bachman and Palmer (1996, p. 29) saw "impact" as operating on two levels:

1. "a socio-cultural level, in terms of educational systems and society in general" (macro level);
2. "a local and personal level, in terms of the people who are directly affected by tests and their results" (micro level).

Wall's (1997) and Hamp-Lyons' (1997) concept of impact appears to reflect Bachman and Palmer's (1996), namely test effects on "educational systems and society in general" as well as "the local and personal level." Impact might thus be seen as a superordinate, which subsumes washback. Impact is concerned with "wider influences," with the macro contexts in society, as well as with the micro contexts of the classroom and the school, whereas washback focuses rather more narrowly on the latter (see Hamp-Lyons, 2000; Hawkey, 2006).

We might speculate that the locally produced tests presented in this volume are likely to have had a positive impact on a broad range of stakeholders in a variety of ways. In terms of potential impact at the "macro level," it is clear that the Asian tests are generally designed to be closely linked to local teaching and learning systems as part of a national strategy to raise educational standards, thus taking careful account of local priorities and considerations. The aim in some cases is to improve existing approaches to assessment (adding in a previously absent speaking or listening test) or to promote assessment for learning in school or university (including the provision of diagnostic feedback). At the "micro level," we might choose to highlight the impact of the locally produced tests on teachers, teaching, and learning across Asia. Inviting teachers and teacher trainers to become directly involved in test development, perhaps

208 Cyril J. Weir

through drafting test items or tasks as members of an item-writing team, or by becoming assessors for a speaking or writing test, offers a valuable opportunity to develop assessment literacy within a local teaching/learning context and to enhance language teacher training and ongoing professional development.

Examples of early washback research for the Asian tests under consideration include Yang and Weir (1998), who led a comprehensive validation study of the College English Test (CET) in China in the 1990s where one examination board attempted to generate empirical evidence on the value of its tests as perceived by a variety of its stakeholders, for example, end users of test results in universities and the business world (see also Weir, Yang, & Jin, 2000). The extensive research driven validation of the GEPT is exemplary in its attempt to generate validation evidence for its exams (e.g., see Brunfaut & Harding, 2014; Qian, 2014; Weir, Chan, & Nakatsuhara, 2013; Wu, 2014; Yu & Lin, 2014). Similarly, the development of the new TEAP in Japan had a rich and growing research base to build on (see Green, 2014; Nakatsuhara, 2014a, 2014b; Taylor, 2014; Weir, 2014).

What seems clear from Chapters 2 to 7 and the discussion so far in this section is that as well as addressing many of the linguistic and socio-cultural attributes of their local context, all of our six tests from Asia, just as the global tests at Cambridge and ETS, have sought to meet the requirements of various international standards of assessment (ALTE, 1998; American Educational Research Association et al. Standards, 2014; EALTA Guidelines, 2006; ILTA guidelines, 2007), in terms of operationalizing quality management systems; a concern for positive washback and impact; carrying out validation research; and a commitment to improving their testing products. Furthermore, as we have seen in each of the previous chapters, the local owners of these tests have invariably sought the involvement of internationally recognized language testing experts in the design and development of their tests to complement the global and local perspectives provided by leading domestic educators and scholars.

So, inevitably we are forced to ask ourselves, is the soubriquet *local* the most appropriate label for what these tests are? Would they in fact be better conceived of as testing hybrids: simultaneously both global and local.

"Glocalization": Think Globally, Act Locally

Glocalization has been described as the process of creating a product or service with a global perspective in mind, while customizing it to fit "perfectly" in a local market. The term was originally coined to refer to a business, organization, or community that is ready to think globally and act locally. This blending of global and local vision results in the hybrid glocal , which emphasizes the idea that a product or service is more likely to succeed when it is adapted specifically—*glocalized*—to the locality or culture in which it will be marketed. The Wikipedia entry on glocalization details how:

The concept comes from the Japanese word *dochakuka*, which means global localization. It originally referred to the adaptation of farming techniques to local conditions.

Wikipedia informs that:

> At a 1997 conference on "Globalization and Indigenous Culture," sociologist Roland Robertson [credited with coining this neologism] stated that glocalization means the simultaneity—the co-presence—of both universalizing and particularizing tendencies.

On closer examination of our field, the glocal phenomenon seems to manifest itself in two distinct ways in English language testing.

The first glocalization type refers to a scenario consonant with the definitions of glocal we have just presented, where global test providers have sought to localize their international products in order to provide a better fit with a particular local context. We will consider this variant under the heading *Glocalization Test Type 1*. This first approach involves the direct localization of global products, an approach not taken up by any of the contributors to this volume, but one that is gaining traction in the market place.

Glocalization Test Type 1: Localizing Global Products

Shi Xiuhua describes how (2013, p. 92):

> In this paradigm the local variations of the globalizing phenomena are always a mixture or amalgam produced by the dynamic interaction (glocalization) that takes place between the original global phenomena and the local conditions these phenomena encounter.

The Cambridge English publication *Principles of Good Practice* refers to this first glocal pathway. The handbook notes (2016, p. 6): "Cambridge English Language Assessment works with many national governments and other organizations to develop learning and testing solutions that meet their precise needs. Where these needs cannot be met using our existing services, we develop tailored solutions." The last sentence is perhaps the most telling for our narrative and just as is the case with the British Council's Aptis suite (see O'Sullivan & Dunlea, 2015, pp. 7–8), both organizations now seem well aware (in their professional cadres but perhaps less so in their marketing teams) that localization of their global products may be required to make a test fit for purpose in a particular context. In other words, one size does not fit all.

A similar tailored-solution paradigm shift is taking place in other domains. Global mega brands such as McDonald's have seen the commercial value of localizing their products: Seaweed Shaker Fries in Asia, Kiwi Burger (beef, tomato, fried egg, lettuce, tomato, and beetroot) in New Zealand, McTurco (two beef patties, vegetables, and cayenne pepper sauce on pita) in Turkey, Chicken Maharaja Mac (Big Mac with spicy grilled chicken instead of beef) in India, to name but a few. The ingredients of the products are altered in context-appropriate ways in different countries, but the international standards of McDonald's, with regard to taste, levels of hygiene, product quality, efficient delivery, and customer satisfaction are all maintained.

Most international test providers are prepared, and indeed would very much like, to offer a bespoke language testing service to clients in particular countries as long as numbers, fee structure, and logistics support this. O'Sullivan and Dunlea (2015, p. 8) provide a useful menu of **levels** of localization with specific reference to the Aptis General test developed by the British Council (see Table 0.1 in the Foreword of this volume). The Aptis General test is used in multiple contexts all over the world, but the British Council as a testing agency will make modifications to it in the light of local needs. Localization is used within the Aptis test system to refer to the ways in which particular test instruments are evaluated and, where it is considered necessary, adapted for use in particular contexts with particular populations to allow for particular decisions to be made.

This last variant in the British Council menu in fact seems out of sync with the other Type 1 examples, as, in this scenario, a test is constructed from scratch outside of the Aptis main suite umbrella directly for the local client. Rather than starting with the global (the Aptis General test) as in the other cases cited in this chapter, the starting point in this last option is the local context and global standards are a further layer that would be added on to this localized base. We will deal with this type of glocalization under the label *Glocalization Test Type 2*.

However, before looking at the Glocalization Type 2 tests, we need to consider carefully the issue of validation research in relation to Type 1 tests. To localize a global test is an issue in itself, but to prove the specific localization fits the purpose and introduces positive impact is even more demanding. The importance of validating a global test's localization is a *sine qua non*. It is not clear from its published research whether Aptis has fully investigated the validity of all of their localized versions.

An attempt was certainly made in cases of Taiwan (Wu, Yeh, Dunlea, & Spiby, 2016) and Vietnam (Dunlea et al., 2018) to investigate the suitability of extant Aptis for those local contexts. However, Dunlea (personal communication, April, 2016) admits:

> Where there is a lack of published evidence is on the less high-profile localization projects, which have been targeted at specific local cultural and L1 contexts. In these cases, the tests have been adapted at a Level 2 of localization, not changing the construct of the main test design, but working with local panels of experts to review item content to avoid

items which may disadvantage local candidates due to implicit cultural or background knowledge requirements. These are always project specific for use in one national or sub-national context. While there is a commitment to work with local partners to approach this kind of localization, it would be fair to say there is no public material investigating the impact and impressions of test-takers as with the 2 studies of use of Aptis General in Taiwan and Vietnam cited above . . . more light on these kinds of localization projects would be beneficial for the wider community.

Jessica Wu (personal communication, April, 2018), in fact questions whether the Aptis–GEPT report (Wu et al., 2016) itself presents sufficient evidence of the suitability of Aptis for the Taiwanese context:

> you will find it compares the construct between the two tests and a post-test survey of 140ish test-takers' perceptions of the two tests. There are some clear differences. For example, the findings show that for the listening input, test-takers stated a preference for accents more familiar to the Taiwanese context. See p. 2.
>
> The evidence is far too weak to support Aptis's local appropriateness for the Taiwanese context. I'd feel more comfortable to say that Aptis has made the first move to understand its compatibility with a local context, but it will need to move further to process localization (or make real localization happen) based on the study such as Aptis–GEPT in Taiwan and to continue checking if the localization brings positive impact to the local context.

Rachel Wu (personal communication, April, 2018) observes a number of current differences between GEPT and Aptis in the report (Wu et al., 2016), raising further doubt about the comparability of the two:

Test Results Are Very Different

The GEPT score data indicate that candidates generally scored higher on the listening test than on the reading test, and they scored higher on speaking than on writing. However, the results of the Aptis test indicate that the test-takers in this study received slightly higher scores on Aptis reading than listening, and they received higher scores on Aptis writing than speaking.

ANOVA Is Unable to Distinguish Some CEFR Levels in Aptis

The Aptis listening, reading and writing tests could distinguish between C, B2, and B1 groups successfully, but not A1, A2, and B1 groups. The speaking test could only distinguish among B2, B1, and A2. (p. 14)

212 Cyril J. Weir

Classification Is Inconsistent

Test-takers tended to achieve higher CEFR levels on the Aptis reading, listening, and writing tests than on the GEPT, and they tended to achieve lower CEFR levels on the Aptis speaking test than on the GEPT. (See p. 15, and Table 6 on p. 16)

Content Analyses Show Distinction From Each Other

Speaking: In terms of domains, the GEPT contained a greater variety of speaking tasks as the test level increased, while the Aptis tasks were either personal or public in domain (see p. 26 and Figure 12). In addition to covering more language functions at each level, the GEPT assessed three macro types of language functions: informational, interactional, and interaction-managing, while Aptis focused on the informational functions only (see p. 28, Table 14; also p. 35). Writing: In terms of domain, the GEPT covered the personal, public, and educational domains, while Aptis contained tasks in only the personal and educational domains (see p. 29 and Figure 16). The GEPT writing tasks were considered cognitively more challenging than Aptis since the GEPT was more specific in content and cultural focus, as well as more abstract than Aptis at most levels (see p. 35 and p. 29).

A great deal of work is necessary to establish the suitability of Global Type 1 tests for local use. It is obviously more difficult for an outside agency to conduct such research as it requires numerous research staff on the ground in the country concerned. However, just as we would expect Glocal Type 2 tests to demonstrate validity for the local context (as we have done in this volume), the same applies to Glocal Type 1 tests.

Glocalization Test Type 2: Globalizing Local Products

Type 2 glocal tests, like the tests described in Chapters 2–7, differ from Type 1 glocal tests in that they are rooted in the local context *ab initio*, but they also usually seek to meet the standards for test construction that have been developed internationally (ALTE, 1993/2001; American Educational Research Association et al. Standards, 2014; EALTA Guidelines, 2006; ILTA guidelines, 2007). In many cases they are also aligned to the CEFR (Council of Europe, 2001; Dunlea, 2015; Wu, 2011, 2014; Wu & Wu, 2010) or other external benchmarks (such as global tests at the same level) through rigorous linking procedures, which provides further criterion referenced evidence of their validity. As we see in earlier chapters, their developers invariably avail themselves of international testing expertise and routinely have recourse to current research findings in the testing literature and act upon these. In all these respects they are glocal tests as they conduct business according to both local and global considerations.

Glocal Type 2 tests would seem to differ from a pure form of the local test in a number of significant ways. In "purely" local tests, no consideration is paid to meeting external, "foreign" testing standards; no assistance is sought from outside testing experts or reference made to the international testing research literature and no account is taken of Standard English varieties of the "inner circle" countries. Glocal Type 2 tests to a greater or lesser extent address all of these. Furthermore, in local tests, the focus is almost entirely on indigenous cultural and social norms and situations. Whereas in glocal tests, while the local context prevails at the lower levels of proficiency to avoid the cognitive dissonance of alien cultures, at the higher levels appropriate global content/themes as well as local increasingly have a place perhaps in recognition of the international nature of many jobs/workplaces, international educational opportunities, and the business or geopolitical realities of our age. At higher levels, English in Asia is often used for communicating across cultures.

Dendrinos (2013, p. 8) is one of the first researchers to apply this concept of glocalization Type 2 to language testing, and she comments from a critical language testing perspective:

> Glocalisation involves locally operated schemes, set up to serve domestic social conditions and needs, which are informed by international research and assessment practices. The most obvious benefit of glocal exam suites is that they are low cost alternatives to profit-driven industrialised testing. The less obvious advantage, but perhaps more important, is their socially interested control over forms of knowledge and literacy.

One of the most interesting chapters in Weir and O'Sullivan's book on the involvement of the British Council with language testing 1945–2016 (2017) is the second chapter, which deals with the British Council's support for indigenous language testing projects around the world. Dendrinos (2013) might well have used any of the 19 projects reported in that chapter to support her argument for the value of glocalized tests built with outside support. Indeed, many of the tests discussed in this volume followed a similar pattern. ELPA was developed with the support of the Testing and Evaluation Unit (TEU) at Reading University and Rita Green and Don Porter in particular. TEAP in Japan was helped by professional input from Weir (2014) on writing, Fumiyo Nakatsuhara (2014a, 2014b) on speaking, Tony Green (2014) on washback and impact, and Lynda Taylor (2014) on reading. All of these external consultants are staff members in CRELLA, a world-leading research institute in testing according to HEFCE Panel D in the UK Research Excellence Framework (REF) 2014. Weir and Tony Woods from Reading University were earlier involved in the CET Validation Study in the early 1990s (see Yang & Weir, 1998) and later advice to CET was given by international testing experts such as Liz Hamp-Lyons. Weir was involved in the design and development of GEPT in Taiwan

214 Cyril J. Weir

from the outset particularly for the exams at the Advanced and Superior Levels, and subsequently so too were leading international testing figures such as Charles Alderson, Lyle Bachman, Antony Kunnan, and Tim McNamara. The TEPS test in Korea benefited from the input of J. D. Brown, and VSTEP in Vietnam from Fred Davidson and Mary Jane Hogan. In many cases then, the local tests discussed in this volume have benefited from outside assistance from leading language testers who have brought a global perspective to the local test development, which has complemented the global and local perspectives provided, by leading domestic educators and scholars.

Dendrinos (2013, p. 14) is at pains to point out, however:

> While glocal tests take into consideration international research findings and abide by supranational structures such as the CEFR, they make decisions regarding the test papers, which are meaningful for the specific society for which they are developed. Test developers in a glocal system know (through intuition and relevant research) candidates' cultural experiences, areas of lifeworld knowledge, types of literacies and social needs. Inevitably, they take all this into account when making decisions regarding test form and content, given that there is central concern about the types of competences, skills and strategies the groups of language learners they address need to develop. In other words, one of the most important characteristics of glocal testing, the KPG exams in particular, is that attention is relocated: from the language itself (as an abstract meaning system) to the user (as a meaning-maker).

Questions of Perception

Elder and Harding (2008, p. 34.3) make a strong case for ensuring an internationally appropriate dimension in all language testing. They argue for retaining some aspects of global English norms especially the use of a Standard English (such as Standard American or Standard British English):

> While there are increasing numbers of locally developed and administered tests of English like the College English Test (CET) in China (Zheng & Cheng, 2008), all of them, to our knowledge, draw on SE as their reference point, even though the test-takers share the same L1 and could feasibly be assessed according to local English norms. . . . The fallback position, clearly safer and more practical, has been to stay with the standard varieties. The appeal of SE lies in its neutrality, in the sense that it is the variety most likely to be equally familiar to all test-taker groups.

Elder and Harding argue that to do otherwise (2008, p. 34.3) might be unfair to test-takers, who could not be certain about the language varieties that should guide their test preparation and be acceptable to their examiners:

Global, Local, or "Glocal" **215**

This is one reason why the default model for language testing is still often Standard English (SE) as used in "inner circle" countries and as codified in English grammars, dictionaries and the like. It allows for greater certainty about what is being assessed.

They point out that there are inherent dangers in a test being seen as too local and quote Elder and Davies (2006):

> local non-standard varieties of English have strong appeal in identity terms, but are often stigmatized by the users themselves who prefer to learn and be tested in high prestige varieties. As a case in point, an early attempt by Brown and Lumley (1998) to develop a test which is sensitive to local norms and uses of English in Indonesia has never been used. . . . Similar problems have been faced in Hong Kong, where the GSLPA, a context-sensitive exit test which mirrors the demands for English in the Hong Kong employment context (Lumley & Qian, 2003) has long struggled for due recognition because tests from the inner circle are often viewed by local stakeholders as "the gold standard."

Local norms are clearly often seen as less useful or portable than those of SE as in the cases of tests in Indonesia and Hong Kong cited earlier. There is clearly an issue here for localized tests in some countries, and the perceptions of stakeholders of local tests may be less positive.

Wu (2015) examines this issue in relation to language tests in use in Taiwan. She describes how a questionnaire survey, supplemented by interviews, was conducted in Taiwan, to investigate stakeholders' perceptions of the local GEPT and three international standardized examinations (IELTS, TOEFL iBT, and TOEIC). Responses show that the locally produced test, the GEPT, was considered to be the more contextually and culturally appropriate examination and the one that is most relevant to Taiwanese learners' learning or working contexts; however, the international examinations were considered to have "higher quality."

She suggests that the differing perceptions of quality are influenced by *country image* (Chao, 1993; Han, 1989; Nebenzahl, Jaffe, & Lampert, 1997; Srikatanyoo & Gnoth, 2002), which affects the way consumers evaluate product attributes. She argues that consumers develop stereotypical beliefs about products from particular countries and the attributes of those products. Just as consumers might intuitively feel (rightly or wrongly) that wine produced in France is likely to taste better than that produced in India, or cars produced in Germany more efficient than those from Albania, so too according to Wu:

> It seems that Taiwanese stakeholders are more confident in the quality of the examinations developed in English-speaking countries.

216 Cyril J. Weir

Wu offers a way out of this quandary that accords closely with our depiction of the glocalized Type 2 test:

> Although a locally-produced examination may be disadvantaged due to the effect of country image, the effect may be mitigated by enhancing the exam's validity. In this way, a better examination image may result. . . . To face the challenge, it is essential for a local examination developer to enrich its examination service by adopting internationally accepted codes of ethics and practice in language assessment (e.g., ILTA, 2007) and present its validation efforts at an international level. These efforts will result in a greater opportunity for international recognition of its examination quality, which will then have a positive impact on perceptions of its examination image by stakeholders in the home country.

The tests discussed in this volume are all primarily local in design, but as Chapters 2 to 7 illustrate, all are to varying degrees glocal hybrids. We have seen the global aspect of these tests in relation to operationalizing quality management systems, a concern for positive washback and impact, use of innovation, and a commitment to validation research. We also noted the willingness to draw on international testing expertise and available research literature in the design and development of the tests. Their adoption of Standard English varieties in test content has also helped them avoid the extreme cases of rejection cited by Elder and Davies (2006). Finally, at the upper proficiency levels of these examinations, accessible, appropriate global as well as local themes are addressed. The number of candidates the tests in this volume attract seems to suggest they are seen by many as appropriate for the use that is made of them (Roever & Pan in relation to GEPT, 2008; Zheng & Cheng for CET, 2008).

Questions of Test Use

O'Sullivan (2011) makes a strong case for the localization of assessment systems (e.g., in the use of local curricula; visuals with local social, cultural or geographic reference; specific language with appropriate local linguistic, social, or cultural references and appropriate use of world knowledge), but he feels that "scores should only be used to make decisions that are applicable to a specific field where there is evidence to support their use, i.e. evidence that the tests are indeed locally appropriate. We have to avoid the idea that local tests cannot be globally appropriate. They can be if there is evidence to support this claim" (personal communication, February, 2018).

The tests in this volume have all been localized to meet the specific needs of learners in the country concerned, so test scores are clearly meaningful within that context. A potential problem occurs when test owners in these local contexts would like people to use their local tests in similar but different situations abroad, perhaps to recognize a home-grown test for university admissions purposes in America or Europe as well as for entry to institutions in their own country. In fact, reviewers often encourage Asian tests to seek such international recognition (Shih, 2008).

Presumably in this case a reverse localization argument then applies. Are the localized tests discussed in this volume appropriate for the norms and language features in other contexts than the ones for which they were originally designed? Are they too country specific and not sufficiently generic? Are they construct-valid and fit for use in those external contexts? Do they contain sufficient test content in a Standard English format to make them useful in an overseas context? Are the contextual and cognitive parameters that underlie these localized tests both appropriate and comprehensive enough for the target contexts beyond the country of origin?

The authors of the chapters in this book are aware of the apparent paradox test localization creates when questions of test use beyond the original design parameters are raised. As discussed earlier, they can refer to the glocal nature of their tests by arguing that the following factors do in fact extend the significance and reach of their tests beyond the local context for which they were initially developed: meeting international standards; involving international testing expertise in test development; being alert and responsive to the findings of the appropriate research literature on language testing in the development of their tests; and use of Standard English variants.

Indeed, it could be argued that many have already gone much further than this and carried out empirical research into the equivalence of their tests with those already designed for and being used in those external contexts. The chapter on the TEPS test in Korea evidences a number of studies where TEPS has been compared empirically with TOEFL (Lee & Lee, 2003; Yi, 2013a, 2013b). The Taiwanese GEPT higher level tests have been compared statistically but also in terms of the comparability of their cognitive and contextual parameters with IELTS (Weir, Chan et al., 2013) and TOEFL (Kunnan & Carr, 2015), both used globally for university entrance. Numerous research studies into the validity of the GEPT higher levels have been published in recent years (e.g., Brunfaut & Harding, 2014; Qian, 2014; Weir, Chan et al., 2013; Wu, 2014; Yu & Lin, 2014), demonstrating evidence in support of using GEPT scores as a means of measuring the English language proficiency of Taiwanese applicants for university admissions purposes in the U.S. or the UK. Eiken has carried out a number of studies comparing it with TOEFL for the purposes of entry to U.S. universities (Brown, Davis, Takahashi, Nakamura, 2012; Hill, 2010). At the end of the day, if content and statistical equivalence is established empirically with external tests, then glocal tests can make a sound case for being used externally as well as locally.

On top of this, a number of the tests in this volume have also gone through the rigorous process of linkage to the CEFR in order to establish more precisely

218 Cyril J. Weir

the levels of proficiency which the tests measure. Dunlea's (2015) doctoral thesis deals with the alignment of the EIKEN test with the CEFR, and Rachel Wu's (2011) thesis examines the comparability of GEPT tests with such international benchmarks (for GEPT alignment see also Brunfaut & Harding, 2014; Green, Inoue, & Nakatsuhara, 2017; Knoch, 2016; Wu & Wu, 2010; Wu, 2014 for comparison of GEPT with CEFR).

In these ways, the global relevance of these glocal tests has been strengthened, and such research provides an empirical base for their use outside of the original local context for which the tests were designed.

Endnote

In this discussion we have encountered a global-local dichotomy for language tests: on one side sits the broad-spectrum general international English-language proficiency tests (such as the Cambridge English examinations, IELTS, and TOEFL iBT described in the first part of this chapter); and on the other side sit tests specifically designed by local agencies, within the local context, specifically for that context with no attention paid to global norms or practice. In between, closer to global, lie Glocal Type 1 external tests; these are originally global tests but now modified in ways similar to that proposed by British Council in their "menu" for localization; and, finally closer to the local side, are Glocal Type 2 tests specifically designed *ab initio* for local purposes but additionally globalized in a number of different ways. Those tests discussed in this volume fall into this category.

Glocalized tests offer a refreshing paradigm for the development of tests in the 21st century. It seems logical that developing glocal tests avoids the sort of "colonial dependence" that can develop when using uniquely global tests. Glocal Type 1 tests are perhaps less satisfactory than Type 2, being originally global tests designed for a non-specific international audience and then modified as far as possible to suit local contexts rather than being designed *ab initio* for a particular context. This notwithstanding, they are clearly more appropriate to a particular society than the all-embracing global test (see O'Sullivan & Dunlea, 2015). Nevertheless, two issues remain with these Glocal Type 1 tests. First, there is the question of what is the evidence base for taking decisions on which parameters appropriate to the local context are to be modified and whether the range of the modifications engineered is comprehensive enough. Secondly, once a global test has been localized, its appropriateness for the local context is never satisfactorily validated.

The Glocal Type 2 tests discussed in this volume are more acceptable to host countries as they are designed *ab initio* to fit with the intended local context by people who are immersed in that context, and are validated specifically for that context. Furthermore, the Glocal Type 2 tests in Chapters 2–7 employ a variety of strategies to ensure they comply with international standards. They

Global, Local, or "Glocal" **219**

are nevertheless an indigenous product and as Dendrinos (2013) argues, they are not "tainted by the linguistic hegemony of global international knowledge products run and owned by external commercial condominiums" (see also McNamara, 2002; Templer, 2004).

As a final thought, we should perhaps remember that Glocal Type 2 tests are not restricted to English, and a number of the contributors to this volume have been developing glocalized tests in languages other than English. There appears to be an increasing demand for developing second foreign language teaching, learning, and assessment in Asia. In Taiwan, second foreign language education has been increasingly promoted by the government in recent years. To respond to the increasing need, the LTTC also develops glocalized tests in major European languages and Japanese. This trend is true for China, too. The CET Committee has been developing and administering tests of Japanese (CJT), Russian (CRT), German (CGT), and French (CFT) since the 1990s, in addition to the CET test. It is the case for Vietnam also. The expertise gained in glocalizing English language tests is transferable to other L2 tests. As a result, the content of this volume has clear implications for language testing research and test development for languages other than English.

> "Glocalized tests are a good news story; they contribute to a narrative of creativity and progress in the field of language testing and assessment"
> *(Lynda Taylor, personal communication, January, 2018)*

References

Abad Florescano, A., Dunne, R. A., & Grounds, M. (2004). A local alternative to international proficiency tests: The EXAVER project. In J. Pender (Ed.), *Ten years of collaboration in ELT: Accounts from Mexico* [CD-ROM edition] (pp. 156–166). Mexico City: British Council.

Alderson, J. C. (2002). *Common European Framework of Reference for Languages: Learning, teaching, assessment; Case studies.* Strasbourg: Council of Europe.

Alderson, J. C., & Wall, D. (1993). Does washback exist? *Applied Linguistics, 14*(2), 115–129.

Al-Fallay, I. (1994). *Limiting bias in the assessment of English as a foreign language: The impact of background knowledge on the proficiency of Saudi Arabian students learning English as a foreign language* (Unpublished doctoral dissertation). University of New Mexico, Albuquerque.

American Educational Research Association, American Psychological Association & National Council on Measurement in Education. (2014). *Standards for educational and psychological testing.* Washington, DC: American Educational Research Association.

Association of Language Testers in Europe. (1993/2001). *Principles of good practice for ALTE examinations.* Retrieved from www.testdaf.de/fileadmin/Redakteur/PDF/ TestDaF/ALTE/ALTE_good_practice.pdf

Association of Language Testers in Europe. (1994). *Code of practice.* Retrieved from www.alte.org/resources/Documents/code_practice_en.pdf

220 Cyril J. Weir

Association of Language Testers in Europe. (1998). *Handbook of language examinations and examination systems*. Strasbourg.

Association of Language Testers in Europe. (2007). *Minimum standards for establishing quality profiles in ALTE examinations*. Retrieved from www.alte.org/resources/Documents/minimum_standards_en.pdf

Association of Language Testers in Europe/Council of Europe. (1997). *Users' guide for examiners*. Strasbourg.

Bachman, L. F., & Palmer, A. S. (1996). *Language testing in practice*. Oxford: Oxford University Press.

Balourdi, A. (2012). *World representations in language exam batteries: Critical discourse analysis of texts used to test reading comprehension* (Doctoral dissertation). Retrieved from http://thesis.ekt.gr/thesisBookReader/id/31673#page/1/mode/2up

Biber, D., Conrad, S., Reppen, R., Byrd, P., Helt, M., Clark, V., . . . Urzua, A. (2004). *Representing language use in the university: Analysis of the TOEFL 2000 spoken and written academic language corpus*. TOEFL Monograph Series MS-25. Princeton, NJ: Educational Testing Service.

British Council. (2013). *The English effect: The impact of English, what it's worth to the UK and why it matters to the world*. London: Author. Retrieved from www.britishcouncil.org/sites/default/files/english-effect-report-v2.pdf

Brown, A., & Lumley, T. (1998). Linguistic and cultural norms in language testing: A case study. *Melbourne Papers in Language Testing*, 7(1), 80–96.

Brown, J. D., Davis, J. McE., Takahashi, C., & Nakamura, K. (2012). *Upper-level EIKEN examinations: Linking, validating, and predicting TOEFL iBT scores at advanced proficiency EIKEN levels*. Tokyo: Eiken Foundation of Japan. Retrieved from www.eiken.or.jp/eiken/group/result/pdf/eiken-toeflibt-report.pdf

Brunfaut, T., & Harding, L. (2014). *Linking the GEPT listening test to the Common European Framework of Reference* (LTTC–GEPT Research Report No. RG-05). Taipei: The Language Training and Testing Center.

Brutt-Griffler, J. (2002). *World English: A study of its development*. Clevedon: Multilingual.

Cambridge English Language Assessment. (2016). *Principles of good practice*. Retrieved from www.cambridgeenglish.org/Images/22695-principles-of-good-practice.pdf

Canagarajah, S. (2006). Changing communicative needs, revised assessment objectives: Testing English as an international language. *Language Assessment Quarterly*, 3(3), 229–242.

Chao, P. (1993). Partitioning country of origin effects: Consumer evaluations of a hybrid product. *Journal of International Business Studies*, 24, 291–306.

Chihara, T., Sakurai, T., & Oller, J. (1989). Background and culture as factors in EFL reading comprehension. *Language Testing*, 6(2), 143–151.

Clyne, M., & Sharifian, F. (2008). English as an international language: Challenges and possibilities. *Australian Review of Applied Linguistics*, 31(3), 28.1–28.16.

Council of Europe. (2001). *Common European Framework of Reference for Languages: Learning, teaching and assessment*. Cambridge, UK: Cambridge University Press.

Cumming, A., Grant, L., Mulcahy-Ernt, P., & Powers, D. (2004). A teacher-verification study of speaking and writing prototype tasks for a new TOEFL. *Language Testing*, 21(2), 107–145.

Cumming, A., Kantor, R., Baba, K., Erdosy, U., Eouanzoui, K., & James, M. (2005). Differences in written discourse in independent and integrated prototype tasks for next generation TOEFL. *Assessing Writing*, 10, 5–43.

Global, Local, or "Glocal" **221**

Davies, A. (Ed.). (2008). *Assessing academic English: Testing English proficiency, 1950–1989 – The IELTS solution*. Studies in Language Testing, 23. Cambridge, UK: Cambridge University Press.

Dendrinos, B. (2006). Mediation in communication, language teaching and testing. *Journal of Applied Linguistics, 22*, 9–35. Thessaloniki: Hellenic Association of Applied Linguistics.

Dendrinos, B. (Ed.). (2011). The role of language testing in supporting multilingualism. In *European Union civil society platform on multilingualism: Policy recommendations for the promotion of multilingualism in the European Union* (pp. 50–54). Retrieved from http://old.enl.uoa.gr/pgs/files/Testing%20position%20paper.pdf

Dendrinos, B. (2013). Social meanings in global-glocal language proficiency exams. In D. Tsagari, S. Papadima-Sophocleous, & S. Ioannu-Georgiou (Eds.), *International experiences in language testing and assessment* (pp. 33–57). Frankfurt am Main: Peter Lang.

Dunlea, J. (2015). *Validating a set of Japanese EFL proficiency tests: Demonstrating locally designed tests meet international standards* (Unpublished doctoral dissertation). University of Bedfordshire, UK.

Dunlea, J., Spiby, R., Nguyen, T. N. Q., Nguyen, T. Q. Y., Nguyen, T. M. H., Nguyen, T. P. T., & Thai, H. L. T. (2018). *Aptis–VSTEP comparability study: Investigating the usage of two EFL tests in the context of higher education in Vietnam*. British Council Validation Series No. VS/2018/001. London: British Council.

Elder, C., & Davies, A. (2006). Assessing English as a lingua franca. *Annual Review of Applied Linguistics, 26*, 282–304. doi:10.1017/S0267190506000146

Elder, C., & Harding, L. (2008). Language testing and English as an international language: Constraints and contributions. *Australian Review of Applied Linguistics, 31*(3), 34.1–34.11. doi: 10.2104/aral0834

Enright, M., Grabe, W., Koda, K., Mosenthal, P., Mulcany-Ernt, P., & Schedl, M. (2000). *TOEFL 2000 reading framework: A working paper*. TOEFL Monograph Series MS-17. Princeton, NJ: Educational Testing Service.

European Association for Language Testing and Assessment. (2006). *Guidelines for good practice in language testing and assessment*. Retrieved from www.ealta.eu.org/guidelines.htm

Geranpayeh, A., & Taylor, L. (Eds.). (2013). *Examining listening: Research and practice in assessing second language listening*. Studies in Language Testing, 35. Cambridge, UK: Cambridge University Press.

Glocalization. (n.d.). In *Cambridge online dictionary*. Retrieved from https://dictionary.cambridge.org/dictionary/english/globalization

Gray, J. (2002). The global coursebook in English language teaching. In D. Block & D. Cameron (Eds.), *Globalization and language teaching* (pp. 151–167). London: Routledge.

Green, A. (2014). *The Test of English for Academic Purposes (TEAP) impact study*. Retrieved from www.eiken.or.jp/teap/group/pdf/teap_washback_study.pdf

Green, A., Inoue, C., & Nakatsuhara, F. (2017). *GEPT speaking–CEFR benchmarking* (LTTC–GEPT Research Report No. RG-09). Taipei: The Language Training and Testing Center.

Hamp-Lyons, L. (1997). Washback, impact and validity: Ethical concerns. *Language Testing, 14*(3), 295–303.

Hamp-Lyons, L. (2000). Social, professional and individual responsibility in language testing. *System, 28*(4), 579–591.

Hamp-Lyons, L., & Kroll, B. (1997). *TOEFL 2000—writing: Composition, community, and assessment*. TOEFL Monograph Series MS-05. Princeton, NJ: Educational Testing Service.

Han, C. M. (1989). Country image: Halo or summary construct? *Journal of Marketing Research, 26,* 222–229.

Hawkey, R. (2006). *Impact theory and practice: Studies of the IELTS test and Progetto Lingue 2000.* Studies in Language Testing, 24. Cambridge, UK: Cambridge University Press.

Hawkey, R., & Milanovic, M. (2013). *Cambridge English exams—The first hundred years. A History of English language assessment from the University of Cambridge 1913–2013.* Cambridge, UK: Cambridge University Press.

Hill, Y. Z. (2010). *Validation of the STEP EIKEN test for college admission* (Unpublished doctoral dissertation). Manoa, Hawai'i: University of Hawai'i at Manoa.

Hino, N. (2016). Negotiation between east Asian values and anglophone culture in the teaching of English in Japan. In H. H. Liao (Ed.), *Critical reflections on foreign language education: Globalization and local interventions* (pp. 29–45). Taipei: The Language Training and Testing Center.

Howatt, A. P. R., & Widdowson, H. G. (2004). *A history of English language teaching* (2nd ed.). Oxford: Oxford University Press.

Hudson, T. (1996). *Assessing second language academic reading from a communicative competence perspective: Relevance for TOEFL 2000.* TOEFL Monograph Series MS-4. Princeton, NJ: Educational Testing Service.

Hughes, A. (Ed.). (1988). *Testing English for university study.* ELT Documents 127. Oxford: Modern English Publications.

International Language Testing Association. (2000/2018). *Code of ethics.* Retrieved from https://cdn.ymaws.com/www.iltaonline.com/resource/resmgr/docs/ILTA_2018_CodeOfEthics_Engli.pdf

International Language Testing Association. (2007). *Guidelines for practice.* Retrieved from www.iltaonline.com/page/ITLAGuidelinesforPra

Jones, N. (2000). Background to the validation of the ALTE can do project and the revised common European framework. *Research Notes, 2,* 11–13.

Jones, N. (2001). The ALTE can do project and the role of measurement in constructing a proficiency framework. *Research Notes, 5,* 5–8.

Jones, N. (2002). Relating the ALTE framework to the Common European Framework of Reference. In J. C. Alderson (Ed.), *Common European Framework of Reference for Languages: Learning, teaching, assessment; Case studies* (pp. 167–183). Strasbourg: Council of Europe.

Jones, N., & Hirtzel, M. (2001). The ALTE Can Do project, English version: Articles and Can Do statements produced by the members of ALTE 1992–2002, appendix D. In Council of Europe (Eds.), *Common European Framework of Reference for Languages.* Cambridge, UK: Cambridge University Press.

Kachru, B. (2005). *Asian Englishes: Beyond the canon.* Hong Kong: Hong Kong University Press.

Kantarcıoğlu, E., Thomas, C., O'Dwyer, J., & O'Sullivan, B. (2010). The COPE linking project: A case study. In W. Martyniuk (Ed.), *Aligning tests with the CEFR: Reflections on using the Council of Europe's draft manual.* Studies in Language Testing, 33. Cambridge, UK: Cambridge University Press.

Khalifa, H., & Weir, C. J. (2009). *Examining reading: Research and practice in assessing second language reading.* Studies in Language Testing, 29. Cambridge, UK: Cambridge University Press.

Knoch, U. (2016). *Linking the GEPT writing sub-test to the Common European Framework of Reference (CEFR)* (LTTC–GEPT Research Report No. RG-08). Taipei: The Language Training and Testing Center.

Kumaravadivelu, B. (2008). *Cultural globalization and language education*. New Haven, CT: Yale University Press.

Kunnan, A., & Carr, N. (2015). *Comparability study between the General English Proficiency Test—Advanced and the Internet-Based Test of English as a Foreign Language (iBT TOEFL)* (LTTC–GEPT Research Report No. RG-06). Taipei: The Language Training and Testing Center.

Lee, H., & Lee, S. (2003). A study on the relationship between the scores of TOEFL, TOEIC and TEPS, and college academic performance. *English Language & Literature Teaching, 9*(1), 153–171.

Lowenberg, P. (2002). Assessing English proficiency in the expanding circle. *World Englishes, 21*(3), 431–435.

Lumley, T., & Qian, D. (2003). Assessing English for employment in Hong Kong. In C. A. Coombe & N. Hubley (Eds.), *Assessment practices: Case studies in TESOL. Practice Series* (pp. 135–147). Alexandria, VA: TESOL.

Malaysian Examinations Council. (2015). *Regulations, test specifications, test format and sample questions*. Selangor, Malaysia: Author.

McNamara, T. (2002). *Language testing*. Oxford: Oxford University Press.

Moore, T., Morton, J., Hall, D., & Wallis, C. (2015). *Literacy practices in the professional workplace: Implications for the IELTS reading and writing tests* (IELTS Research Reports Online Series 2015/1). IELTS Partners: Australia and the UK.

Morrow, C. (2017). Assessing entry-level academic literacy with IELTS in the U.A.E. In R. Al-Mahrooqi, C. Coombe, F. Al-Maamari, & V. Thakur (Eds.), *Revisiting EFL assessment* (pp. 151–169). New York, NY: Springer.

Nakatsuhara, F. (2014a). *A research report on the development of the Test of English for Academic Purposes (TEAP) speaking test for Japanese university entrants—Study 1 & study 2.* Retrieved from www.eiken.or.jp/teap/group/pdf/teap_speaking_report1.pdf

Nakatsuhara, F. (2014b). *A Research report on the development of the Test of English for Academic Purposes (TEAP) speaking test for Japanese university entrants—Study 3 & study 4.* Retrieved from www.eiken.or.jp/teap/group/report.html

Nebenzahl, I. D., Jaffe, E. D., & Lampert, S. I. (1997). Toward a theory of country image effect on product evaluation. *Management International Review, 37*(1), 27–49.

North, B. (2000). *The development of a common framework scale of language proficiency*. New York, NY: Peter Lang Publishing.

North, B. (2002). Developing descriptor scales of language proficiency for the CEF common reference levels. In J. C. Alderson (Ed.), *Common European Framework of Reference for Languages: Learning, teaching, assessment: Case studies* (pp. 87–105). Strasbourg: Council of Europe.

O'Dwyer, J. (2008). *Formative evaluation for organisational learning*. Frankfurt am Main: Peter Lang.

O'Sullivan, B. (2005). *Levels specification project report* (Internal report). Zayed University, United Arab Emirates.

O'Sullivan, B. (Ed.). (2006). *Issues in testing business English: The revision of the Cambridge business English certificates*. Studies in Language Testing, 17. Cambridge, UK: Cambridge University Press.

O'Sullivan, B. (2011). Introduction—Professionalisation, localisation and fragmentation in language testing. In B. O'Sullivan (Ed.), *Language testing: Theories and practices* (pp. 1–12). Basingstoke: Palgrave Macmillan.

O'Sullivan, B., & Dunlea, J. (2015). Aptis general technical manual, version 1.0. *Technical Report* (TR/2015/005). London: British Council.

Qian, D. (2014). *A register analysis of the GEPT advanced level examinees' written production* (LTTC–GEPT Research Report No. RG-04). Taipei: The Language Training and Testing Center.

Read, J. (2015). *Assessing English proficiency for university study.* Basingstoke: Palgrave MacMillan.

Read, J., & Wette, R. (2009). *Achieving English proficiency for professional registration: The experience of overseas qualified health professionals in the New Zealand context* (IELTS Research Reports, Vol. 10, pp. 181–222). London: IELTS Australia: Canberra and British Council.

Robertson, R. (1997). Comments on the "Global Triad" and "Glocalization." In N. Inoue (Ed.), *Globalization and indigenous culture.* Retrieved from www2.kokugakuin.ac.jp/ijcc/wp/global/15robertson.html

Roever, C., & Pan, Y. C. (2008). Test review: GEPT: General English Proficiency Test. *Language Testing, 25*(3), 403–418.

Sasaki, M. (2000). Effects of cultural schemata on students' test-taking processes for cloze tests: A multiple data source approach. *Language Testing, 17,* 85–114.

Sawyer, W., & Singh, M. (2011). *Learning to play the 'classroom tennis' well: IELTS and international students in teacher education* (IELTS Research Reports, Vol. 11, pp. 1–54). London: IELTS Australia: Canberra and British Council.

Shaw, S., & Weir, C. J. (2007). *Examining writing: Research and practice in assessing second language writing.* Studies in Language Testing, 26. Cambridge, UK: Cambridge University Press.

Shi, X. (2013). The glocalization of English: A Chinese case study. *Journal of Developing Societies, 29*(2), 89–122.

Shih, C. M. (2008). Critical language testing: A case study of the General English Proficiency Test. *English Teaching and Learning, 32*(3), 1–34.

Srikatanyoo, M., & Gnoth, J. (2002). Country image and international tertiary education. *Brand Management, 10*(2), 139–146.

Steffensen, M., Joag-Dev, C., & Anderson, R. (1979). A cross-cultural perspective on reading comprehension. *Reading Research Quarterly, 15,* 10–29.

Taylor, L. (Ed.). (2011). *Examining speaking: Research and practice in assessing second language speaking.* Studies in Language Testing, 30. Cambridge, UK: Cambridge University Press.

Taylor, L. (2014). *A report on the review of test specifications for the reading and listening papers of the Test of English for Academic Purposes (TEAP) for Japanese University Entrants.* Retrieved from www.eiken.or.jp/teap/group/report.html

Templer, B. (2004). High-stakes testing at high fees: Notes and queries on the international English proficiency assessment market. *Journal for Critical Education Policy Studies, 2*(1). Retrieved from www.jceps.com/?pageID=articleand articleID=21

Tsou, W. (2015). Globalization to glocalization: Rethinking English language teaching in response to the ELF phenomenon. *English as a Global Language Education (EaGLE) Journal, 1*(1), 47–63.

Van Avermaet, P., Kuijper, H., & Saville, N. (2004). A code of practice and quality management system for international examinations. *Language Assessment Quarterly, 1*(2), 137–150.

Wall, D. (1997). Impact and washback in language testing. In C. Clapham & D. Corson (Eds.), *Encyclopedia of language and education: Volume 7. Language testing and assessment* (pp. 291–302). Dordrecht: Kluwer Academic.

Weir, C. J. (2013). An overview of the influences on English language testing. In C. J. Weir, I. Vidaković, & E. D. Galaczi (Eds.), *Measured constructs: A history of the constructs underlying Cambridge English Language (ESOL) examinations 1913–2012* (pp. 1–102). Studies in Language Testing, 37. Cambridge, UK: Cambridge University Press.

Weir, C. J. (2014). *A research report on the development of the Test of English for Academic Purposes (TEAP) writing test for Japanese university entrants*. Retrieved from www.eiken.or.jp/teap/group/report.html

Weir, C. J., Chan, S. H. C., & Nakatsuhara, F. (2013). *Examining the criterion related validity of the GEPT advanced reading and writing tests: Comparing GEPT with IELTS and real life academic performance* (LTTC–GEPT Research Report No. RG-01). Taipei: The Language Training and Testing Center

Weir, C. J., & O'Sullivan, B. (2017). *Assessing English on the global stage: A history of the British Council's involvement in language testing 1941–2016*. London: Equinox.

Weir, C. J., Vidaković, I., & Galaczi, E. D. (2013). *Measured constructs: A history of the constructs underlying Cambridge English Language (ESOL) examinations 1913–2012*. Studies in Language Testing, 37. Cambridge, UK: Cambridge University Press.

Weir, C. J., Yang, H., & Jin, Y. (2000). *An empirical investigation of the componentiality of L2 reading in English for academic purposes*. Studies in Language Testing, 12. Cambridge, UK: Cambridge University Press.

Wu, J. R. W. (2015, May). *Choosing an international and locally-produced English tests: Stakeholders' attitude and perception*. Paper presented at 12th annual EALTA conference, Copenhagen, Denmark.

Wu, J. R. W., & Wu, R. Y. F. (2010). Relating the GEPT reading comprehension tests to the CEFR. In W. Martyniuk (Ed.), *Aligning tests with the CEFR: Reflections on using the Council of Europe's draft manual* (pp. 204–224). Studies in Language Testing, 33. Cambridge, UK: Cambridge University Press.

Wu, R. Y. F. (2011). *Establishing the validity of the General English Proficiency Test reading component through a critical evaluation of alignment with the Common European Framework of Reference* (Unpublished doctoral dissertation). University of Bedfordshire, UK.

Wu, R. Y. F. (2014). *Validating second language reading examinations: Establishing the validity of the GEPT through alignment with the Common European Framework of Reference*. Studies in Language Testing, 41. Cambridge, UK: Cambridge University Press.

Wu, R. Y. F., Yeh, H., Dunlea, J., & Spiby, R. (2016). *Aptis-GEPT comparison study: Looking at two tests from multiple perspectives using the socio-cognitive model* (British Council Validation Series No. VS/2016/002). London: British Council.

Yang, H., & Weir, C. J. (1998). *The validation study of the College English Test*. Shanghai: Shanghai Foreign Language Education Press.

Yi, Y.-S. (2013a). Investigating the comparability of academic texts in TOEFL and TEPS. *Modern Studies in English Language & Literature, 57*(4), 321–340.

Yi, Y.-S. (2013b). On the optimal text length of reading comprehension tests. *The Jungang Journal of English Language and Literature, 55*(4), 505–530.

Yu, G., & Lin, S. W. (2014). *A comparability study on the cognitive processes of taking GEPT (advanced) and IELTS (academic) writing tasks using graph prompts* (LTTC–GEPT Research Report No. RG-02). Taipei: The Language Training and Testing Center.

Zafar Khan, S. (2009). Imperialism of international tests: An EIL perspective. In F. Sharifian (Ed.), *English as an international language: Perspectives and pedagogical issues* (pp. 190–205). Bristol: Multilingual Matters.

Zheng, Y., & Cheng, L. (2008). Test review: College English Test (CET) in China. *Language Testing, 25*(3), 408–417.

INDEX

Page numbers in italics indicate figures; page numbers in bold indicate tables.

AALA *see* Asian Association for Language Assessment (AALA)
Academic Forum on English Language Testing in Asia (AFELTA) 3, 21, 86, 96n1, 205; members of 7n1
AFELTA *see* Academic Forum on English Language Testing in Asia (AFELTA)
Alderson, Charles 14, 214
ALTE *see* Association of Language Testers in Europe (ALTE)
Aptis General test, British Council xvii, xxiv, **xxv**, 210–211
ASEAN Economic Community (AEC) 71
Asian Association for Language Assessment (AALA) 86, 205, 206
assessment use argument (AUA) 84, 86, 87, 93, 124
Association of Language Testers in Europe (ALTE) 21, 151, 208; Can-do Project of 195–196

Bachman, Lyle 14, 214
Bachman's Communicative Language Ability 80
British Council 86, 93, 102, 163, 200, 209, 210, 213; Aptis test xvii, xxiv, **xxv**, 210–211; Aptis listening 211–212; English Proficiency Test Battery (EPTB) xiii–xiv
Brown, J. D. *xvi*, 214

Cambridge Assessment English 2, 75, 79, 106, 169, 199; Examinations 195–196
Cambridge English Qualifications 73, 80, 90, 139
Carr, Nathan 96n5
CEFR *see* Common European Framework of Reference for Languages (CEFR)
Center for Research in English Language Learning and Assessment (CRELLA) 144, 213
Certificate of Proficiency in English (CPE) xiii, 195, 199
CET *see* College English Test (CET)
China: College English Test (CET) in 101, 124–125; *see also* College English Test (CET)
China's Standards of English Language Ability (CSE) *xv*, 108
College English Curriculum Requirements 107
College English Test (CET) 1, 5, 75, 78; banded system of 106–107; comparison of speaking tests 108–111, **110**; ensuring the fairness of 115–116; features unique to local English language test 105–111; high-stakes uses of 119–120; innovation in 121–122; input materials in CET in past decades **104**; intended purposes of 117; interface between teaching, learning

and testing 106–108; latest version of **105**; milestones of 101–105; procedure of CET item writing *112*; quality control of test items 112–113; rating of constructed-response items 113–115; research agenda for 123–124; revision of test content and format 103–105; stages of CET managerial system **103**; sub-skills assessed in **129–130**; test development and management 102–103; validation studies of 120–121; washback on teaching and learning 117–119; website 7n2, 117

College Entrance Examination Center, Taiwan 18

Collins COBUILD English Dictionary 18

Common Chinese Framework of Reference for English (CCFR-E) 92

Common European Framework of Reference for Languages (CEFR) 9, 72, 140–143, 169, 188, 195–196

Davidson, Fred 214

Davies, Alan xiii

Diagnostic English Language Assessment (DELA) 200

Diagnostic English Language Needs Assessment (DELNA) 200

EALTA *see* European Association for Language Testing and Assessment (EALTA)

Educational Testing Service (ETS) United States xiii, 2, 75, 106

EFL *see* English as Foreign Language (EFL)

EIKEN 1, 5–6; acronym for test system 131; Action Plan 136–137; balance between local and global 155; impact 150; improvements needed 153–155; increasing acceptance and use in period 3 135; innovation 150; intention of impact 134–135; Jitsuyo Eigo Gino Kentei 131; lessons learned 153–155; localized test 201; looking inside test 140–143; model of validation 132–133; overview 138; overview of proficiency levels of grades **140**; peripheral features of test system 138–140; quality assurance 153; responding to changing needs in period 4 135–136; social, educational and political context 133–134; test format **159–161**; testing system 5–6;

validation 150–152; website 7n2, 135–136, 151; *see also* Test of English for Academic Purposes (TEAP)

Eiken Foundation 5–6, 75, 131, 144, 151

ELPA *see* English Language Proficiency Assessment (ELPA)

English as Foreign Language (EFL) 4, 10, 12, 36, 42, 47, 48, 56, 60, 73, 75, 78, 80 , 86, education in Taiwan 12, 28–31; in Japan 132, 133, 144; *see also* General English Proficiency Test (GEPT)

English for the Malaysian Civil Service (EMCS) project 162

English Language Proficiency Assessment (ELPA) 1, 6; critical analysis of 189–190; developing 162–165; different uses of 175–176; digitizing 187; early test development phase 163; ELPA 1.0 165–167, **168**; ELPA 2.0 167, **168**, 169; emerging competencies 188; evolution of 162; extrapolation 180–181; generalizability 178–180; inference evidence 177, *180*; interpretive argument approach **181**, 182; interpretive argument for trait interpretation 177, **178**; item writing 164; localization 165–170; maintaining quality and fairness 176–182; problems and challenges of 174–175; purpose of test 162; qualitative approaches to test validity 188–189; reporting 164–165; research and innovation 186–189; scoring procedures 178, *179*; testing needs analysis 163; testing reading 173–174; testing speaking 172–173; testing writing 170–172; test use and impact 181, 181–182, 182–186; using multiple rating instruments 186; utilizing pre-ELPA screening test 187

English language testing 1–3, 6–7; glocalization 4–5; localization 3–4

English Proficiency Test Battery (EPTB) xiii–xiv

English as Second Language (ESL) 2, 4, 42, 46

European Association for Language Testing and Assessment (EALTA) 21

European Economic Community 195

General English Proficiency Test (GEPT) 1, 2, 5, 9–11, 75, 78, 201; administering tests 37n5; aligning with local curriculum

228 Index

35; alignment with CEFR (Common European Framework of Reference) 13; a posteriori validation of 22–28; challenges going forward 34–36; consequential validity 27–28; LTTC English learner corpus 33; context and cognitive validity 22–24; criterion-related validity 25–27; enhancing transparency and quality 35–36; feasibility of automatic scoring 34; level framework **10**; government support of 13; impact on EFL education in Taiwan 28–31; innovation 31–34; international institutions recognizing GEPT scores 13; Language Training and Testing Center (LTTC) as developer 9; linking scores into common score scale 33–34; local features of 14–18; means to change in EFL education in Taiwan 12; monitoring effectiveness of policy implementation 30; new task design concepts 31–32; ongoing quality monitoring 21; overview of development 11–13; overview of validation studies *23*; promoting assessment for learning 29–30; quality control and test fairness 19–21; results of GEPT–CEFR linking studies **26**; scoring 20; scoring validity 24–25; Self-Assessment Scales and Tests 29; stimulating interest in language assessment research 31; supporting professional development of assessment literacy 30–31; supporting self-directed learning 36; task design 14–15; test formats and passing standards of **16–17**; test paper production 19–20; topic selection 15, 18; website 7n2; wordlists 18

General English Proficiency Test–Advanced (GEPT–A) 123
GEPT *see* General English Proficiency Test (GEPT)
globalization 198
globalized test 193–201; Cambridge Assessment English Examinations 195–196; International English Language Testing System (IELTS) 196–197; Internet-based test of English as a Foreign Language (TOEFL iBT) *xiv*, 194–195; purposes of 197–201
glocal 193
glocalization 208–219; globalization and localization 4; glocalization test type 1, 209–212, 218; glocalization test type 2, 212–214, 218–219; paradigm

of testing 218–219; questions of perception 214–216; questions of test use 216–218; testing 4–5
Green, Rita 213
Green, Tony 213

Hamp-Lyons, Liz 213
Hogan, Mary Jane 214
Huang Shuming 31
Hue University 74
Human Resource Development Strategy 71

impact 89
INTAN *see* National Institute of Public Administration (INTAN)
International English Language Testing System (IELTS) xiv, xxiii–xxiv, 1, 2, 13, 73, 75, 80, 106, 166, 176, 188; comparison of speaking tests 108–111, **110**; global test 196–197; purpose of 199–201
Item Response Theory (IRT) 20, 33, 34, 49, 51, 52, 60, 64

Japan: EIKEN in 131; Ministry of Education, Culture, Sports, Science and Technology (MEXT) 136–137, 140–141, 146–148; periods for English education in 133–134; Test of English for Academic Purposes (TEAP) 131
Japan Language Testing Association (JLTA) 21
Jitsuyo Eigo Gino Kentei *see* EIKEN
JLTA *see* Japan Language Testing Association (JLTA)
Journal of Language Testing (journal) 2

Korea Institute for Curriculum and Evaluation (KICE) 75, 78
Korea Research Institute for Vocational Education and Training (KRIVET) 42
Kunnan, Antony 14, 214

Language Education Institute (LEI) 42
Language Testing (journal) 105, 119
Language Testing Research Colloquium (LTRC) 21, 121, 205
Language Training and Testing Center (LTTC) 2–3, 5, 219; English Learner Corpus (LTTC–ELC) 33; local English test in Taipei 123; mandate of 36n1; research grants program 31; website 36n1
localization: levels of 210; localized test 201–203; testing 3–4

local tests 1–2; context of development xix; context of use xx; expertise for local test development *xx*; features of xx–xxiii; impact and washback 207–208; implications of xxiii–xxvi; innovation 206–207; linguistic features 202–203; quality management 204–205; validation research 205–206
LTRC *see* Language Testing Research Colloquium (LTRC)

McNamara, Tim 14, 214
Malaysian Public Service 1, 190, 201; *see also* English Language Proficiency Assessment (ELPA)
Malaysian University English Test (MUET) 169, 200
Measures to Enhance the English Proficiency of Civil Servants (Taiwan) 13
Ministry of Education, Culture, Sports, Science and Technology (MEXT) Japan 136–137, 140–141, 146–148
Ministry of Education and Training (MOET): Vietnam 94, 97n10, 97n11; VSTEP test 74

Nakatsuhara, Fumiyo 213
National Centre Test for University Admissions 134, 135, 145
National College English Testing Committee (NCETC) 102, 107, 114, 116, 118, 120, 121
National College English Testing Syllabuses 5
National Education Examinations Authority (NEEA) 103, 107, 108, 116, 117, 120
National English Ability Test (NEAT) 75, 78
National Institute of Public Administration (INTAN) 6, 162, 163, 167, 174, 182, 186–190
National Taiwan University 29, 33
NFL (National Foreign Language) Project 3, 72, 74, 78, 90

Pearson Test of English 123
Porter, Don *xvi*, 213
Principles of Good Practice (Cambridge) 199, 209

quality control: College English Test (CET) 112–113; EIKEN 153; English Language Proficiency Assessment (ELPA) 176–182; General English Proficiency Test (GEPT) 19–21; Test of English for Academic Purposes (TEAP) 153; Test of English Proficiency by Seoul National University (TEPS) 49–55; Vietnamese Standardized Test of English Proficiency (VSTEP) 83–89
Quality Management System (QMS) 204, 208, 216

Robertson, Roland 209

Seoul National University (SNU) 42
Shanghai Jiao Tong University 102
SNUCREPT (Seoul National University Criterion Referenced English Proficiency Test) 44, 57–59
SNULT (Seoul National University Language Tests) 44, **45**
Sophia University 6, 131, 144
Standard American English (SAE): Internet-based test of English as a Foreign Language (TOEFL iBT) 194
Standard English (SE): perception 214–216
Studies in Language Testing (SiLT) 197

Taiwan: College Entrance Examination Center 18; English as Foreign Language (EFL) education in 12, 28–31; *see also* General English Proficiency Test (GEPT)
target language use (TLU) 82, 142, 146, 169
Taylor, Lynda 213, 219
Teaching and Learning Foreign Languages in the National Education System 72
TEAP *see* Test of English for Academic Purposes (TEAP)
TEPS *see* Test of English Proficiency by Seoul National University (TEPS)
testing: expertise for local test development *xx*; globalized test 193–201; glocalization of 4–5; localization of 3–4; localized test 201–203; questions of perception 214–216; questions of use 216–218; Revised Test Validation Model *xvii*
Test of English as a Foreign Language (TOEFL) 1, 2, 12, 73, 75, 80, 118, 166, 176, 188; comparison of speaking tests 108–111, **110**; Internet-based test of (TOEFL iBT) *xiv*, 26–27, 194–195, 202, 218

230 Index

Test of English for Academic Purposes (TEAP) 131, 200, 202; impact of 149–150; improvements needed 153–155; innovation 150; introduction of 137–138; lessons learned 153–155; looking inside test 146–148; overview 138; peripheral features of test system 143–146; quality assurance 153; social, educational and political context 133–134; test format **161**; validation 152–153; *see also* EIKEN

Test of English for International Communication (TOEIC) 12, 27, 43, 56–57, 73, 79, 83, 90, 169, 188, 215

Test of English Proficiency by Seoul National University (TEPS) 1, 5, 42–43, 217; family of tests **45**, **63**; going forward 64–66; item format and item writing procedures 48–49; localized nature of tests 46–49; overview of development and revision of 44–46; pattern of total scale scores *53*; psychometric and statistical item analysis 51; quality control and fairness of 49–55; reliability 51–52; research and innovation 57–64; research on development of **58**; research on maintenance of **61–62**; research on revision of and family of tests **63**; research on stabilization of **59–60**; score comparability 52–53; structure of 47–48; *TEPS Item Writer's Guide* 50; *TEPS Reviewer's Guide* 50; test use and impact 55–57; validity 53–55; website 7n2

TOEFL *see* Test of English as a Foreign Language (TOEFL)

TOEIC *see* Test of English for International Communication (TOEIC)

University of Auckland 200
University of Cambridge Local Examinations Syndicate (UCLES) xiii–xiv, 195–196

University of Da Nang 74
University of Languages and International Studies (ULIS): Center for Language Testing and Assessment 88–89; Vietnam National University 3, 5, 73, 82

University of Melbourne 200
University of Reading 102, 162, 163

Vietnam National University (VNU) 3, 5, 96n2

Vietnamese Standardized Test of English Proficiency (VSTEP) 1, 3, 5; context-specific peculiarities 81–83; dilemmas of local tests 83; education reform in Vietnam and 71–75; equity = fairness in accessibility 89–90; equity = fairness in tests 87–89; future directions 94–96; impacts of 89–92, 96–97n6; introduction of 71–75; localization of 75, 78–83; localization *vs* internationalization 80–81; "localized" 80–83; "locally produced" 78–80; made by the Vietnamese 79–80; a Made-in-Vietnam test 78–79; practicality of 87; quality assurance and quality control 83–89; research and contribution 92–94; sustainability 90–91; test formats of **76–77**; transparency of 85–87; validity of 84–85; website 7n2

VSTEP *see* Vietnamese Standardized Test of English Proficiency (VSTEP)

washback: impact and 207–208; term 207

Weir, Cyril 14, 102, 213
Woods, Tony 102, 213
World Bank 71
Wu, Jessica 211
Wu, Rachel 211, 218

Yang Huizhong 102